BILLIONAIRE ISLAND

ISLAND

VOLUME ONE

MARK RUSSELL

STEVE PUGH

CHRIS CHUCKRY

ROB STEEN

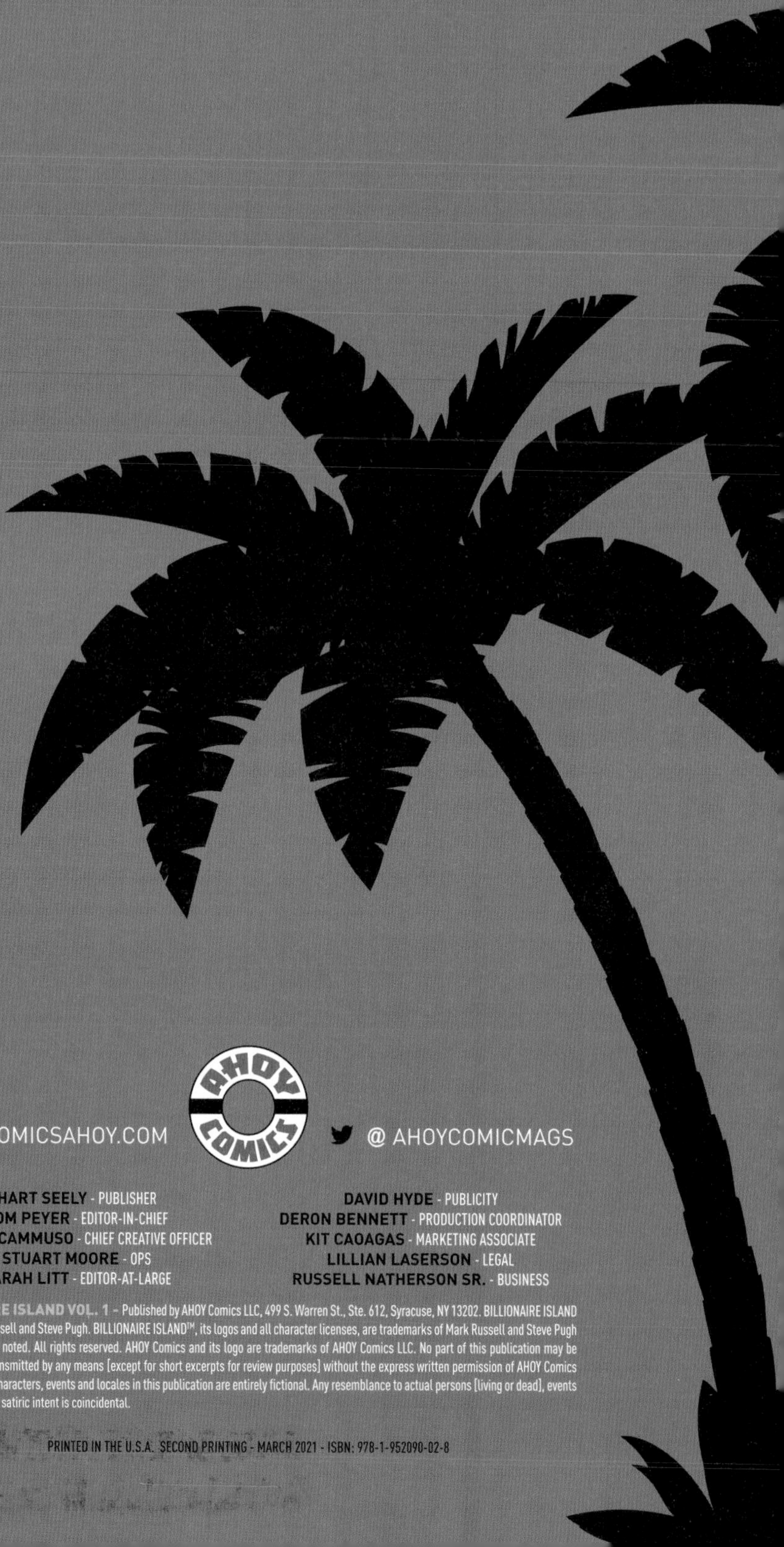

COMICSAHOY.COM

@ AHOYCOMICMAGS

HART SEELY - PUBLISHER
TOM PEYER - EDITOR-IN-CHIEF
FRANK CAMMUSO - CHIEF CREATIVE OFFICER
STUART MOORE - OPS
SARAH LITT - EDITOR-AT-LARGE

DAVID HYDE - PUBLICITY
DERON BENNETT - PRODUCTION COORDINATOR
KIT CAOAGAS - MARKETING ASSOCIATE
LILLIAN LASERSON - LEGAL
RUSSELL NATHERSON SR. - BUSINESS

PRINTED IN THE U.S.A. SECOND PRINTING - MARCH 2021 - ISBN: 978-1-952090-02-8

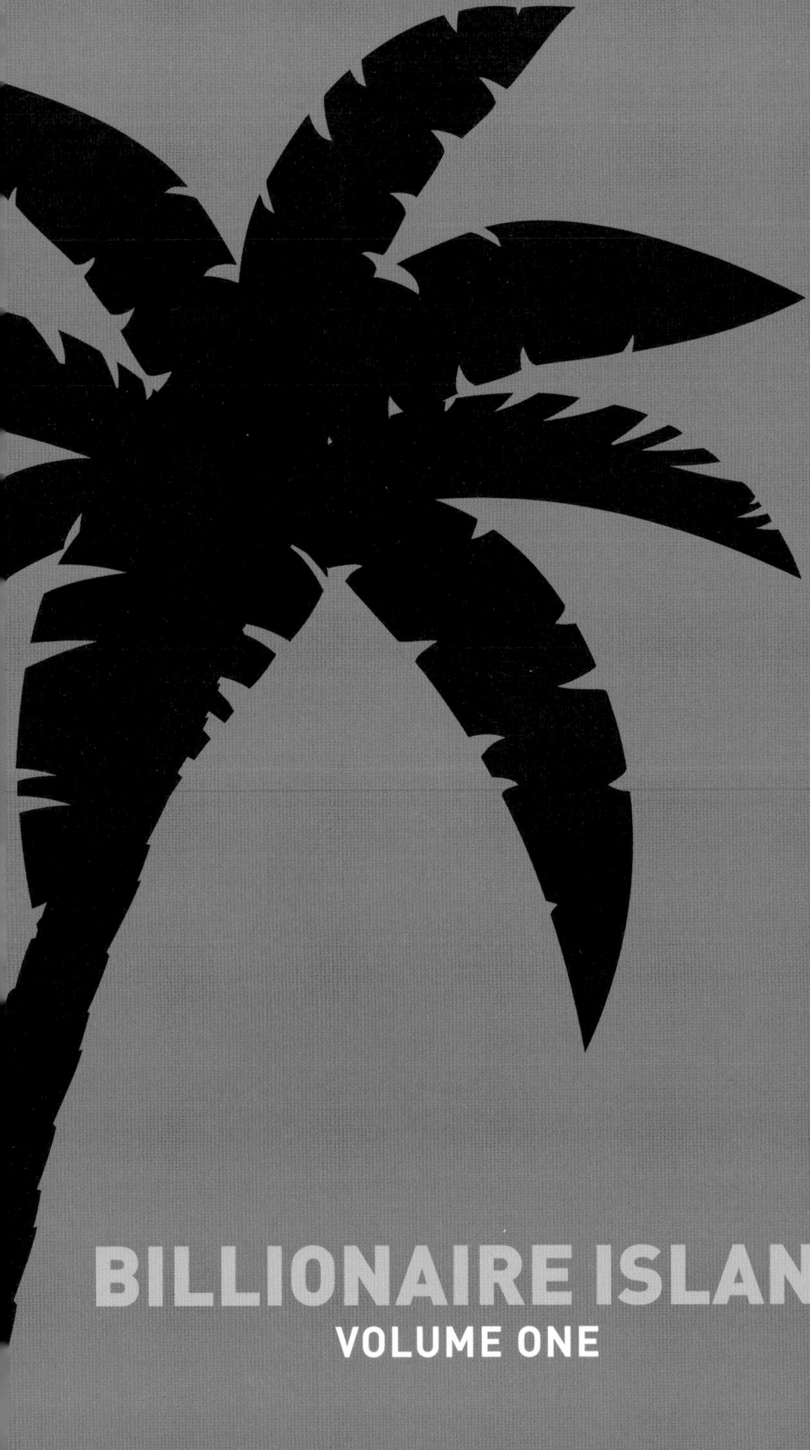

BILLIONAIRE ISLAND

VOLUME ONE

MARK RUSSELL WRITER
STEVE PUGH ARTIST
CHRIS CHUCKRY COLOR
ROB STEEN LETTERS

STEVE PUGH COVER
TODD KLEIN LOGO
JOHN J. HILL DESIGN
SARAH LITT EDITOR
CORY SEDLMEIER COLLECTION EDITOR

CREATED BY MARK RUSSELL AND STEVE PUGH

C O N T E N T S

BILLIONAIRE ISLAND

CHAPTER ONE 8

CHAPTER TWO 30

CHAPTER THREE 52

CHAPTER FOUR 74

CHAPTER FIVE 96

CHAPTER SIX 118

INTRODUCTION

Not long ago on my, ugh, Twitter feed, I saw a lot of people discussing the idea that one of our most famous billionaires, a relatively new billionaire, should-would-could step in and fix some of the world's biggest and obvious problems. I'm not going to mention which billionaire as it is someone I may be working for at the moment. The back and forth was rather optimistic towards the idea of a Savior billionaire until others chimed in. One post, in particular, stayed with me: *Why would he? Why would this billionaire help any of us? If I was a billionaire I wouldn't help anybody. That's the whole point of being a billionaire.*

"If I was a billionaire I wouldn't help anybody."

It got me thinking and, yeah, in the history of the universe, since the terrible invention of billionaires, not one of them has ever actually done right by the rest of us.

No one has ever taken their massive accumulated power and wealth and turned it around and fixed the world's obvious ills.

Not once. Never. It's never happened.

They've talked about it. It doesn't last long enough to actually, you know, work. It usually ends up with one of the billionaires trying to run for office or putting their name on something. The end.

Billionaires are SUCH a dumb idea. They should not be. They do not make for a better world and often actively get in the way of a better world. It's true. Google it. (And by doing so, about five billionaires get .00312 cents richer.)

Billionaires! What DO they do? ALL they do is make the world better for billionaires while at the same time trying really hard not to EVER create ANY more billionaires.

Listen, no lie, as I write this the world is teetering on the brink of madness and it's mostly billionaires that put us here. So, I'm feeling extra grumpy about the whole thing.

Or, I should say I was. Then I read and fell in LOVE with *BILLIONAIRE ISLAND*.

I'm so mad about the world I couldn't find the funny again until Mark Russell and Steve Pugh showed it to me. In THIS world where irony has been all but ruined? That is GREAT satire.

Oh, I am a huge fan of Mark Russell. I am a BIG fan of Steve Pugh. I'm also a big fan of the specific collaboration between Mark and Steve. I think this is just another brick in what will be a VERY long and varied collaboration. I love how high they reach and how often they get there.

The second I walked into DC Comics and had a writing gig to give someone I called Mark Russell.

I haven't discussed this with Mark Russell but I bet the movie *Network* was a huge influence on this material. I thought about it a lot when reading. All of us highfalutin'

writers of a certain age look up to Paddy Chayefsky for the ultimate inspiration. The highest inspiration. Paddy Chayefsky is synonymous with excellent writing that only a few people have been able to achieve (Charlie Kaufman, the Coen brothers...), some unique distillation of real emotion in the broadest of satire pulled together in a way that only they could do.

In the movie *Network* — please stop what you're doing and go watch it, we'll wait — Paddy Chayefsky was able to conjure a world for the 1970s audience of wildly over-the-top media satire. Today? It's a mirror. Every single thing in the movie has come true! Every single thing. Every maddening, horrible, over the top, unthinkable moment of that movie is actually happening in real life right now.

As I said, many of us in the storytelling racket look to that movie as the ultimate achievement. To create a piece of work that changes and evolves its meaning as time goes on. So much art is of a moment (and that is a special thing). But to transcend the moment in any way, shape, or form is out of the artist's hands and can be truly beautiful.

I think that's what Mark and Steve and everyone else associated have accomplished here. I think this is masterful satire and it's ALL GOING TO COME TRUE!! Probably by the end of this sentence.

Congratulations to the entire team on accomplishing the highest artistic achievement especially in the middle of our craziest time.

Wait! Hold on... *BILLIONAIRE ISLAND*, *Snagglepuss*, *Flintstones*, *Wonder Twins*... yeah.

Okay, I'll say it. Mark Russell IS comics' Paddy Chayefsky.

(Shit, I hope he likes Paddy Chayefsky.)

Bendis!
What's left of Portland, Oregon
September 2020

Brian Michael Bendis is an award-winning comics creator, Amazon and New York Times bestseller, and one of the most successful writers working in mainstream comics. For the last twenty years, Brian's books have consistently sat on top of the nationwide comic and graphic novel sales charts.

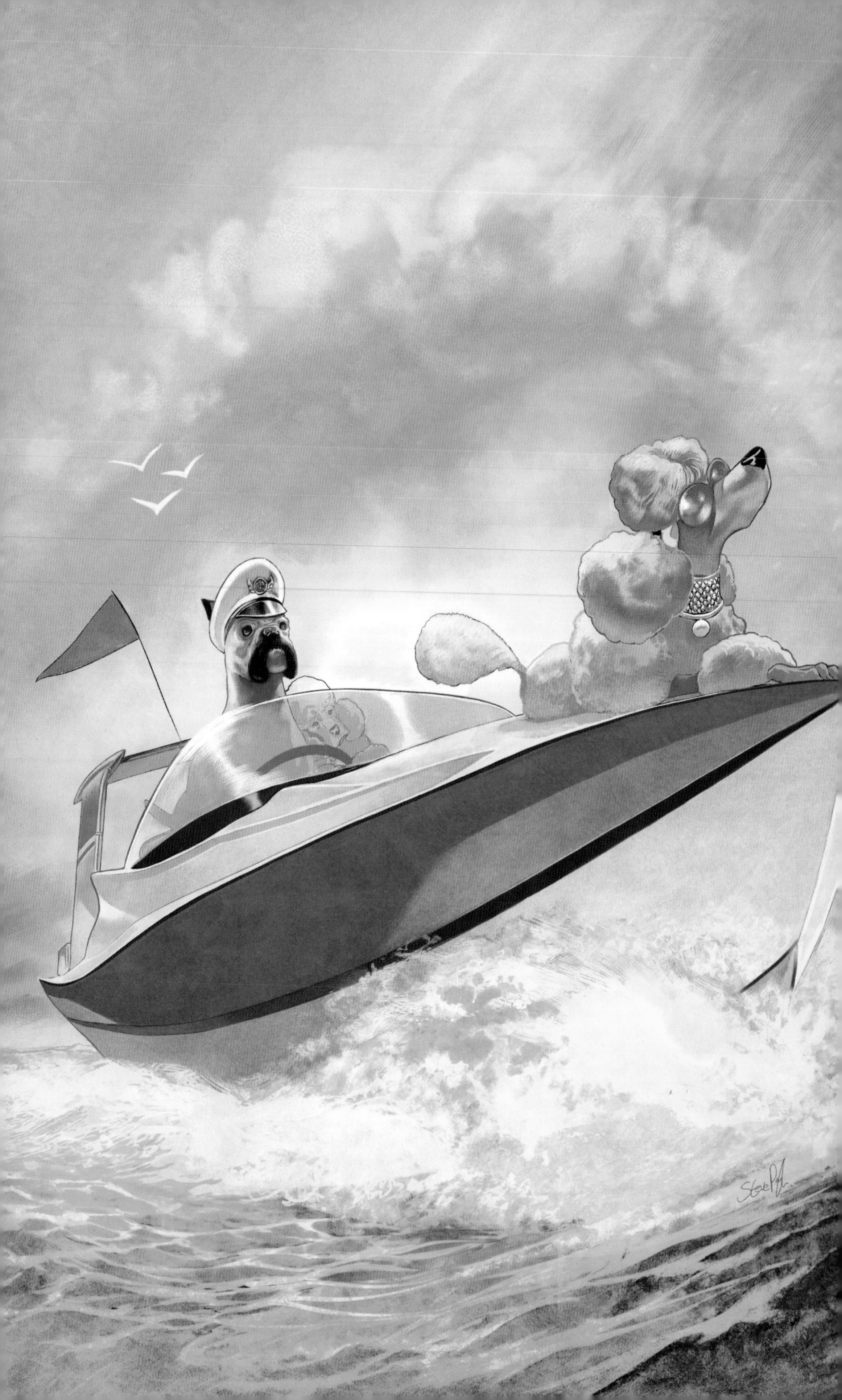

F O R E W O R D

BILLIONAIRE ISLAND is, to put it bluntly, about the end of the world. Or, at least, the end of the world as we know it. Whatever your political persuasion, your socio-economic background, we all seem to have intuitively grasped that the end is coming. That there's a time limit to sucking all the resources out of the planet and we are quickly approaching the buzzer.

From the days when we were hunter-gatherers, we have basically come up with two strategies to handle such disasters—sharing and working together for our collective survival...and hoarding.

The inhabitants of Freedom Unlimited (or Billionaire Island, as it is colloquially known) have, like most of us, opted for hoarding. Hoarding has proven so popular a solution that even people with little or nothing seem to have settled on it. Climate change, the depletion of our natural resources, and the desertification of 75% of the Earth's land surface is an existential threat to the entire human race, one which directly or indirectly creates millions of refugees every year. It is a collective danger. And yet, the reaction of most of the world has been to huddle around the flag of their small chunk of the human race. To break out their guns to protect themselves from those who have already slipped off the edge in a violent prayer that they won't be next. Whether they've been successfully propagandized against their own interests, or they simply imagine that their overlords will show them the mercy they deny to everyone else, many people have chosen to deal with the world going sideways by turning to nationalism. For that's essentially what nationalism is...another word for hoarding.

But whether by walling off borders and imprisoning refugees, or by heading to a well-provisioned bunker with your billions, the poor person's hoarding and the rich person's hoarding are predicated on the same fallacy. That even though the water in the aquarium is turning to poison, you'll somehow be safe hiding in your little pewter castle.

Given that **BILLIONAIRE ISLAND** is about the end of the world, about the calamity that surely awaits at the end of business as usual, it was with some irony that its publication was itself interrupted by a global pandemic. A dress rehearsal, of sorts, for what will inevitably be the main production, should we continue dumping the world's resources into offshore banks and getaway yachts. So I hope it is, if nothing else, a reminder that there is another way. That the human race does not have an artificial island to escape to. That we must survive where we stand.

And that, like it or not, we must do it together.

Sincerely,
Mark Russell
Portland, Oregon
August 2020

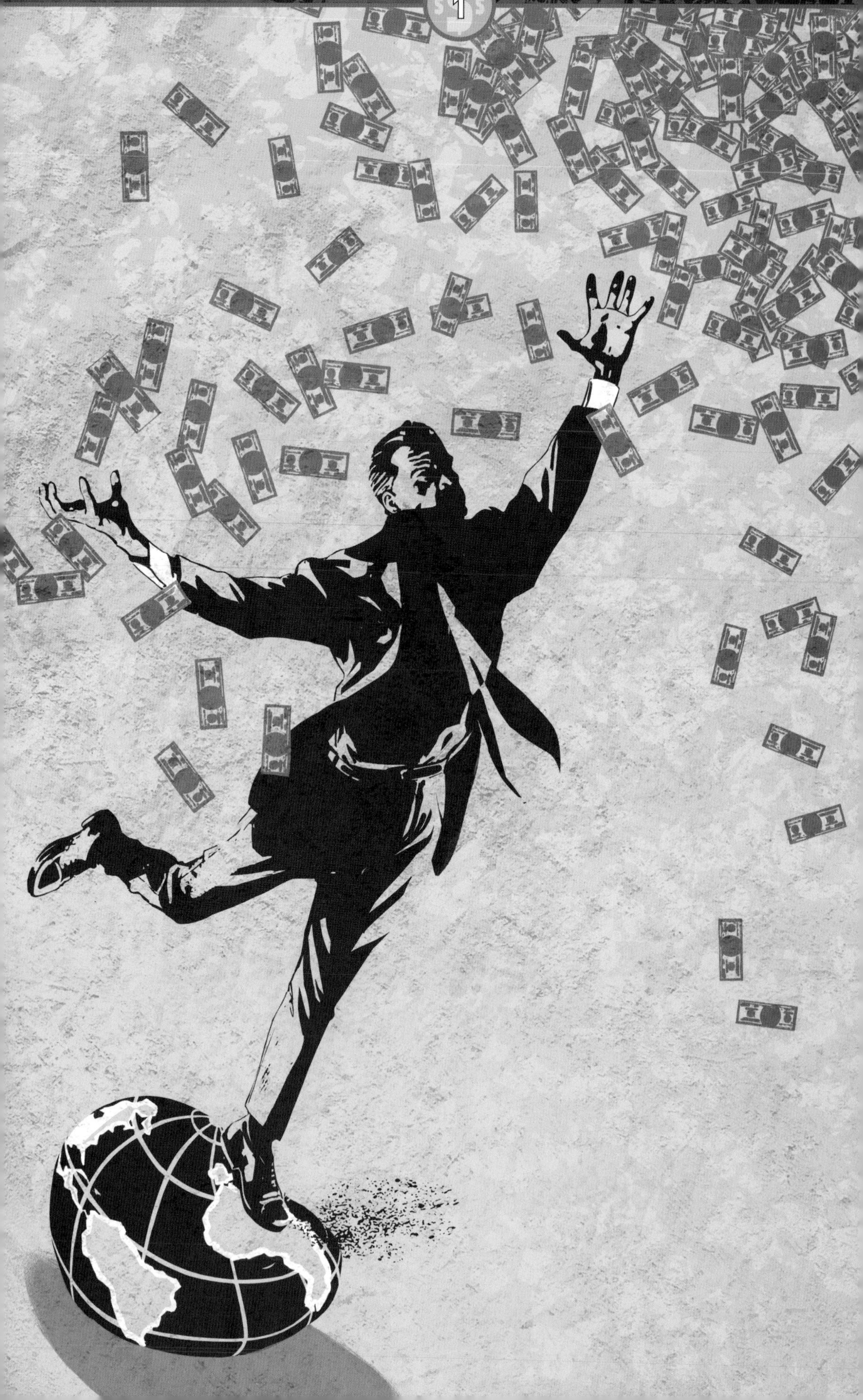

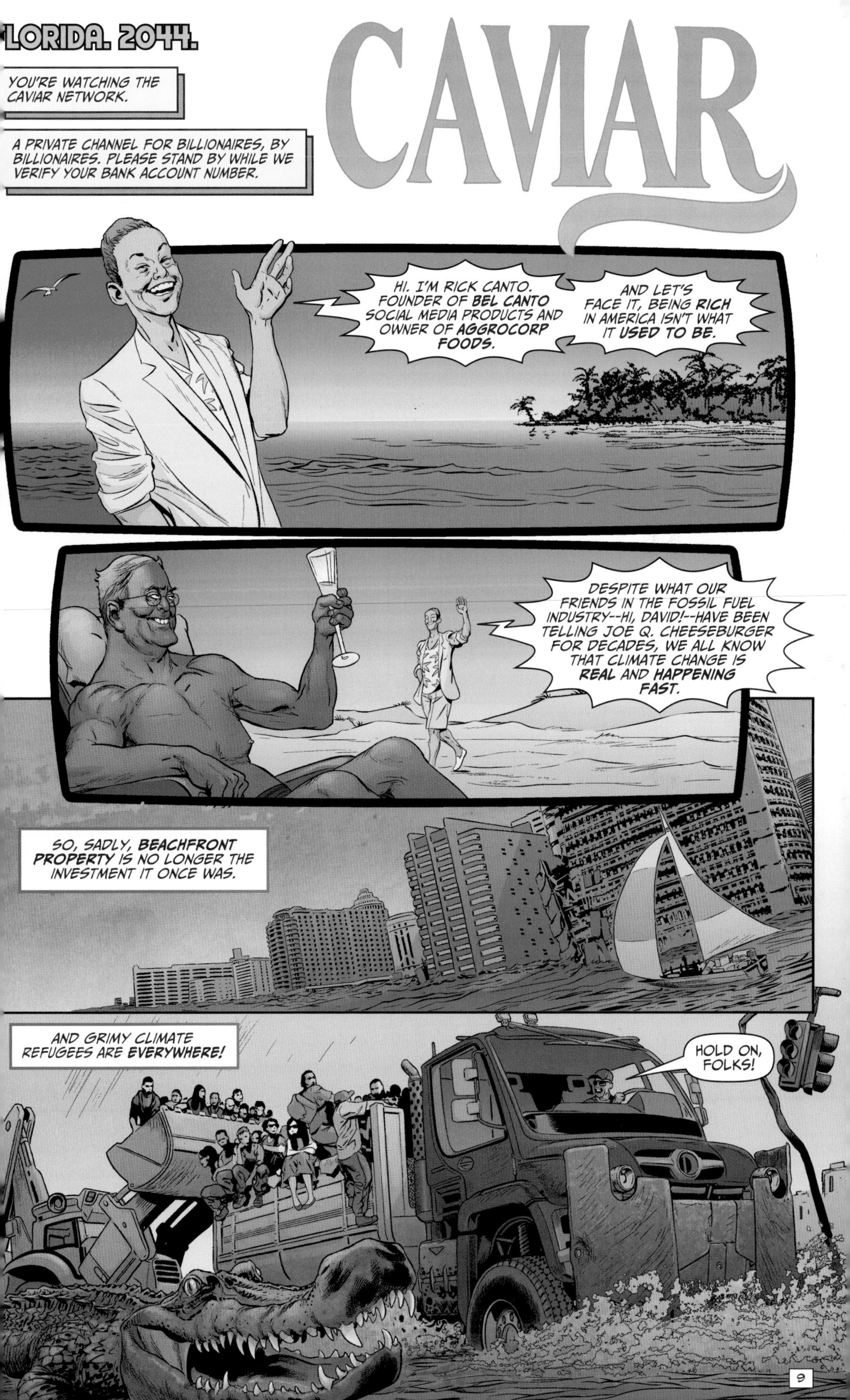
LORIDA. 2044.
CAVIAR
YOU'RE WATCHING THE CAVIAR NETWORK.
A PRIVATE CHANNEL FOR BILLIONAIRES, BY BILLIONAIRES. PLEASE STAND BY WHILE WE VERIFY YOUR BANK ACCOUNT NUMBER.
HI. I'M RICK CANTO. FOUNDER OF BEL CANTO SOCIAL MEDIA PRODUCTS AND OWNER OF AGGROCORP FOODS.
AND LET'S FACE IT, BEING RICH IN AMERICA ISN'T WHAT IT USED TO BE.
DESPITE WHAT OUR FRIENDS IN THE FOSSIL FUEL INDUSTRY--HI, DAVID!--HAVE BEEN TELLING JOE Q. CHEESEBURGER FOR DECADES, WE ALL KNOW THAT CLIMATE CHANGE IS REAL AND HAPPENING FAST.
SO, SADLY, BEACHFRONT PROPERTY IS NO LONGER THE INVESTMENT IT ONCE WAS.
AND GRIMY CLIMATE REFUGEES ARE EVERYWHERE!
HOLD ON, FOLKS!

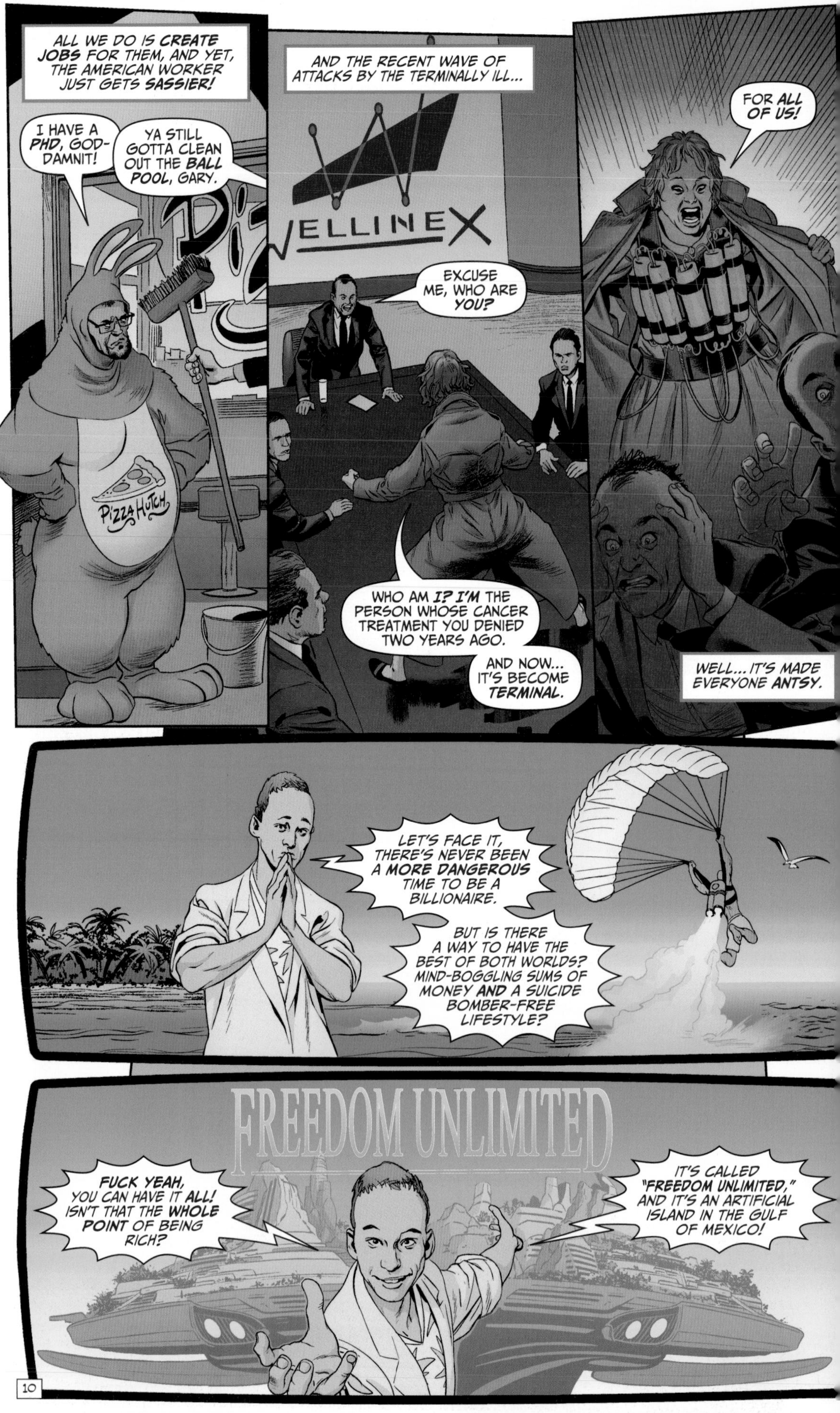

ALL WE DO IS CREATE JOBS FOR THEM, AND YET, THE AMERICAN WORKER JUST GETS SASSIER!
I HAVE A PHD, GOD-DAMNIT!
YA STILL GOTTA CLEAN OUT THE BALL POOL, GARY.
PIZZA HUTCH
AND THE RECENT WAVE OF ATTACKS BY THE TERMINALLY ILL...
WELLINEX
EXCUSE ME, WHO ARE YOU?
WHO AM I? I'M THE PERSON WHOSE CANCER TREATMENT YOU DENIED TWO YEARS AGO.
AND NOW... IT'S BECOME TERMINAL.
FOR ALL OF US!
WELL... IT'S MADE EVERYONE ANTSY.
LET'S FACE IT, THERE'S NEVER BEEN A MORE DANGEROUS TIME TO BE A BILLIONAIRE.
BUT IS THERE A WAY TO HAVE THE BEST OF BOTH WORLDS? MIND-BOGGLING SUMS OF MONEY AND A SUICIDE BOMBER-FREE LIFESTYLE?
FREEDOM UNLIMITED
IT'S CALLED "FREEDOM UNLIMITED," AND IT'S AN ARTIFICIAL ISLAND IN THE GULF OF MEXICO!
FUCK YEAH, YOU CAN HAVE IT ALL! ISN'T THAT THE WHOLE POINT OF BEING RICH?

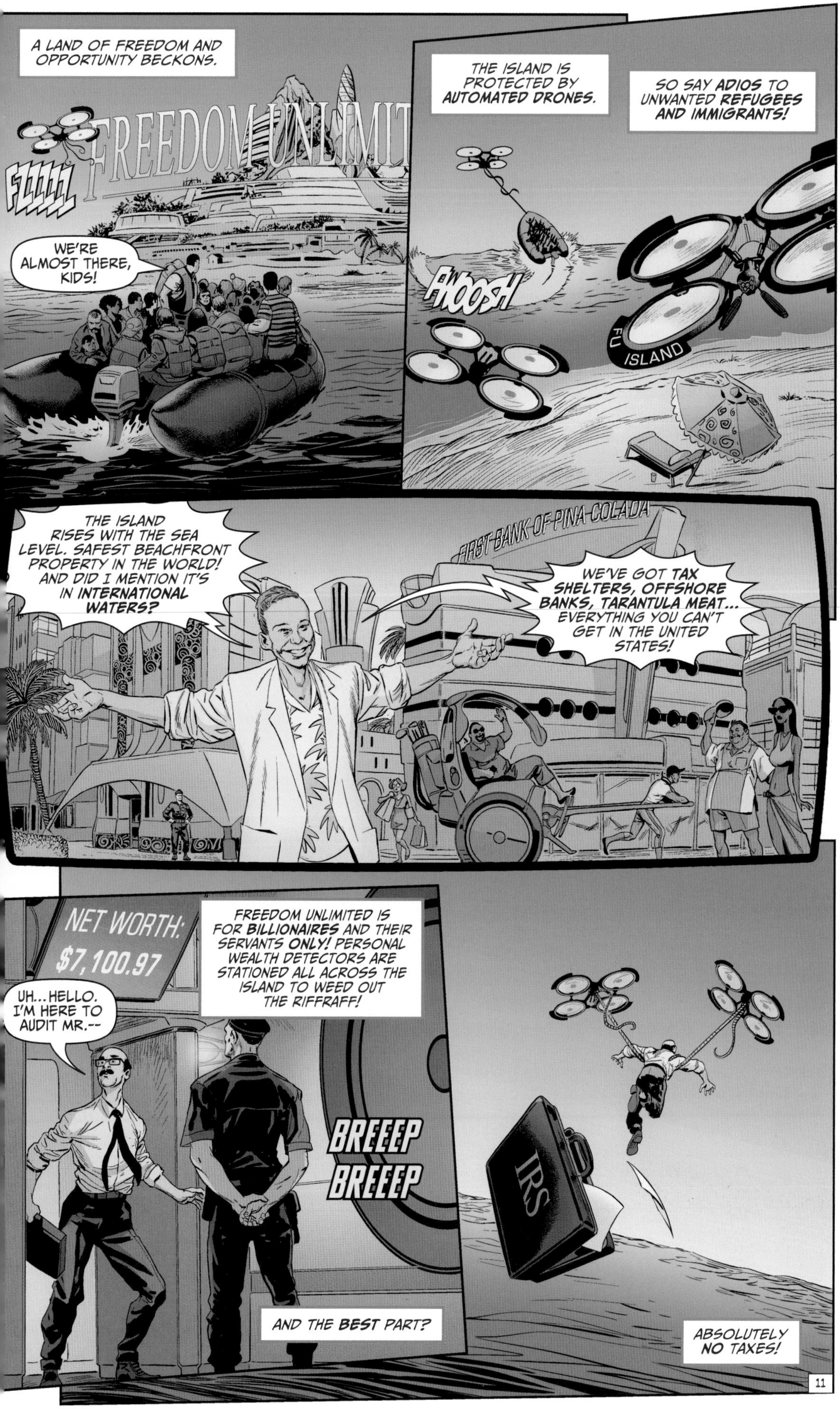
A LAND OF FREEDOM AND OPPORTUNITY BECKONS.
FREEDOM UNLIMIT
FZZZZZ
WE'RE ALMOST THERE, KIDS!
THE ISLAND IS PROTECTED BY AUTOMATED DRONES.
SO SAY ADIOS TO UNWANTED REFUGEES AND IMMIGRANTS!
FWOOSH
FU ISLAND
FIRST BANK OF PINA COLADA
THE ISLAND RISES WITH THE SEA LEVEL. SAFEST BEACHFRONT PROPERTY IN THE WORLD! AND DID I MENTION IT'S IN INTERNATIONAL WATERS?
WE'VE GOT TAX SHELTERS, OFFSHORE BANKS, TARANTULA MEAT... EVERYTHING YOU CAN'T GET IN THE UNITED STATES!
NET WORTH: $7,100.97
FREEDOM UNLIMITED IS FOR BILLIONAIRES AND THEIR SERVANTS ONLY! PERSONAL WEALTH DETECTORS ARE STATIONED ALL ACROSS THE ISLAND TO WEED OUT THE RIFFRAFF!
UH...HELLO. I'M HERE TO AUDIT MR.--
BREEEP BREEEP
AND THE BEST PART?
IRS
ABSOLUTELY NO TAXES!

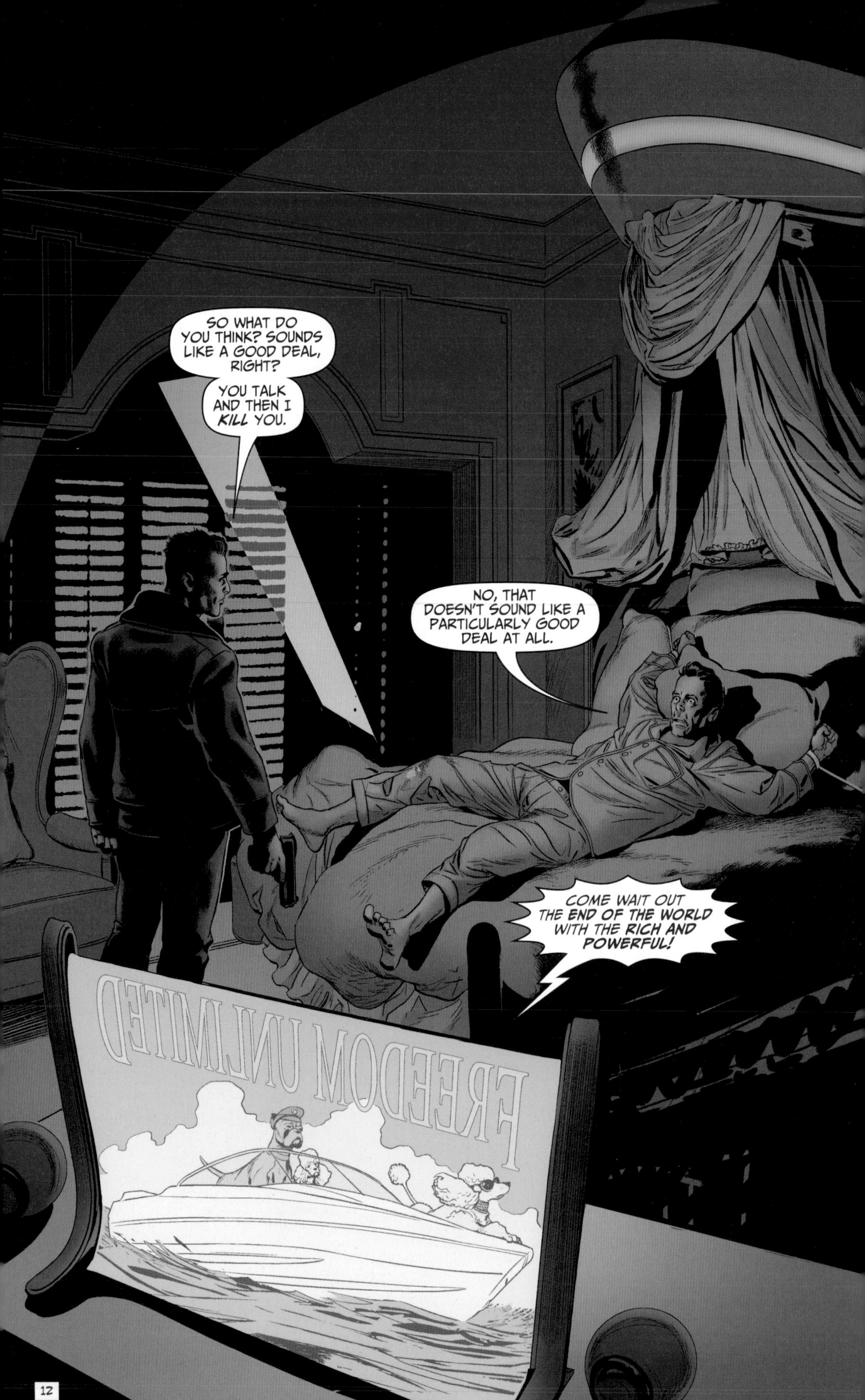
SO WHAT DO YOU THINK? SOUNDS LIKE A GOOD DEAL, RIGHT?
YOU TALK AND THEN I KILL YOU.
NO, THAT DOESN'T SOUND LIKE A PARTICULARLY GOOD DEAL AT ALL.
COME WAIT OUT THE END OF THE WORLD WITH THE RICH AND POWERFUL!
FREEDOM UNLIMITED

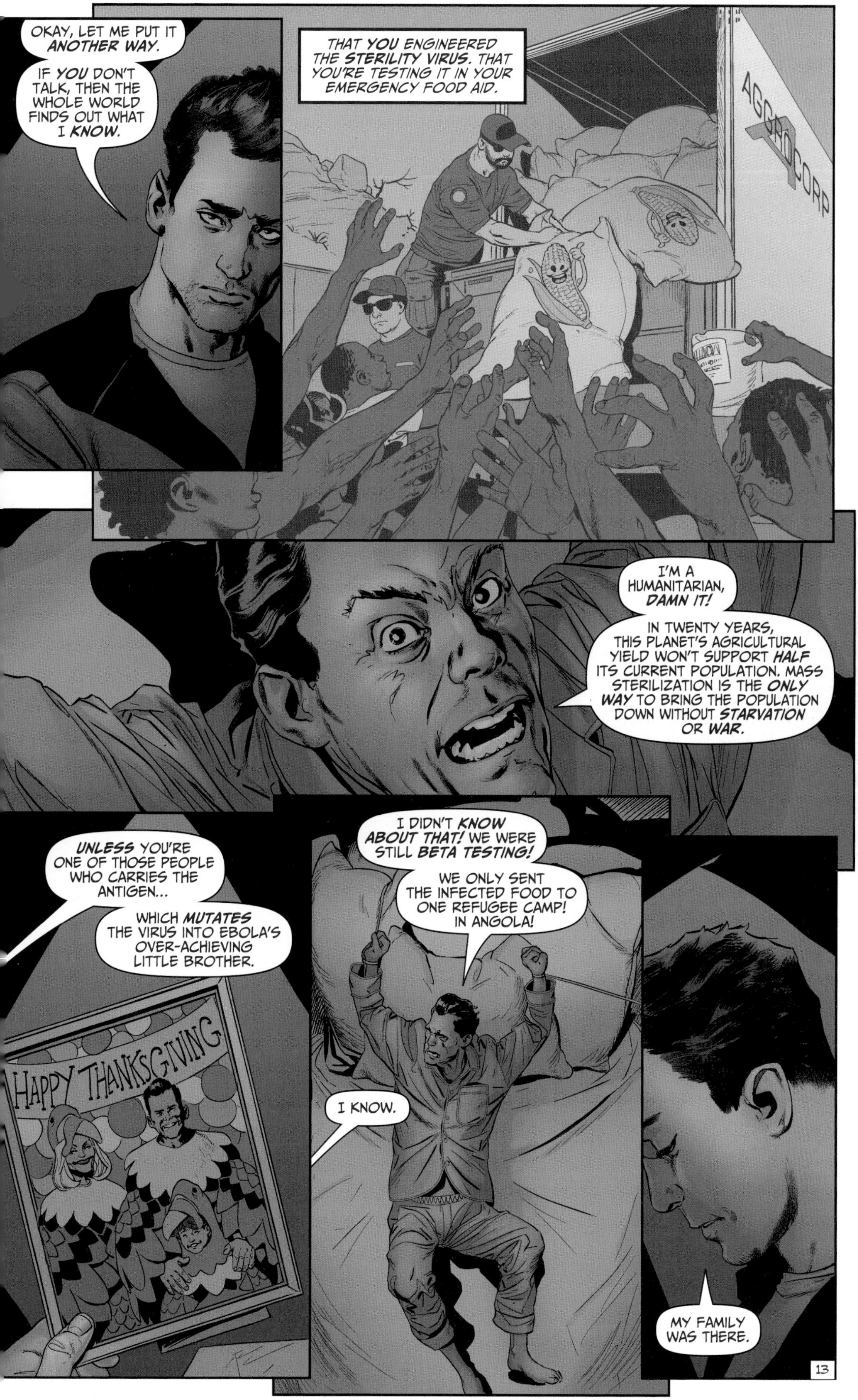
OKAY, LET ME PUT IT ANOTHER WAY.
IF YOU DON'T TALK, THEN THE WHOLE WORLD FINDS OUT WHAT I KNOW.
THAT YOU ENGINEERED THE STERILITY VIRUS. THAT YOU'RE TESTING IT IN YOUR EMERGENCY FOOD AID.
AGGROCORP
I'M A HUMANITARIAN, DAMN IT!
IN TWENTY YEARS, THIS PLANET'S AGRICULTURAL YIELD WON'T SUPPORT HALF ITS CURRENT POPULATION. MASS STERILIZATION IS THE ONLY WAY TO BRING THE POPULATION DOWN WITHOUT STARVATION OR WAR.
UNLESS YOU'RE ONE OF THOSE PEOPLE WHO CARRIES THE ANTIGEN...
WHICH MUTATES THE VIRUS INTO EBOLA'S OVER-ACHIEVING LITTLE BROTHER.
HAPPY THANKSGIVING
I DIDN'T KNOW ABOUT THAT! WE WERE STILL BETA TESTING!
WE ONLY SENT THE INFECTED FOOD TO ONE REFUGEE CAMP! IN ANGOLA!
I KNOW.
MY FAMILY WAS THERE.

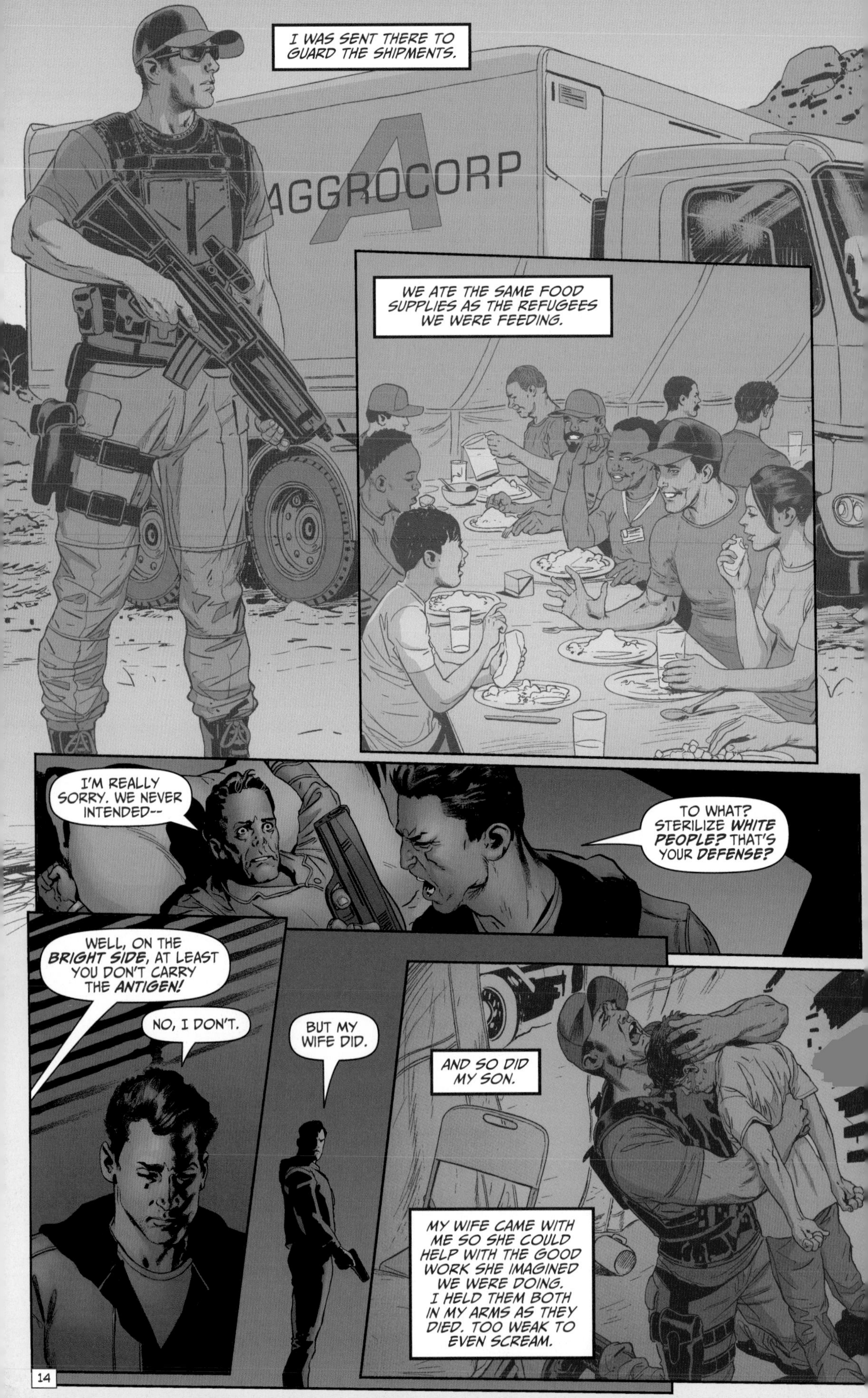
I WAS SENT THERE TO GUARD THE SHIPMENTS.
AGGROCORP
WE ATE THE SAME FOOD SUPPLIES AS THE REFUGEES WE WERE FEEDING.
I'M REALLY SORRY. WE NEVER INTENDED--
TO WHAT? STERILIZE WHITE PEOPLE? THAT'S YOUR DEFENSE?
WELL, ON THE BRIGHT SIDE, AT LEAST YOU DON'T CARRY THE ANTIGEN!
NO, I DON'T.
BUT MY WIFE DID.
AND SO DID MY SON.
MY WIFE CAME WITH ME SO SHE COULD HELP WITH THE GOOD WORK SHE IMAGINED WE WERE DOING. I HELD THEM BOTH IN MY ARMS AS THEY DIED. TOO WEAK TO EVEN SCREAM.

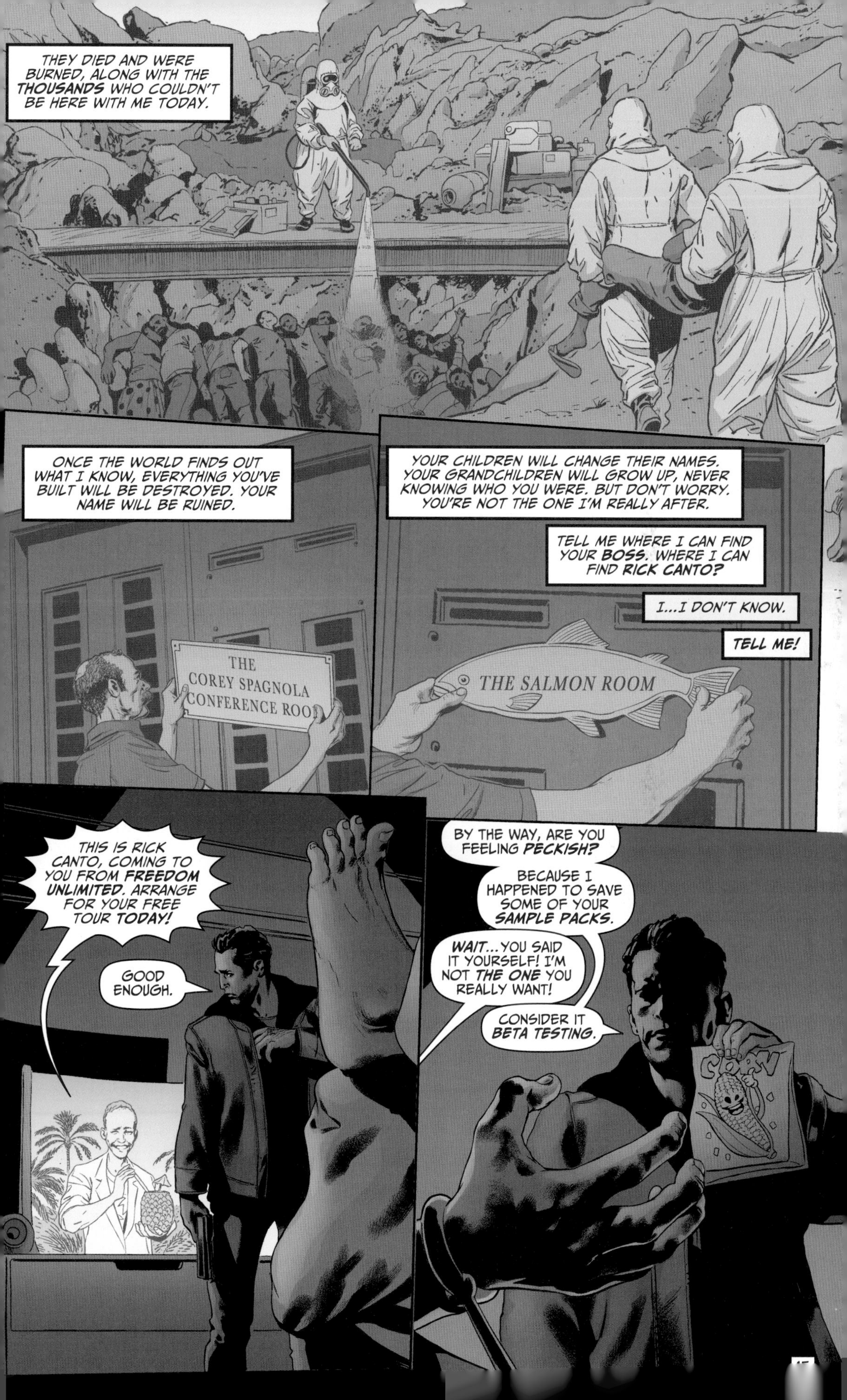
THEY DIED AND WERE BURNED, ALONG WITH THE THOUSANDS WHO COULDN'T BE HERE WITH ME TODAY.
ONCE THE WORLD FINDS OUT WHAT I KNOW, EVERYTHING YOU'VE BUILT WILL BE DESTROYED. YOUR NAME WILL BE RUINED.
THE COREY SPAGNOLA CONFERENCE ROO
YOUR CHILDREN WILL CHANGE THEIR NAMES. YOUR GRANDCHILDREN WILL GROW UP, NEVER KNOWING WHO YOU WERE. BUT DON'T WORRY. YOU'RE NOT THE ONE I'M REALLY AFTER.
TELL ME WHERE I CAN FIND YOUR BOSS. WHERE I CAN FIND RICK CANTO?
I...I DON'T KNOW.
TELL ME!
THE SALMON ROOM
THIS IS RICK CANTO, COMING TO YOU FROM FREEDOM UNLIMITED. ARRANGE FOR YOUR FREE TOUR TODAY!
GOOD ENOUGH.
BY THE WAY, ARE YOU FEELING PECKISH?
BECAUSE I HAPPENED TO SAVE SOME OF YOUR SAMPLE PACKS.
WAIT...YOU SAID IT YOURSELF! I'M NOT THE ONE YOU REALLY WANT!
CONSIDER IT BETA TESTING.

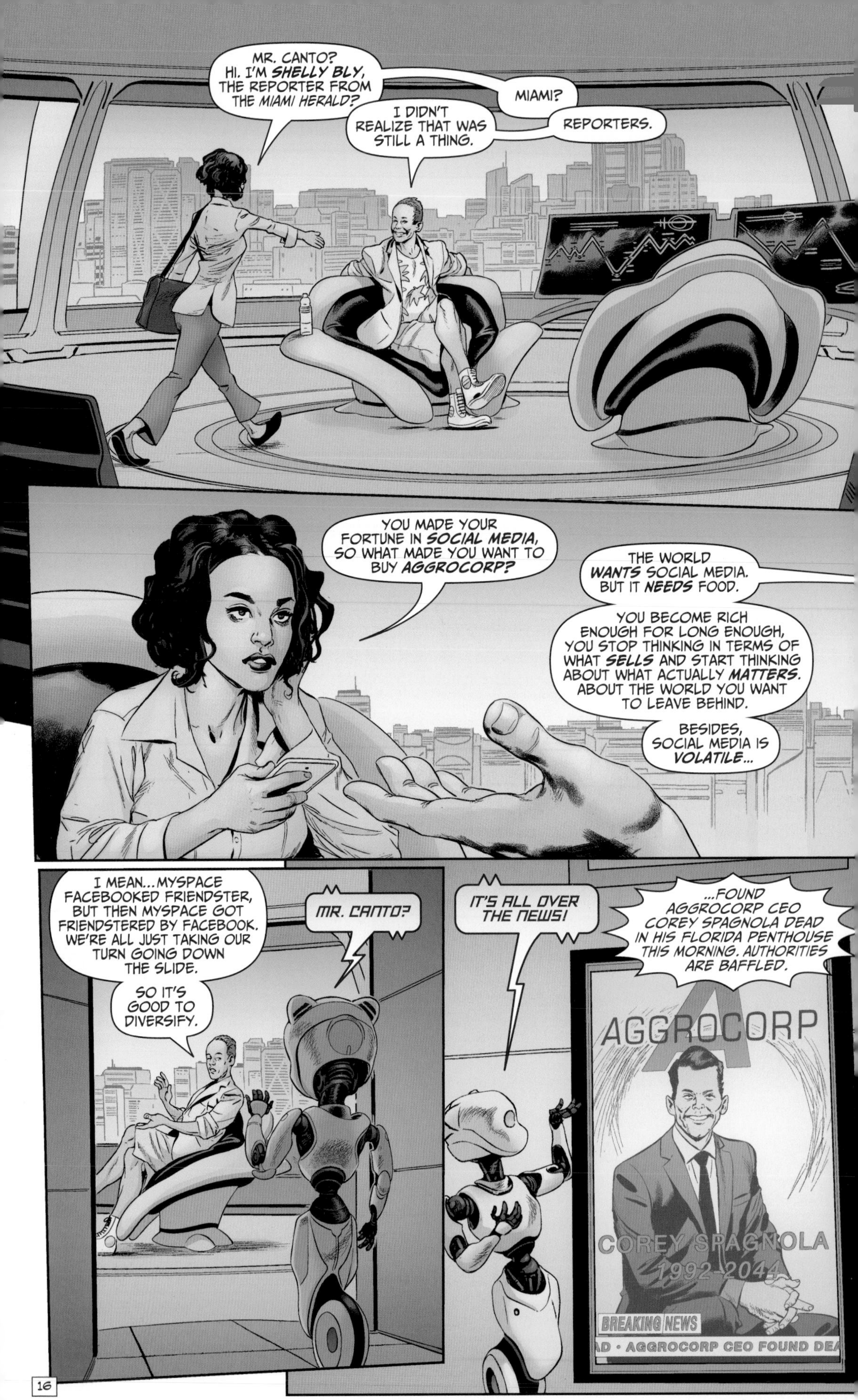

MR. CANTO? HI. I'M SHELLY BLY, THE REPORTER FROM THE MIAMI HERALD?
MIAMI?
I DIDN'T REALIZE THAT WAS STILL A THING.
REPORTERS.
YOU MADE YOUR FORTUNE IN SOCIAL MEDIA, SO WHAT MADE YOU WANT TO BUY AGGROCORP?
THE WORLD WANTS SOCIAL MEDIA. BUT IT NEEDS FOOD.
YOU BECOME RICH ENOUGH FOR LONG ENOUGH, YOU STOP THINKING IN TERMS OF WHAT SELLS AND START THINKING ABOUT WHAT ACTUALLY MATTERS. ABOUT THE WORLD YOU WANT TO LEAVE BEHIND.
BESIDES, SOCIAL MEDIA IS VOLATILE...
I MEAN... MYSPACE FACEBOOKED FRIENDSTER, BUT THEN MYSPACE GOT FRIENDSTERED BY FACEBOOK. WE'RE ALL JUST TAKING OUR TURN GOING DOWN THE SLIDE.
SO IT'S GOOD TO DIVERSIFY.
MR. CANTO?
IT'S ALL OVER THE NEWS!
...FOUND AGGROCORP CEO COREY SPAGNOLA DEAD IN HIS FLORIDA PENTHOUSE THIS MORNING. AUTHORITIES ARE BAFFLED.
AGGROCORP
COREY SPAGNOLA
1992-2044
BREAKING NEWS
AD • AGGROCORP CEO FOUND DEA

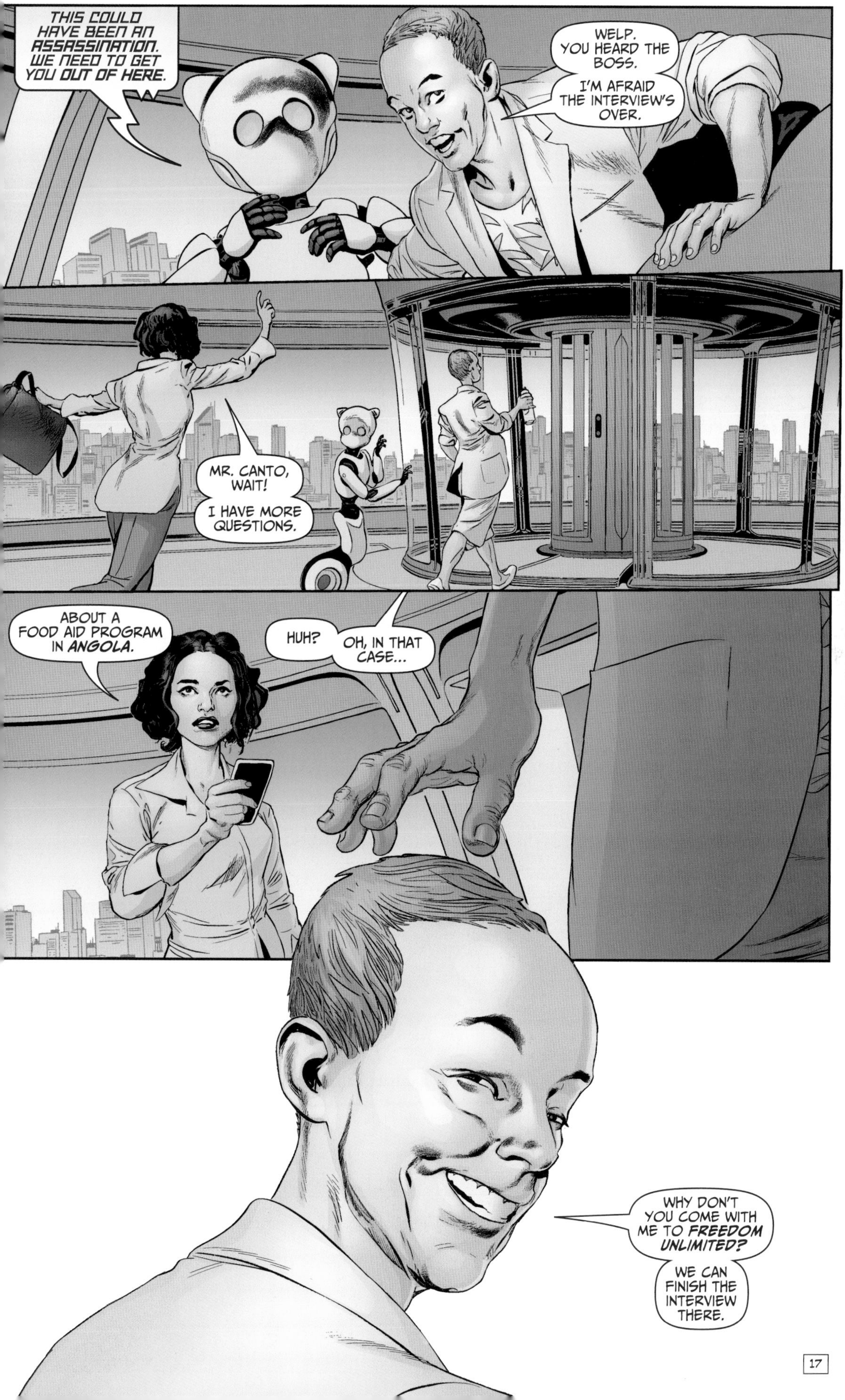
THIS COULD HAVE BEEN AN ASSASSINATION. WE NEED TO GET YOU OUT OF HERE.
WELP. YOU HEARD THE BOSS.
I'M AFRAID THE INTERVIEW'S OVER.
MR. CANTO, WAIT!
I HAVE MORE QUESTIONS.
ABOUT A FOOD AID PROGRAM IN ANGOLA.
HUH?
OH, IN THAT CASE...
WHY DON'T YOU COME WITH ME TO FREEDOM UNLIMITED?
WE CAN FINISH THE INTERVIEW THERE.

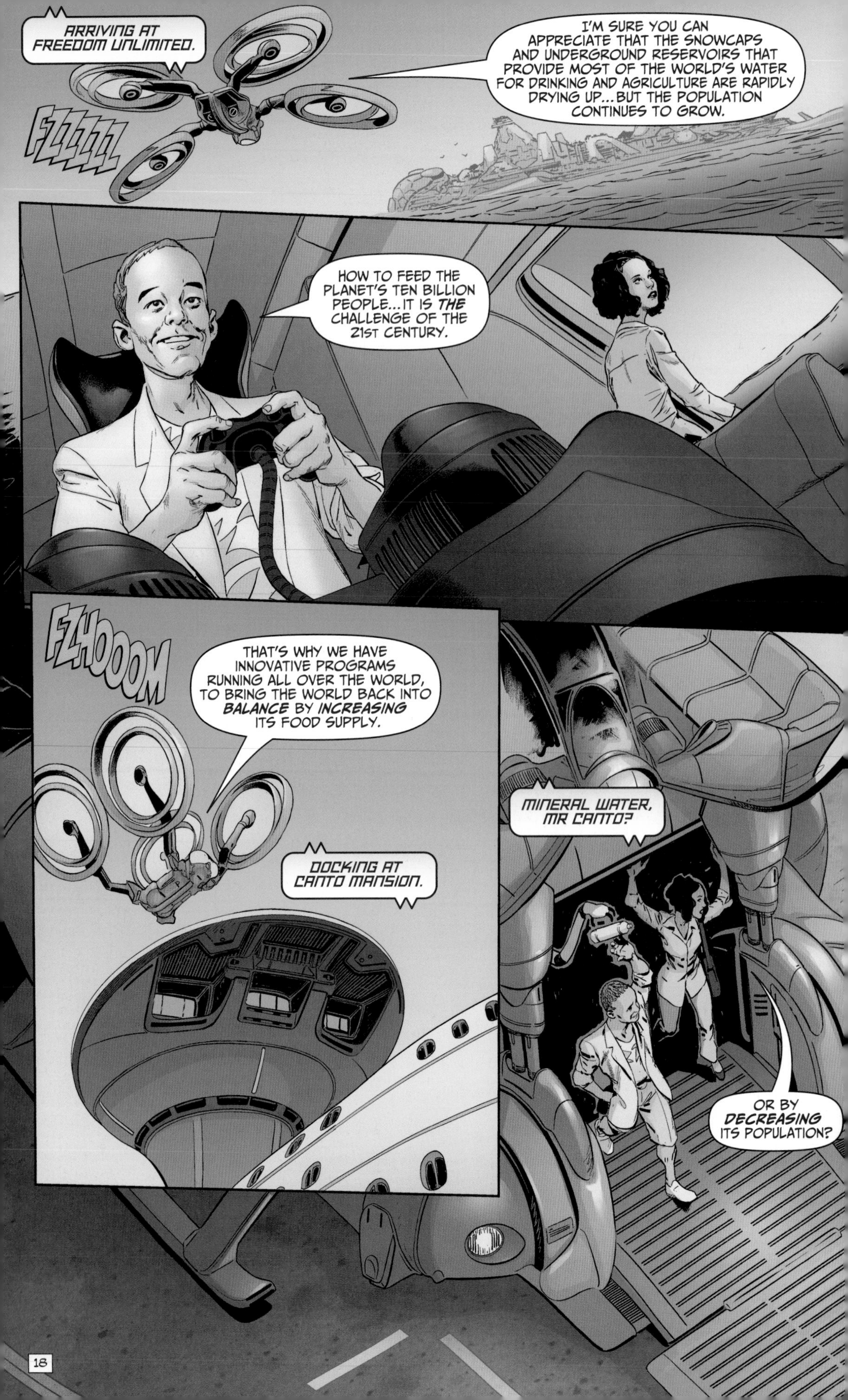
ARRIVING AT FREEDOM UNLIMITED.
I'M SURE YOU CAN APPRECIATE THAT THE SNOWCAPS AND UNDERGROUND RESERVOIRS THAT PROVIDE MOST OF THE WORLD'S WATER FOR DRINKING AND AGRICULTURE ARE RAPIDLY DRYING UP... BUT THE POPULATION CONTINUES TO GROW.
FZZZZZ
HOW TO FEED THE PLANET'S TEN BILLION PEOPLE... IT IS *THE* CHALLENGE OF THE 21ST CENTURY.
FZHOOOM
THAT'S WHY WE HAVE INNOVATIVE PROGRAMS RUNNING ALL OVER THE WORLD, TO BRING THE WORLD BACK INTO *BALANCE* BY *INCREASING* ITS FOOD SUPPLY.
DOCKING AT CANTO MANSION.
MINERAL WATER, MR CANTO?
OR BY *DECREASING* ITS POPULATION?

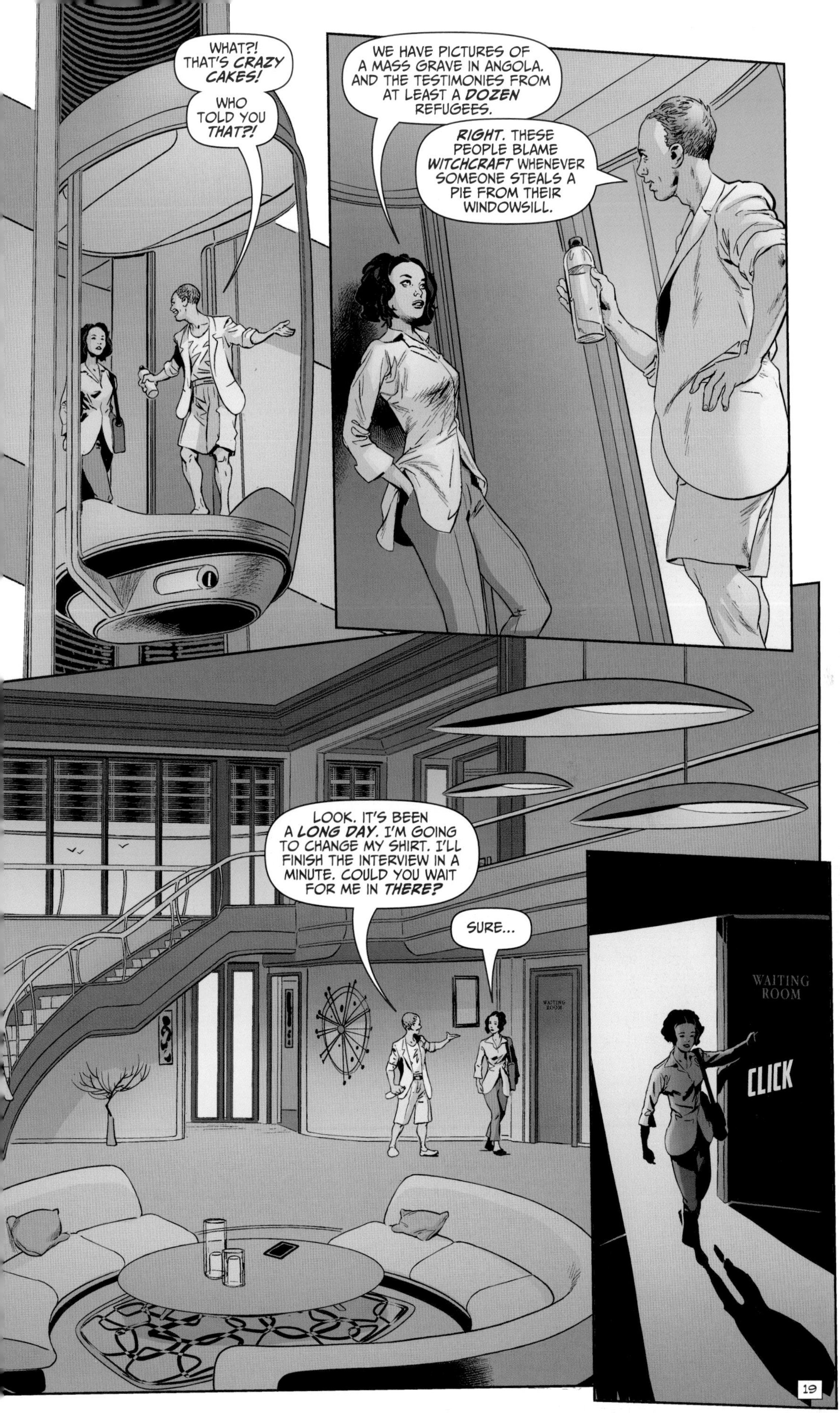
WHAT?! THAT'S CRAZY CAKES!
WHO TOLD YOU THAT?!
WE HAVE PICTURES OF A MASS GRAVE IN ANGOLA. AND THE TESTIMONIES FROM AT LEAST A DOZEN REFUGEES.
RIGHT. THESE PEOPLE BLAME WITCHCRAFT WHENEVER SOMEONE STEALS A PIE FROM THEIR WINDOWSILL.
LOOK. IT'S BEEN A LONG DAY. I'M GOING TO CHANGE MY SHIRT. I'LL FINISH THE INTERVIEW IN A MINUTE. COULD YOU WAIT FOR ME IN THERE?
SURE...
WAITING ROOM
WAITING ROOM
CLICK

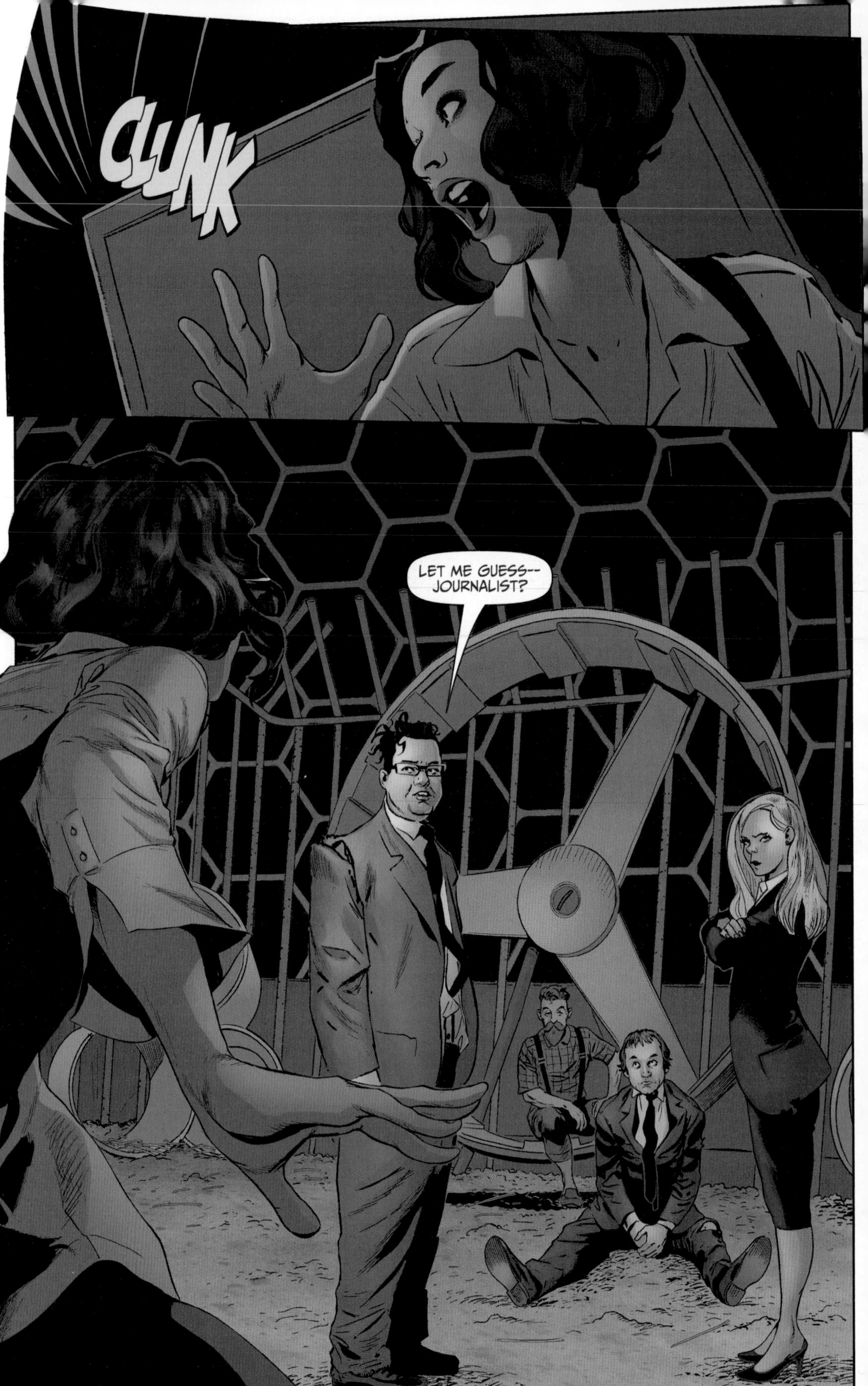
CLUNK
LET ME GUESS-- JOURNALIST?

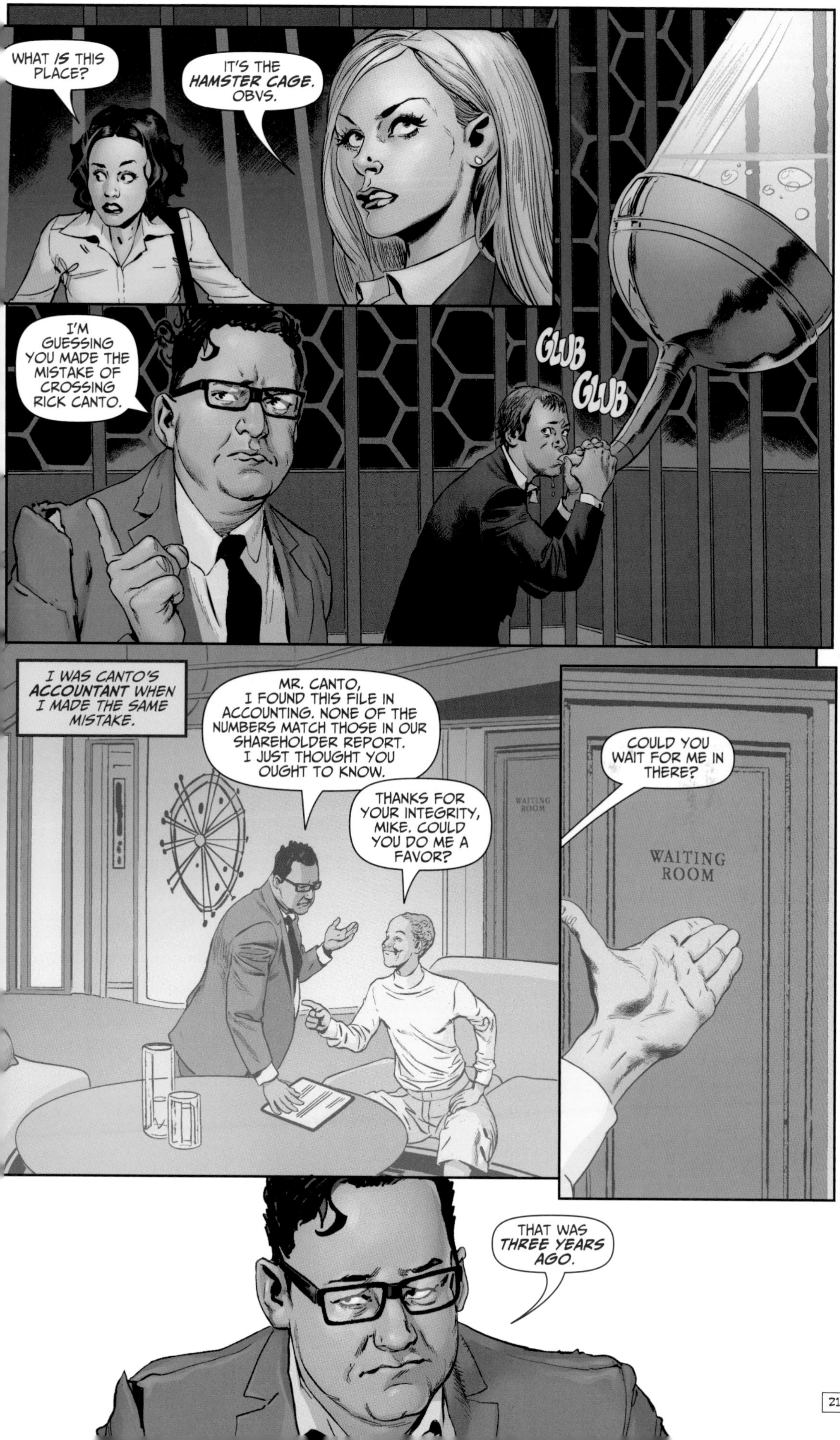
WHAT IS THIS PLACE?
IT'S THE HAMSTER CAGE. OBVS.
I'M GUESSING YOU MADE THE MISTAKE OF CROSSING RICK CANTO.
GLUB GLUB
I WAS CANTO'S ACCOUNTANT WHEN I MADE THE SAME MISTAKE.
MR. CANTO, I FOUND THIS FILE IN ACCOUNTING. NONE OF THE NUMBERS MATCH THOSE IN OUR SHAREHOLDER REPORT. I JUST THOUGHT YOU OUGHT TO KNOW.
THANKS FOR YOUR INTEGRITY, MIKE. COULD YOU DO ME A FAVOR?
WAITING ROOM
COULD YOU WAIT FOR ME IN THERE?
WAITING ROOM
THAT WAS THREE YEARS AGO.

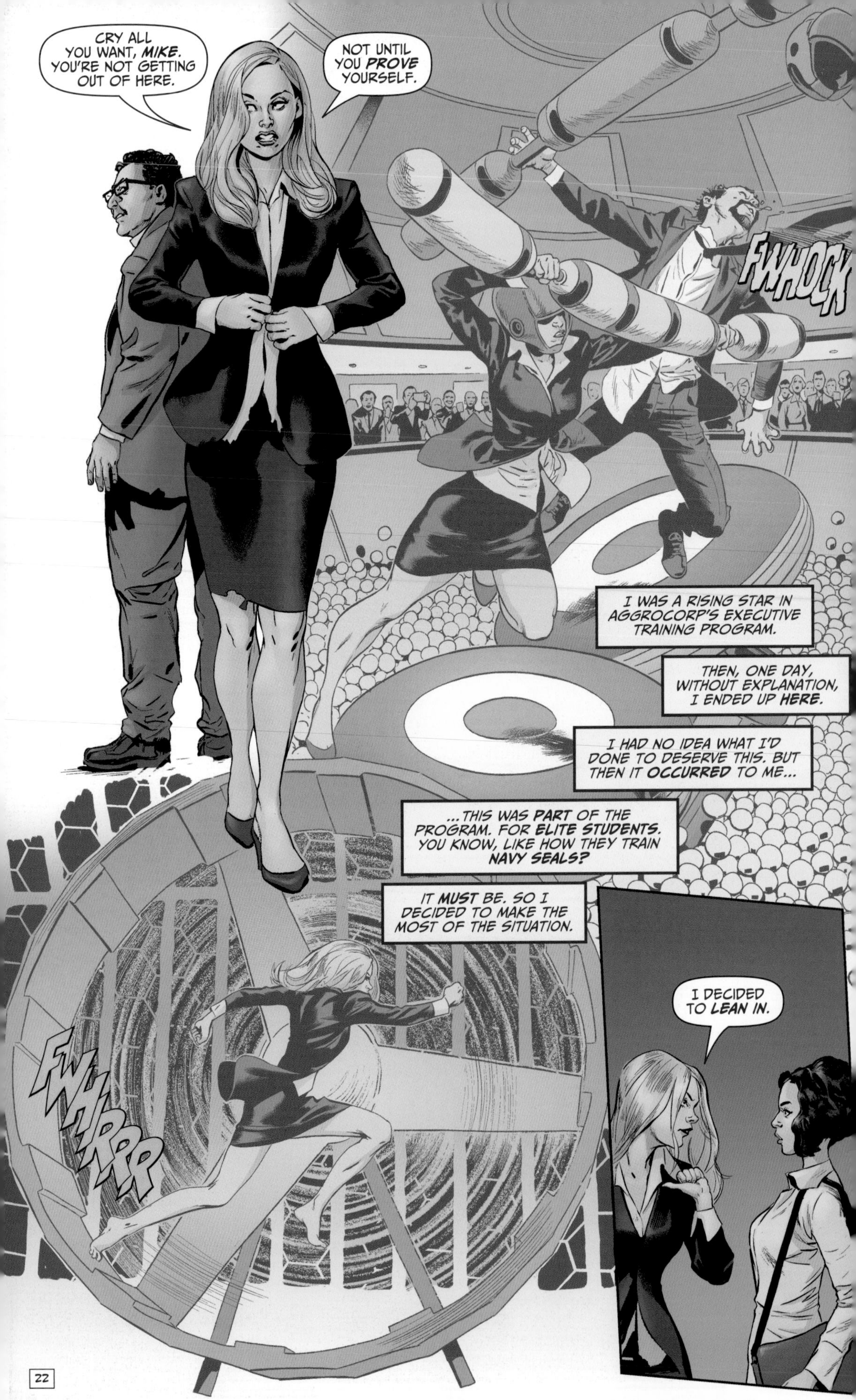
CRY ALL YOU WANT, MIKE. YOU'RE NOT GETTING OUT OF HERE.
NOT UNTIL YOU PROVE YOURSELF.
FWHOCK
I WAS A RISING STAR IN AGGROCORP'S EXECUTIVE TRAINING PROGRAM.
THEN, ONE DAY, WITHOUT EXPLANATION, I ENDED UP HERE.
I HAD NO IDEA WHAT I'D DONE TO DESERVE THIS. BUT THEN IT OCCURRED TO ME...
...THIS WAS PART OF THE PROGRAM. FOR ELITE STUDENTS. YOU KNOW, LIKE HOW THEY TRAIN NAVY SEALS?
IT MUST BE. SO I DECIDED TO MAKE THE MOST OF THE SITUATION.
FWHRRR
I DECIDED TO LEAN IN.

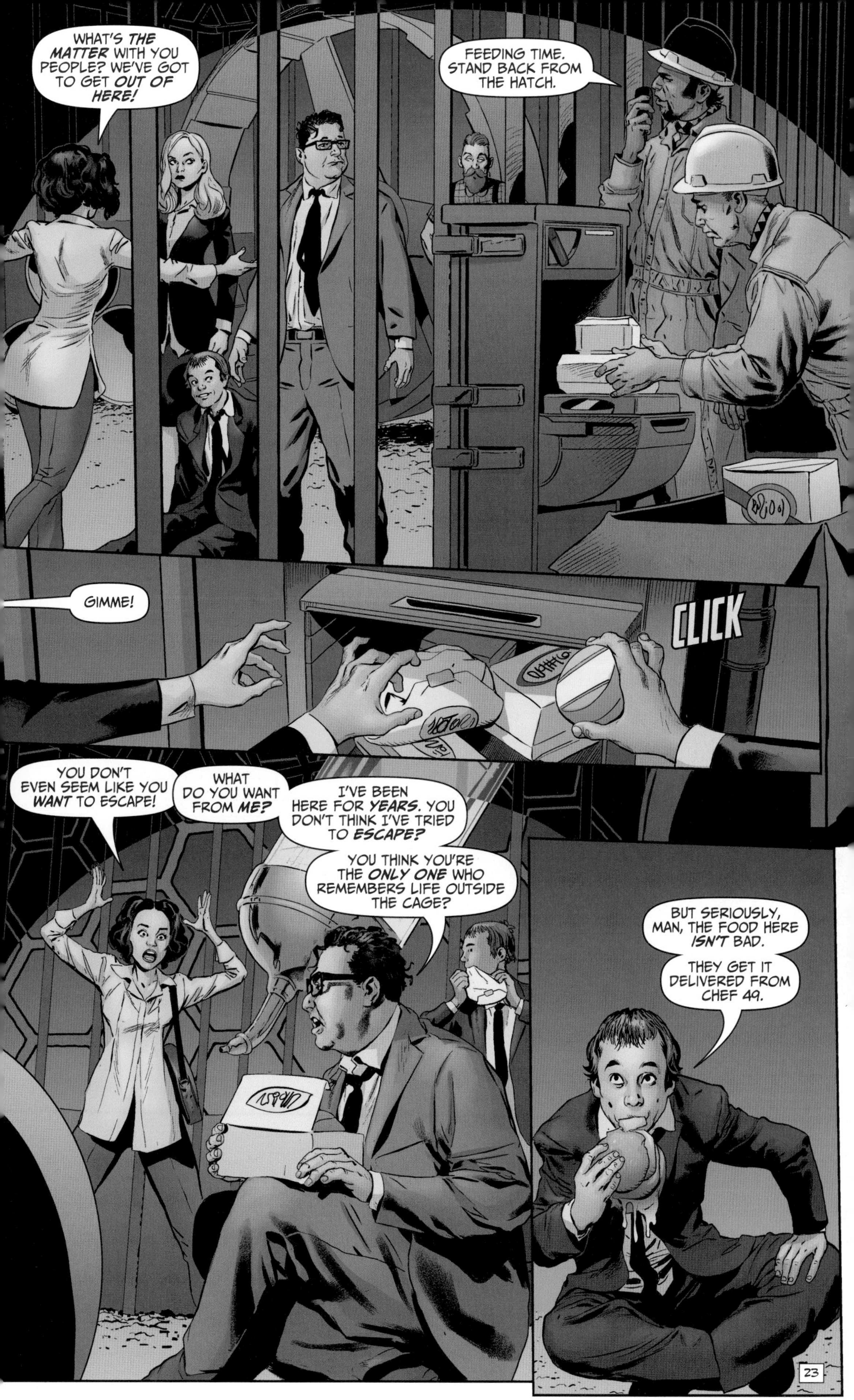
WHAT'S THE MATTER WITH YOU PEOPLE? WE'VE GOT TO GET OUT OF HERE!
FEEDING TIME. STAND BACK FROM THE HATCH.
GIMME!
CLICK
YOU DON'T EVEN SEEM LIKE YOU WANT TO ESCAPE!
WHAT DO YOU WANT FROM ME?
I'VE BEEN HERE FOR YEARS. YOU DON'T THINK I'VE TRIED TO ESCAPE?
YOU THINK YOU'RE THE ONLY ONE WHO REMEMBERS LIFE OUTSIDE THE CAGE?
BUT SERIOUSLY, MAN, THE FOOD HERE ISN'T BAD.
THEY GET IT DELIVERED FROM CHEF 49.

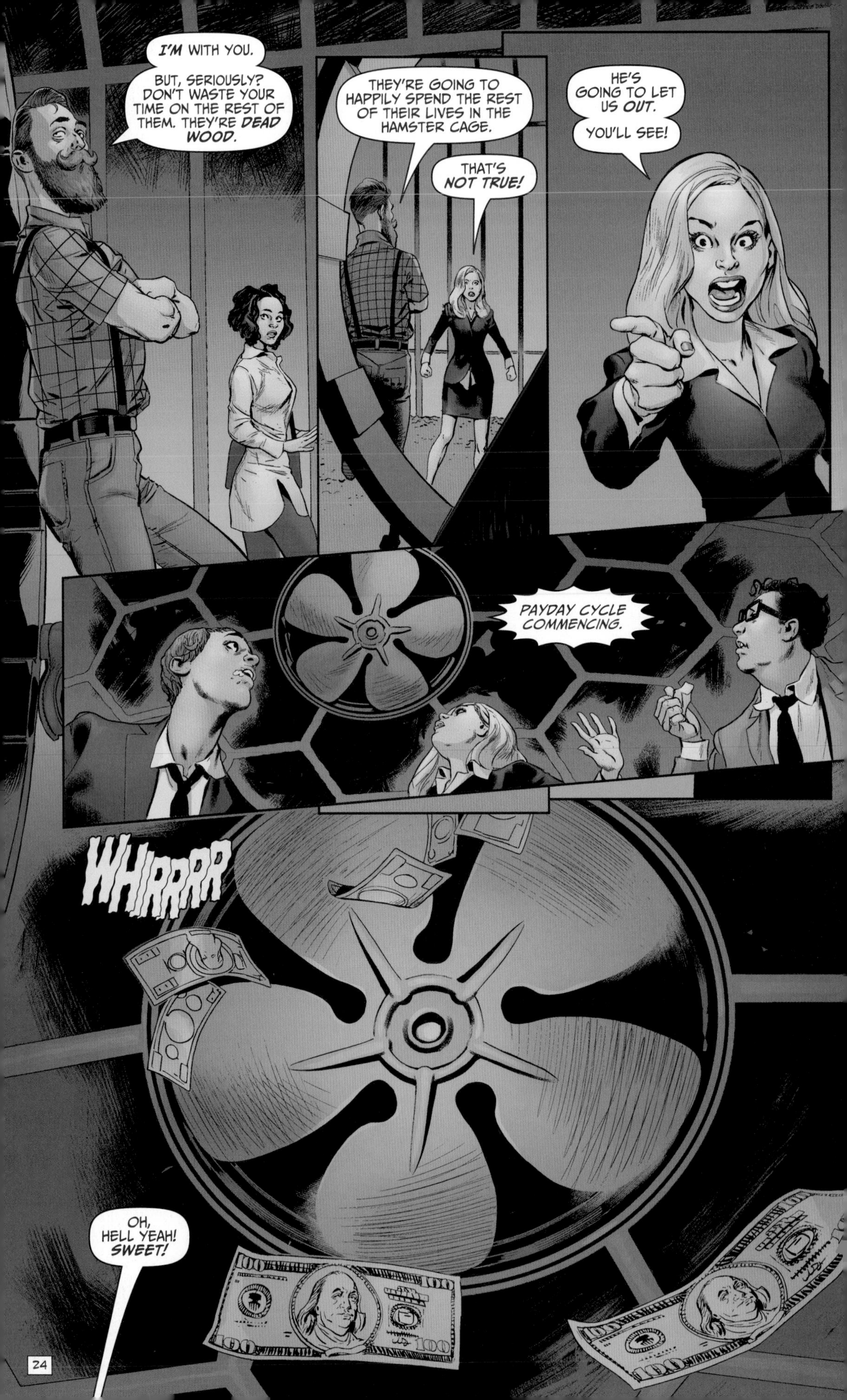
I'M WITH YOU.
BUT, SERIOUSLY? DON'T WASTE YOUR TIME ON THE REST OF THEM. THEY'RE DEAD WOOD.
THEY'RE GOING TO HAPPILY SPEND THE REST OF THEIR LIVES IN THE HAMSTER CAGE.
THAT'S NOT TRUE!
HE'S GOING TO LET US OUT.
YOU'LL SEE!
PAYDAY CYCLE COMMENCING.
WHIRRRR
OH, HELL YEAH! SWEET!

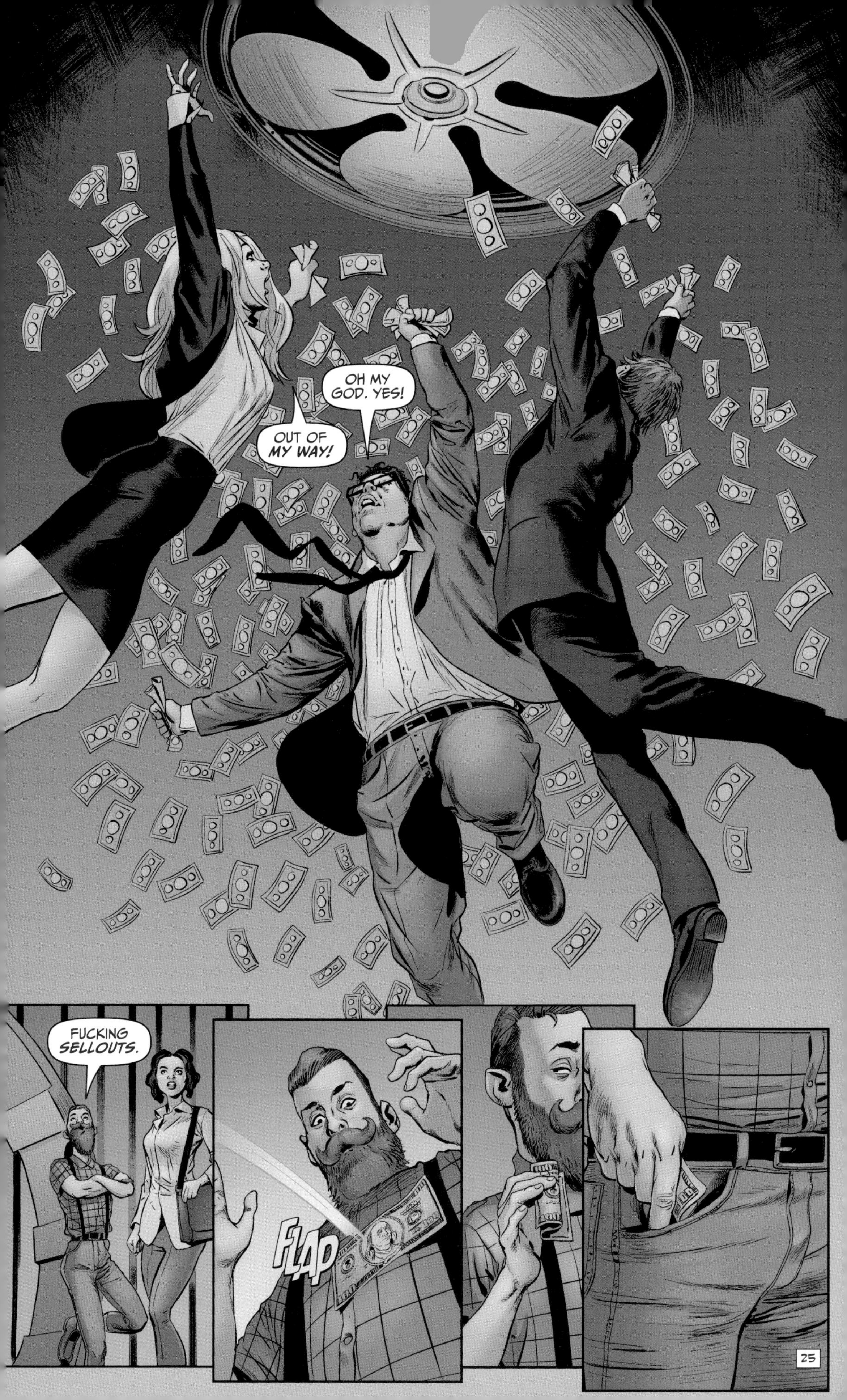
OH MY GOD. YES!
OUT OF MY WAY!
FUCKING SELLOUTS.
FLAP

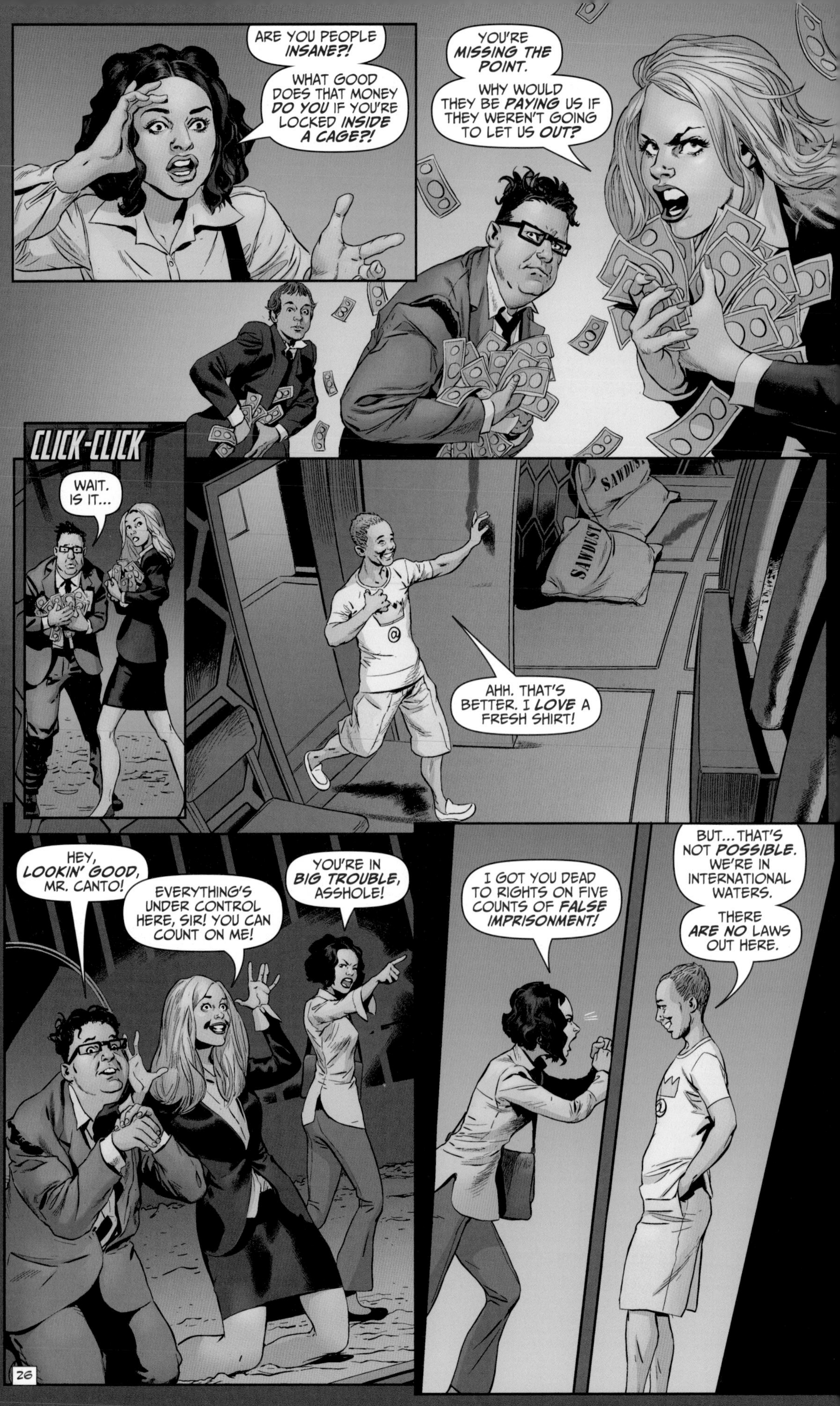

ARE YOU PEOPLE INSANE?!
WHAT GOOD DOES THAT MONEY DO YOU IF YOU'RE LOCKED INSIDE A CAGE?!
YOU'RE MISSING THE POINT.
WHY WOULD THEY BE PAYING US IF THEY WEREN'T GOING TO LET US OUT?
CLICK-CLICK
WAIT. IS IT...
SAWDUST
SAWDUST
AHH. THAT'S BETTER. I LOVE A FRESH SHIRT!
HEY, LOOKIN' GOOD, MR. CANTO!
EVERYTHING'S UNDER CONTROL HERE, SIR! YOU CAN COUNT ON ME!
YOU'RE IN BIG TROUBLE, ASSHOLE!
I GOT YOU DEAD TO RIGHTS ON FIVE COUNTS OF FALSE IMPRISONMENT!
BUT... THAT'S NOT POSSIBLE. WE'RE IN INTERNATIONAL WATERS.
THERE ARE NO LAWS OUT HERE.

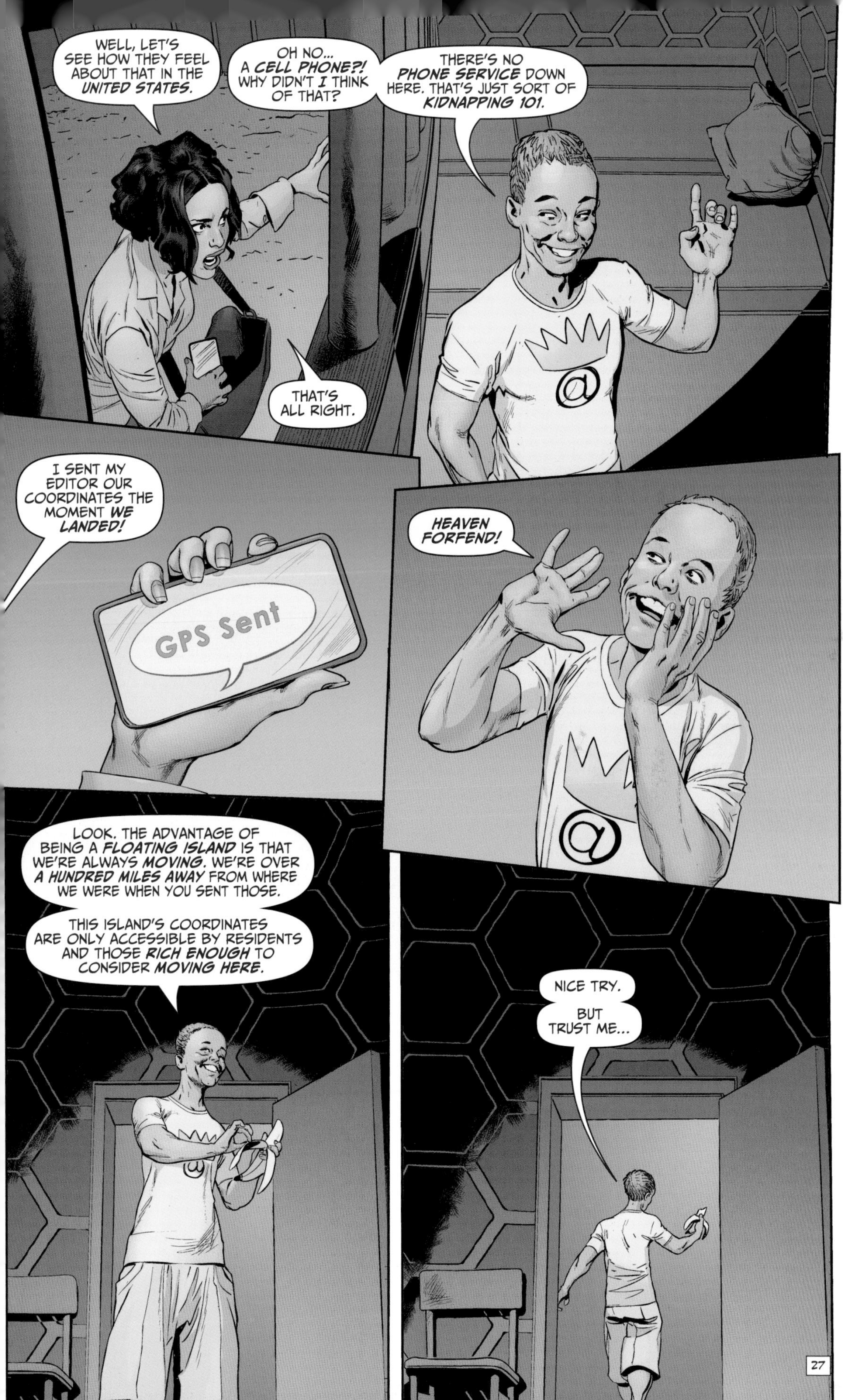

WELL, LET'S SEE HOW THEY FEEL ABOUT THAT IN THE UNITED STATES.
OH NO... A CELL PHONE?! WHY DIDN'T I THINK OF THAT?
THERE'S NO PHONE SERVICE DOWN HERE. THAT'S JUST SORT OF KIDNAPPING 101.
THAT'S ALL RIGHT.
I SENT MY EDITOR OUR COORDINATES THE MOMENT WE LANDED!
GPS Sent
HEAVEN FORFEND!
LOOK. THE ADVANTAGE OF BEING A FLOATING ISLAND IS THAT WE'RE ALWAYS MOVING. WE'RE OVER A HUNDRED MILES AWAY FROM WHERE WE WERE WHEN YOU SENT THOSE.
THIS ISLAND'S COORDINATES ARE ONLY ACCESSIBLE BY RESIDENTS AND THOSE RICH ENOUGH TO CONSIDER MOVING HERE.
NICE TRY.
BUT TRUST ME...

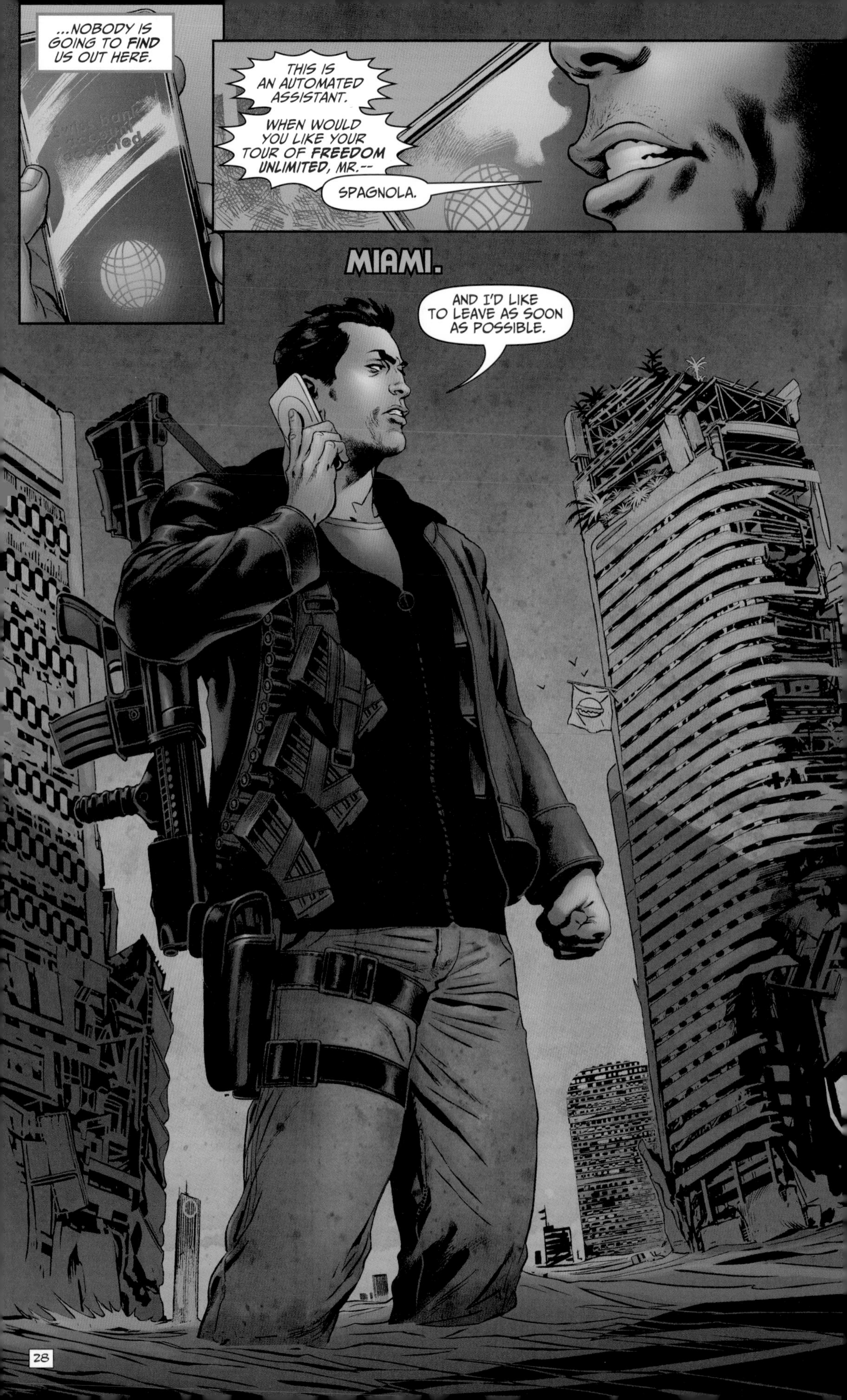
...NOBODY IS GOING TO FIND US OUT HERE.
THIS IS AN AUTOMATED ASSISTANT.
WHEN WOULD YOU LIKE YOUR TOUR OF FREEDOM UNLIMITED, MR.--
SPAGNOLA.
MIAMI.
AND I'D LIKE TO LEAVE AS SOON AS POSSIBLE.

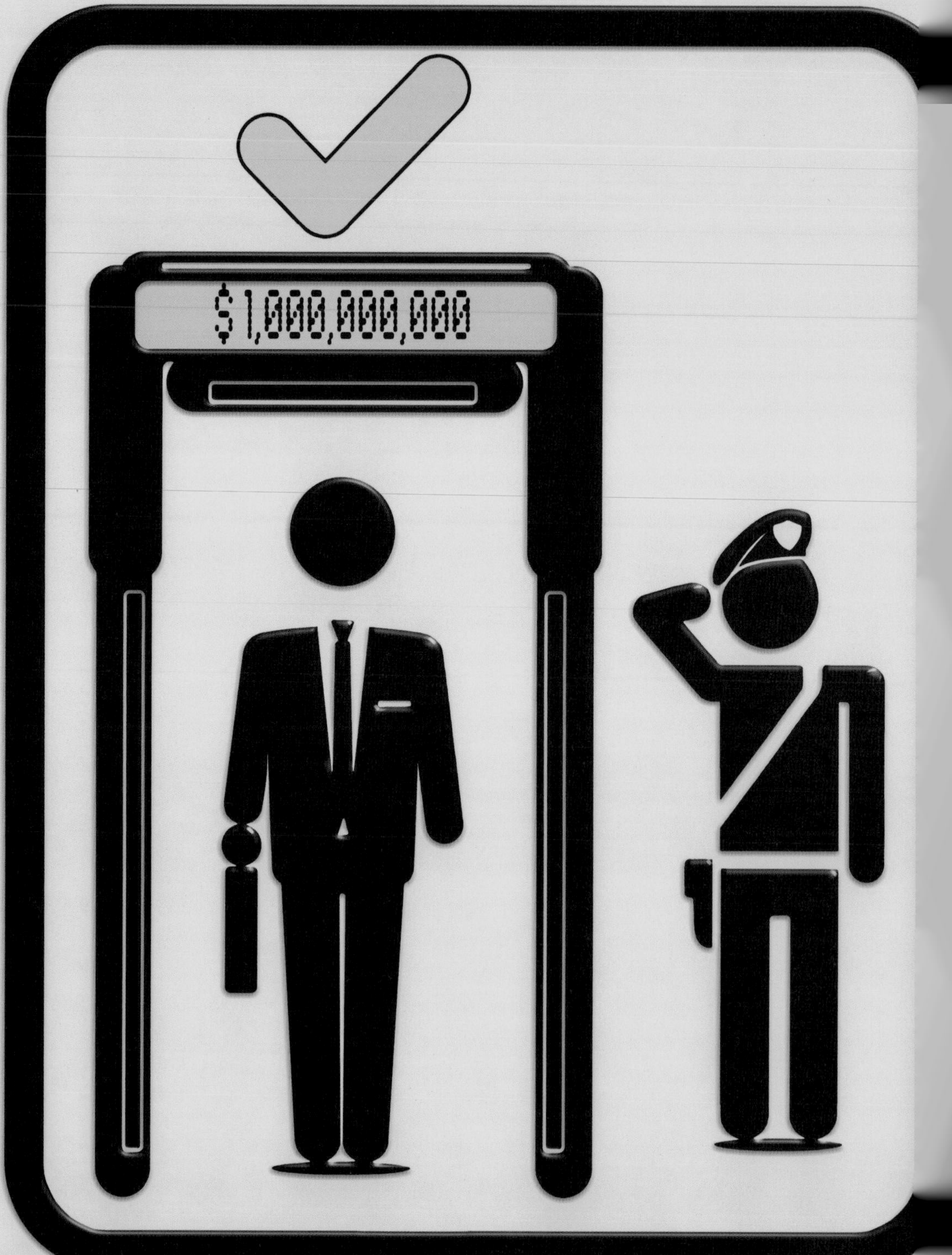
$1,000,000,000

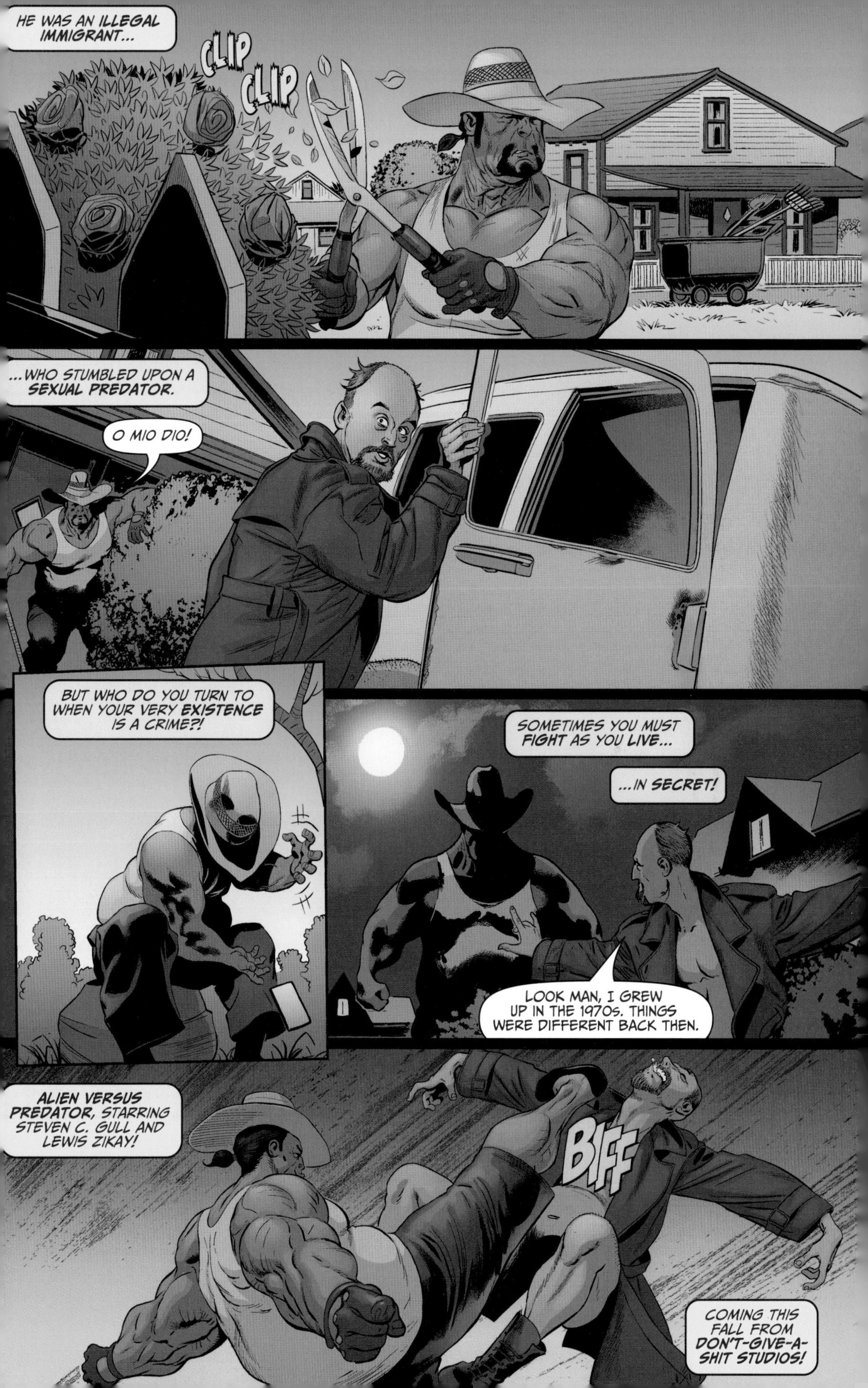
HE WAS AN ILLEGAL IMMIGRANT...
CLIP CLIP
...WHO STUMBLED UPON A SEXUAL PREDATOR.
O MIO DIO!
BUT WHO DO YOU TURN TO WHEN YOUR VERY EXISTENCE IS A CRIME?!
SOMETIMES YOU MUST FIGHT AS YOU LIVE...
...IN SECRET!
LOOK MAN, I GREW UP IN THE 1970s. THINGS WERE DIFFERENT BACK THEN.
ALIEN VERSUS PREDATOR, STARRING STEVEN C. GULL AND LEWIS ZIKAY!
BIFF
COMING THIS FALL FROM DON'T-GIVE-A-SHIT STUDIOS!

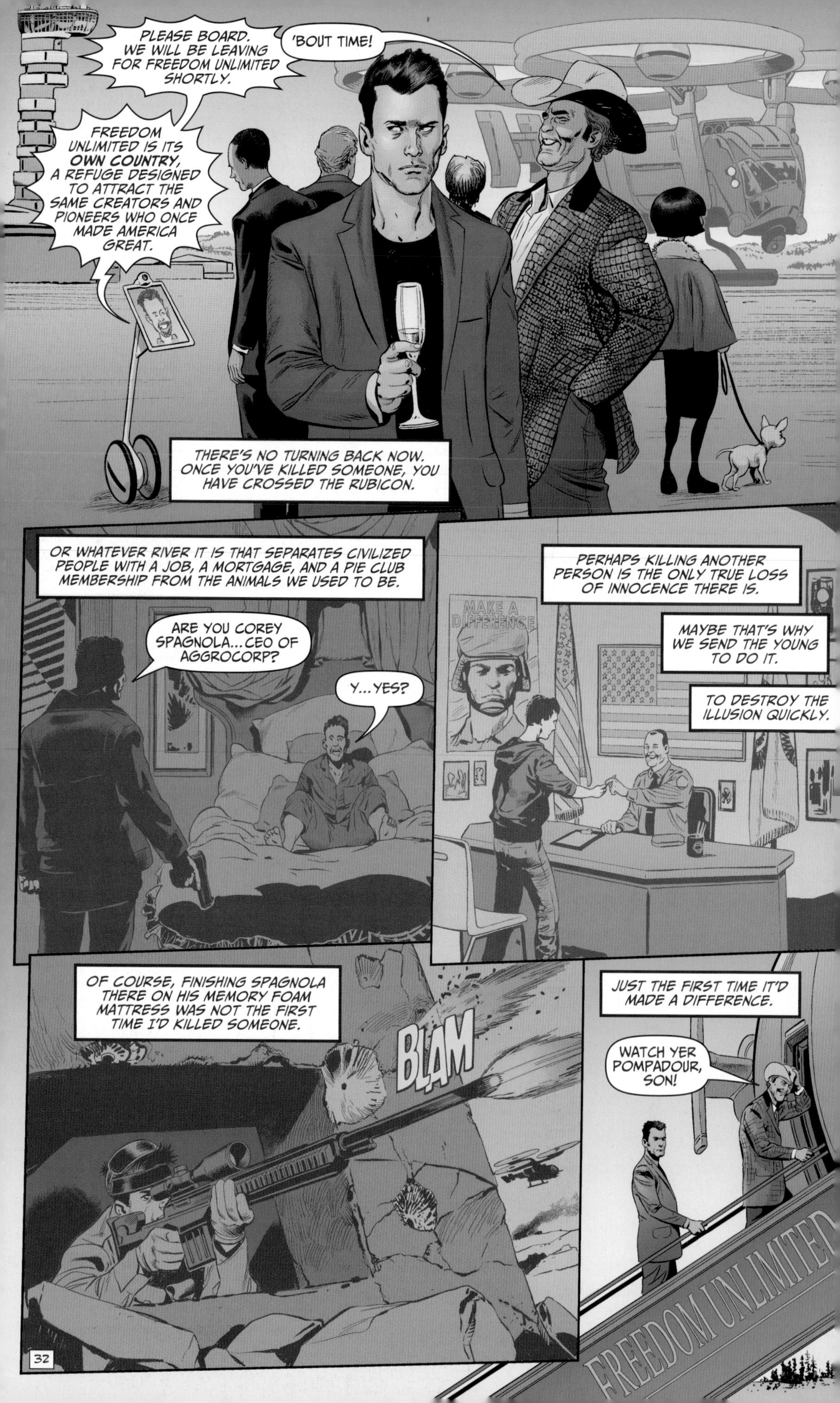
PLEASE BOARD. WE WILL BE LEAVING FOR FREEDOM UNLIMITED SHORTLY.
'BOUT TIME!
FREEDOM UNLIMITED IS ITS **OWN COUNTRY**, A REFUGE DESIGNED TO ATTRACT THE SAME CREATORS AND PIONEERS WHO ONCE MADE AMERICA GREAT.
THERE'S NO TURNING BACK NOW. ONCE YOU'VE KILLED SOMEONE, YOU HAVE CROSSED THE RUBICON.
OR WHATEVER RIVER IT IS THAT SEPARATES CIVILIZED PEOPLE WITH A JOB, A MORTGAGE, AND A PIE CLUB MEMBERSHIP FROM THE ANIMALS WE USED TO BE.
ARE YOU COREY SPAGNOLA...CEO OF AGGROCORP?
Y...YES?
PERHAPS KILLING ANOTHER PERSON IS THE ONLY TRUE LOSS OF INNOCENCE THERE IS.
MAKE A DIFFERENCE
MAYBE THAT'S WHY WE SEND THE YOUNG TO DO IT.
TO DESTROY THE ILLUSION QUICKLY.
OF COURSE, FINISHING SPAGNOLA THERE ON HIS MEMORY FOAM MATTRESS WAS NOT THE FIRST TIME I'D KILLED SOMEONE.
BLAM
JUST THE FIRST TIME IT'D MADE A DIFFERENCE.
WATCH YER POMPADOUR, SON!
FREEDOM UNLIMITED

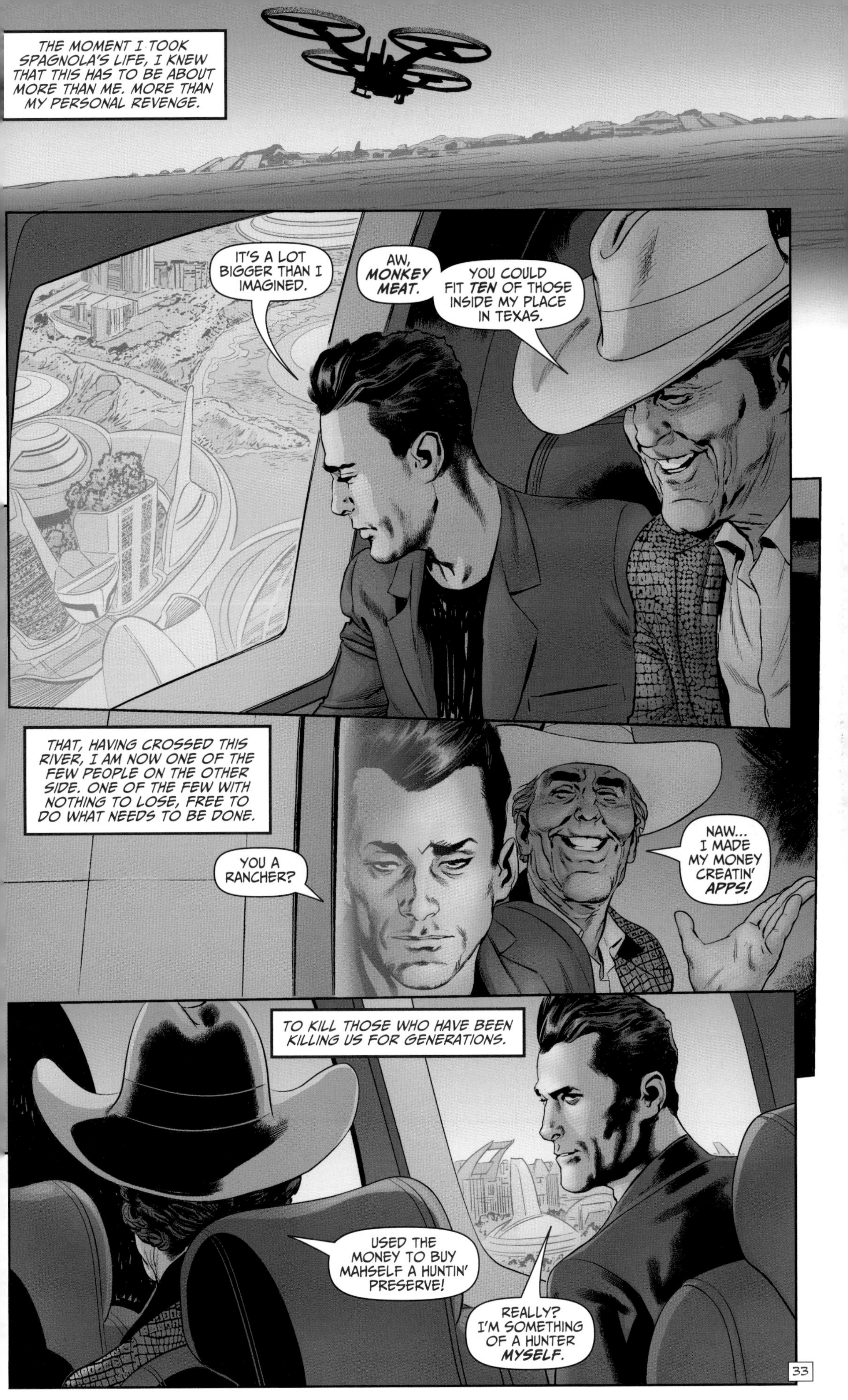
THE MOMENT I TOOK SPAGNOLA'S LIFE, I KNEW THAT THIS HAS TO BE ABOUT MORE THAN ME. MORE THAN MY PERSONAL REVENGE.
IT'S A LOT BIGGER THAN I IMAGINED.
AW, MONKEY MEAT.
YOU COULD FIT TEN OF THOSE INSIDE MY PLACE IN TEXAS.
THAT, HAVING CROSSED THIS RIVER, I AM NOW ONE OF THE FEW PEOPLE ON THE OTHER SIDE. ONE OF THE FEW WITH NOTHING TO LOSE, FREE TO DO WHAT NEEDS TO BE DONE.
YOU A RANCHER?
NAW... I MADE MY MONEY CREATIN' APPS!
TO KILL THOSE WHO HAVE BEEN KILLING US FOR GENERATIONS.
USED THE MONEY TO BUY MAHSELF A HUNTIN' PRESERVE!
REALLY? I'M SOMETHING OF A HUNTER MYSELF.

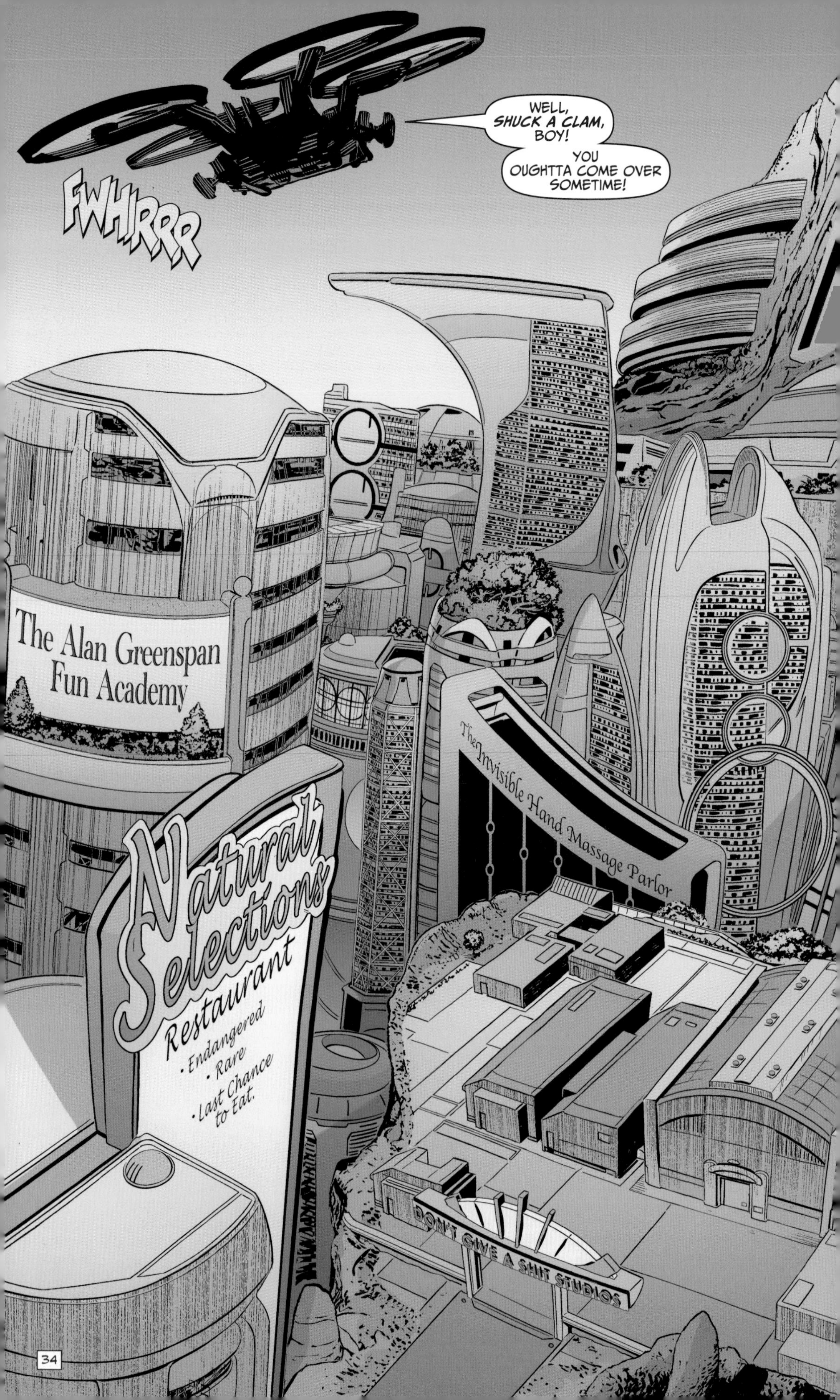
WELL, SHUCK A CLAM, BOY!
YOU OUGHTTA COME OVER SOMETIME!
FWHIRRR
The Alan Greenspan Fun Academy
The Invisible Hand Massage Parlor
Natural Selections Restaurant
· Endangered
· Rare
· Last Chance to Eat.
DON'T GIVE A SHIT STUDIOS

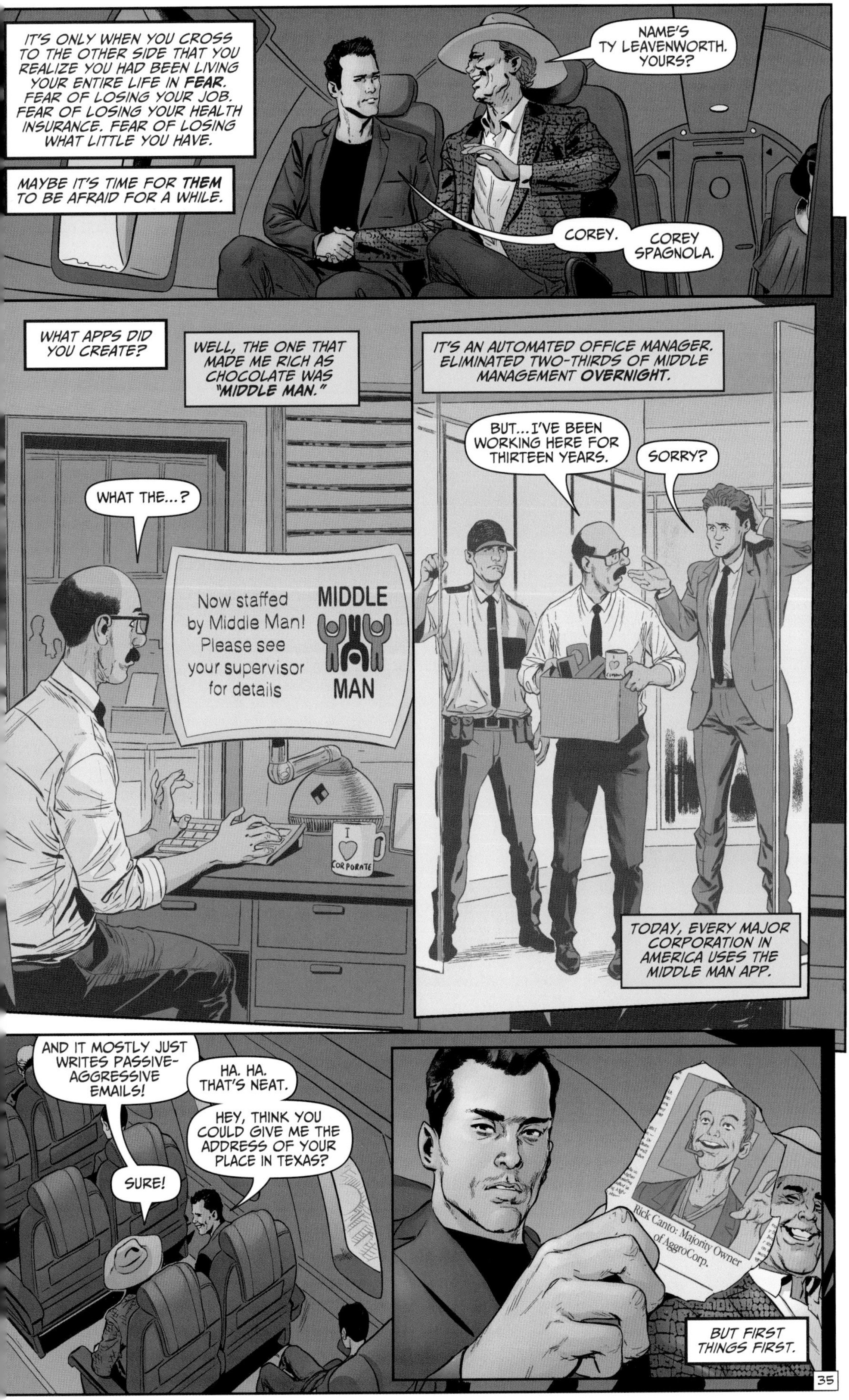
IT'S ONLY WHEN YOU CROSS TO THE OTHER SIDE THAT YOU REALIZE YOU HAD BEEN LIVING YOUR ENTIRE LIFE IN FEAR. FEAR OF LOSING YOUR JOB. FEAR OF LOSING YOUR HEALTH INSURANCE. FEAR OF LOSING WHAT LITTLE YOU HAVE.
MAYBE IT'S TIME FOR THEM TO BE AFRAID FOR A WHILE.
NAME'S TY LEAVENWORTH. YOURS?
COREY.
COREY SPAGNOLA.
WHAT APPS DID YOU CREATE?
WELL, THE ONE THAT MADE ME RICH AS CHOCOLATE WAS "MIDDLE MAN."
WHAT THE...?
Now staffed by Middle Man! Please see your supervisor for details
MIDDLE MAN
I CORPORATE
IT'S AN AUTOMATED OFFICE MANAGER. ELIMINATED TWO-THIRDS OF MIDDLE MANAGEMENT OVERNIGHT.
BUT... I'VE BEEN WORKING HERE FOR THIRTEEN YEARS.
SORRY?
TODAY, EVERY MAJOR CORPORATION IN AMERICA USES THE MIDDLE MAN APP.
AND IT MOSTLY JUST WRITES PASSIVE-AGGRESSIVE EMAILS!
HA. HA. THAT'S NEAT.
HEY, THINK YOU COULD GIVE ME THE ADDRESS OF YOUR PLACE IN TEXAS?
SURE!
Rick Canto: Majority Owner of AggroCorp.
BUT FIRST THINGS FIRST.

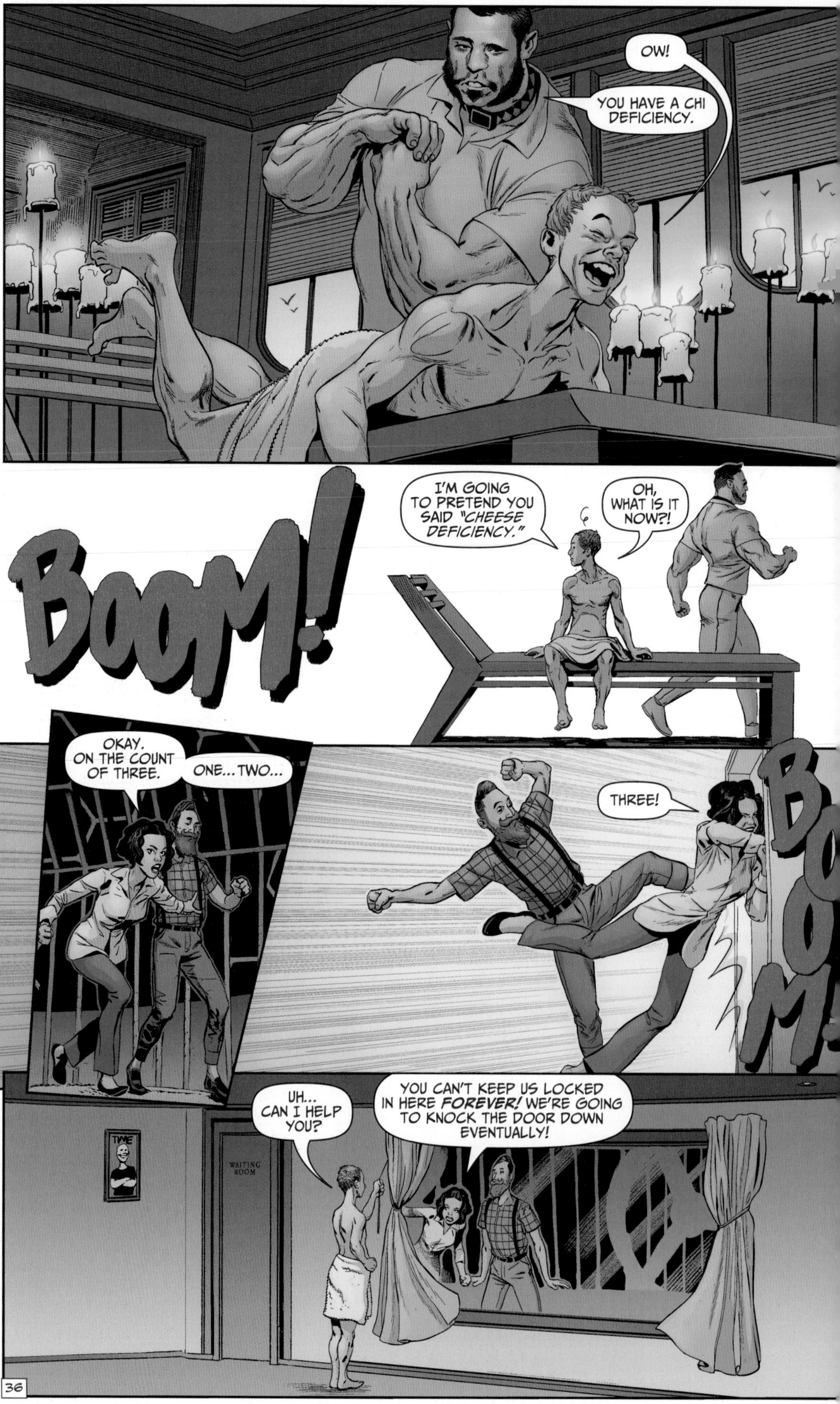
OW!
YOU HAVE A CHI DEFICIENCY.
BOOM!
I'M GOING TO PRETEND YOU SAID "CHEESE DEFICIENCY."
OH, WHAT IS IT NOW?!
OKAY. ON THE COUNT OF THREE.
ONE... TWO...
THREE!
BOOM!
UH... CAN I HELP YOU?
YOU CAN'T KEEP US LOCKED IN HERE FOREVER! WE'RE GOING TO KNOCK THE DOOR DOWN EVENTUALLY!
WAITING ROOM

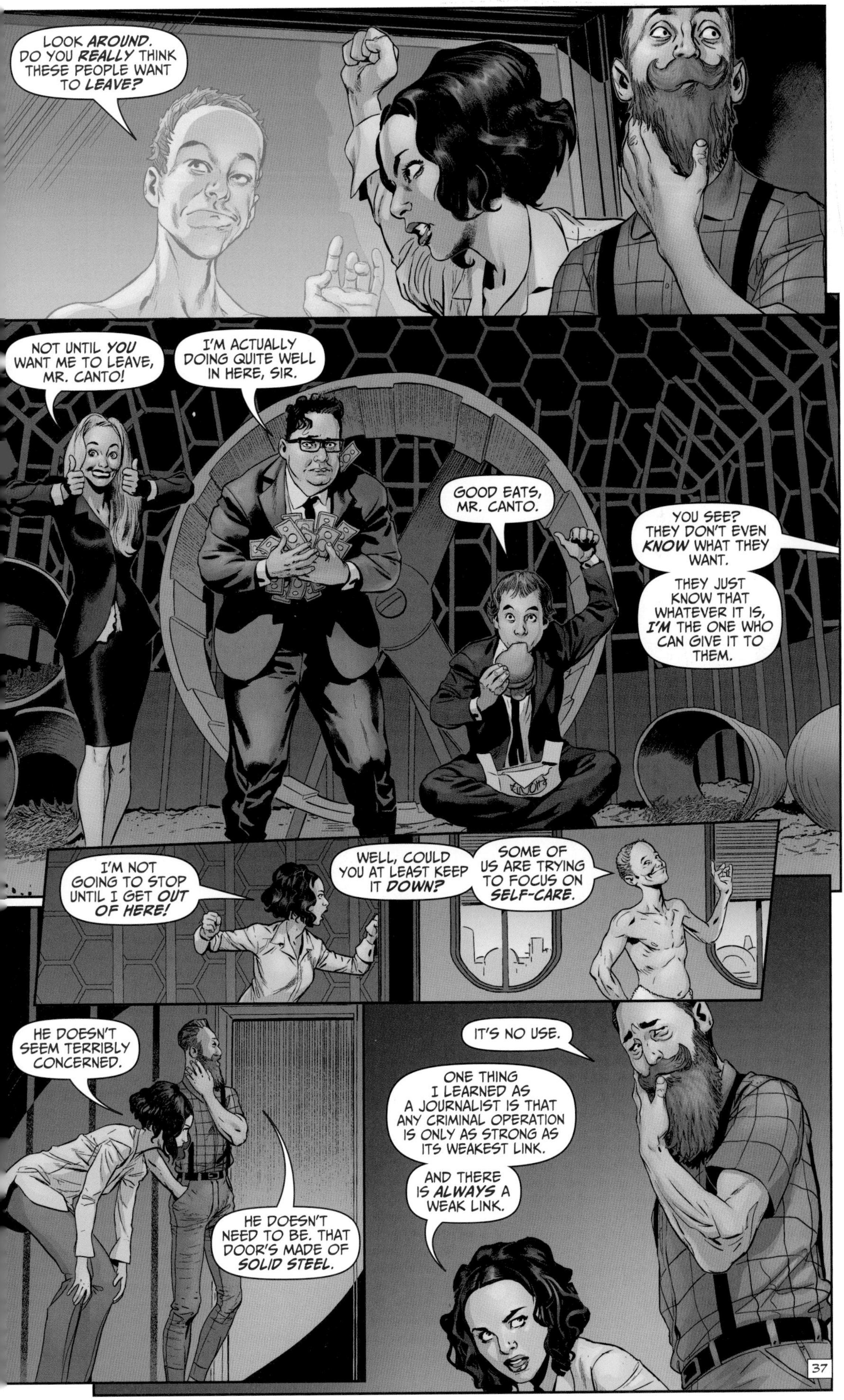
LOOK AROUND. DO YOU REALLY THINK THESE PEOPLE WANT TO LEAVE?
NOT UNTIL YOU WANT ME TO LEAVE, MR. CANTO!
I'M ACTUALLY DOING QUITE WELL IN HERE, SIR.
GOOD EATS, MR. CANTO.
YOU SEE? THEY DON'T EVEN KNOW WHAT THEY WANT.
THEY JUST KNOW THAT WHATEVER IT IS, I'M THE ONE WHO CAN GIVE IT TO THEM.
I'M NOT GOING TO STOP UNTIL I GET OUT OF HERE!
WELL, COULD YOU AT LEAST KEEP IT DOWN?
SOME OF US ARE TRYING TO FOCUS ON SELF-CARE.
HE DOESN'T SEEM TERRIBLY CONCERNED.
HE DOESN'T NEED TO BE. THAT DOOR'S MADE OF SOLID STEEL.
IT'S NO USE.
ONE THING I LEARNED AS A JOURNALIST IS THAT ANY CRIMINAL OPERATION IS ONLY AS STRONG AS ITS WEAKEST LINK.
AND THERE IS ALWAYS A WEAK LINK.

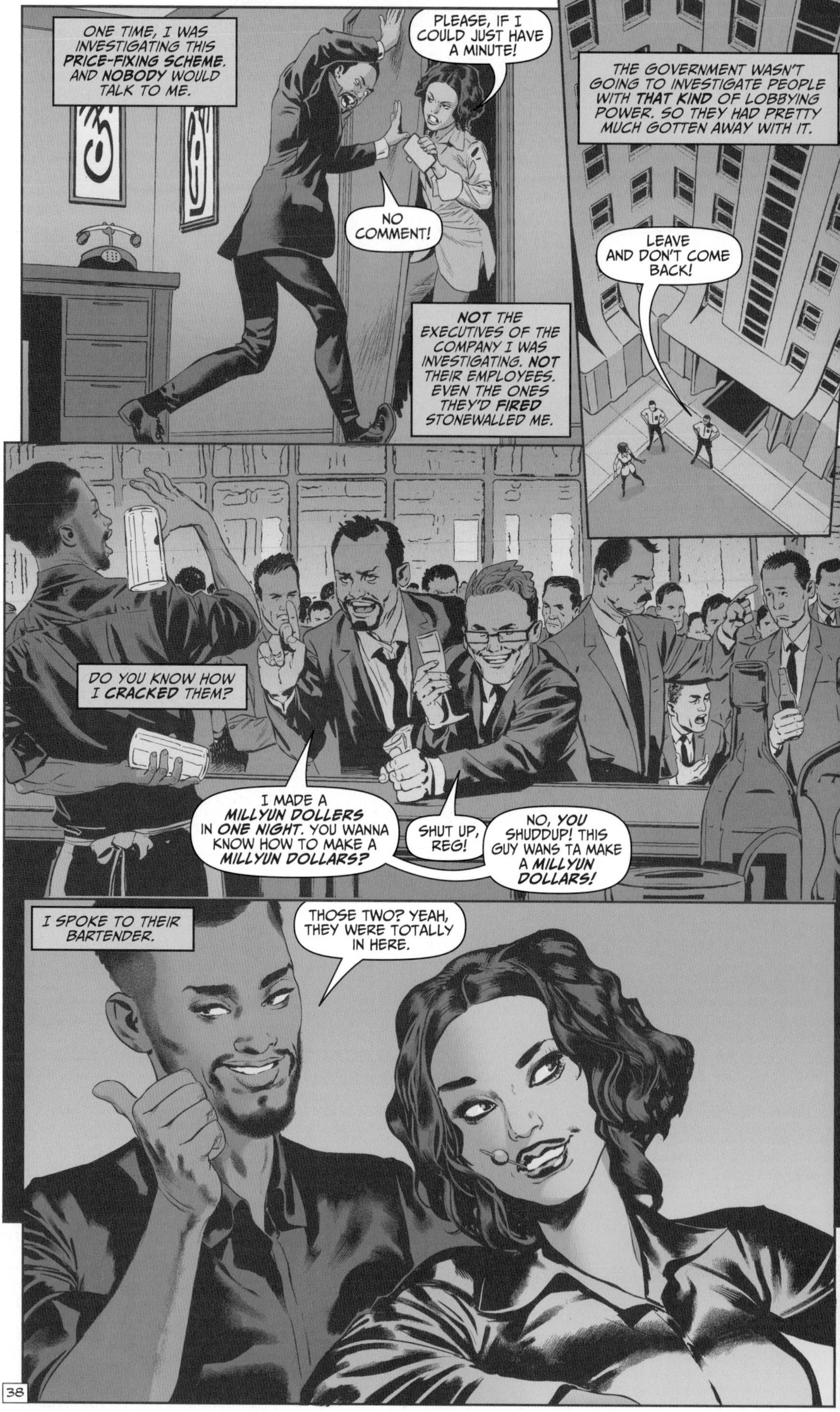

ONE TIME, I WAS INVESTIGATING THIS PRICE-FIXING SCHEME. AND NOBODY WOULD TALK TO ME.
PLEASE, IF I COULD JUST HAVE A MINUTE!
NO COMMENT!
NOT THE EXECUTIVES OF THE COMPANY I WAS INVESTIGATING. NOT THEIR EMPLOYEES. EVEN THE ONES THEY'D FIRED STONEWALLED ME.
THE GOVERNMENT WASN'T GOING TO INVESTIGATE PEOPLE WITH THAT KIND OF LOBBYING POWER. SO THEY HAD PRETTY MUCH GOTTEN AWAY WITH IT.
LEAVE AND DON'T COME BACK!
DO YOU KNOW HOW I CRACKED THEM?
I MADE A MILLYUN DOLLERS IN ONE NIGHT. YOU WANNA KNOW HOW TO MAKE A MILLYUN DOLLARS?
SHUT UP, REG!
NO, YOU SHUDDUP! THIS GUY WANS TA MAKE A MILLYUN DOLLARS!
I SPOKE TO THEIR BARTENDER.
THOSE TWO? YEAH, THEY WERE TOTALLY IN HERE.

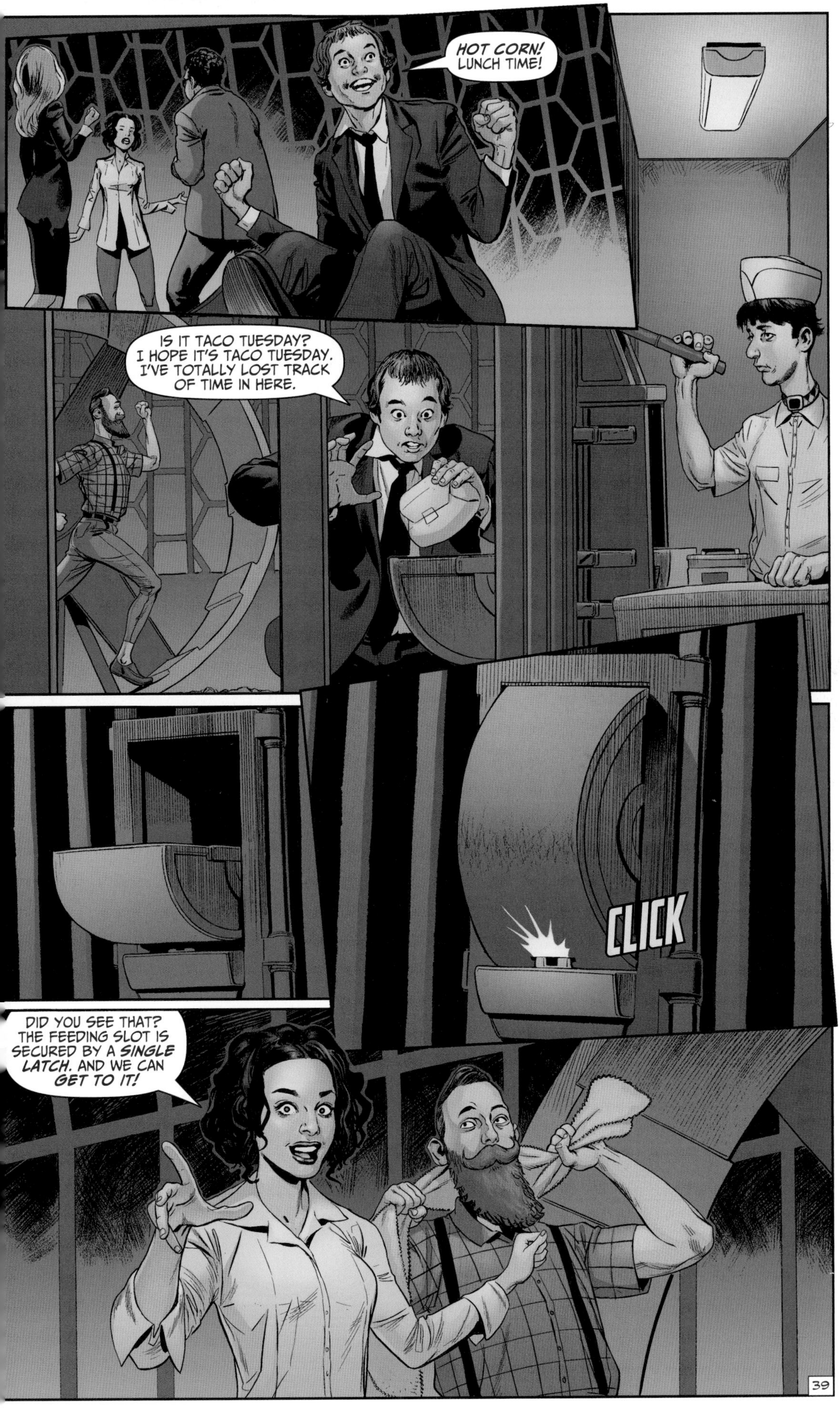
HOT CORN! LUNCH TIME!
IS IT TACO TUESDAY? I HOPE IT'S TACO TUESDAY. I'VE TOTALLY LOST TRACK OF TIME IN HERE.
CLICK
DID YOU SEE THAT? THE FEEDING SLOT IS SECURED BY A SINGLE LATCH. AND WE CAN GET TO IT!

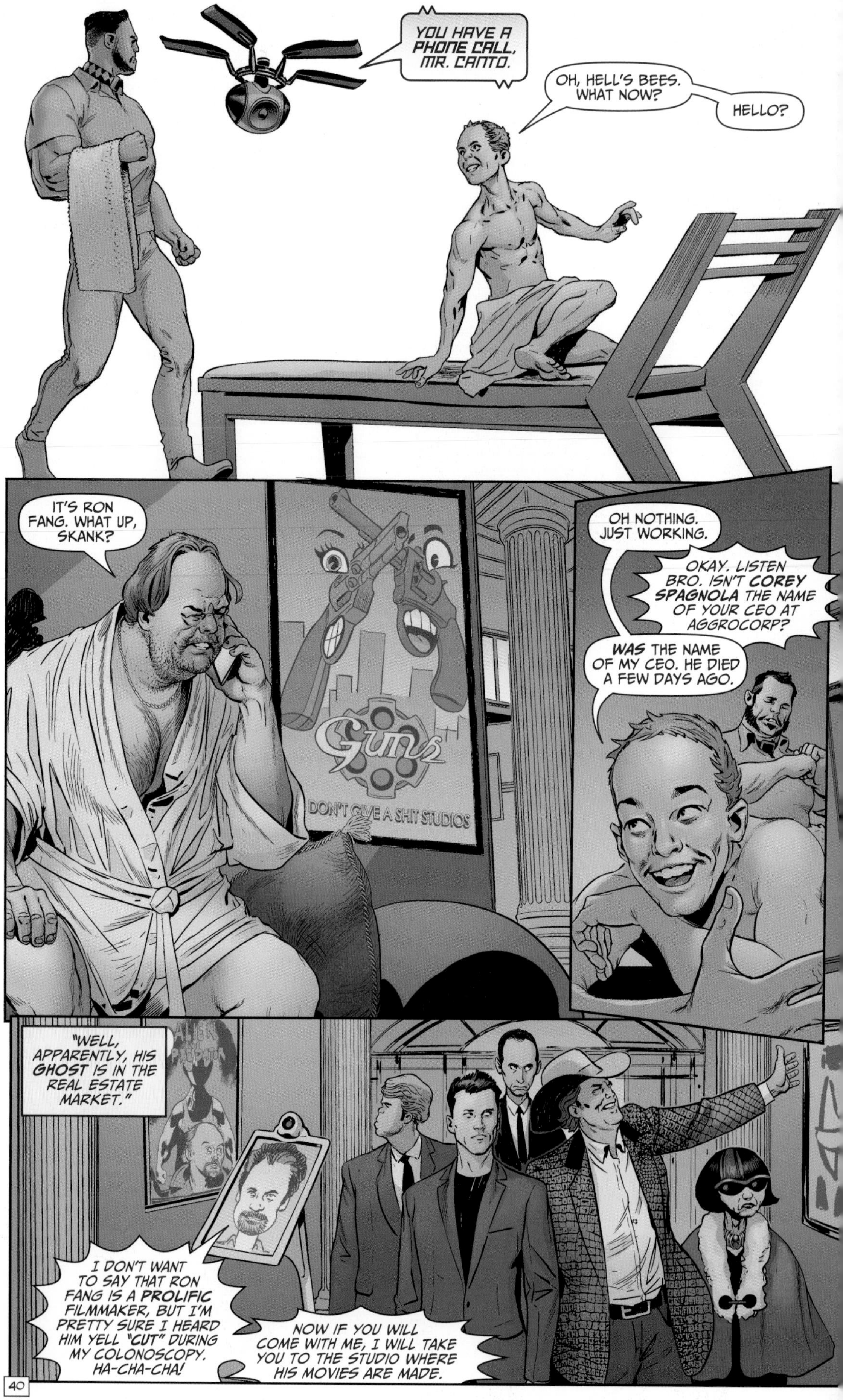
YOU HAVE A PHONE CALL, MR. CANTO.
OH, HELL'S BEES. WHAT NOW?
HELLO?
IT'S RON FANG. WHAT UP, SKANK?
Guns
DON'T GIVE A SHIT STUDIOS
OH NOTHING. JUST WORKING.
OKAY. LISTEN BRO. ISN'T COREY SPAGNOLA THE NAME OF YOUR CEO AT AGGROCORP?
WAS THE NAME OF MY CEO. HE DIED A FEW DAYS AGO.
"WELL, APPARENTLY, HIS GHOST IS IN THE REAL ESTATE MARKET."
I DON'T WANT TO SAY THAT RON FANG IS A PROLIFIC FILMMAKER, BUT I'M PRETTY SURE I HEARD HIM YELL "CUT" DURING MY COLONOSCOPY. HA-CHA-CHA!
NOW IF YOU WILL COME WITH ME, I WILL TAKE YOU TO THE STUDIO WHERE HIS MOVIES ARE MADE.

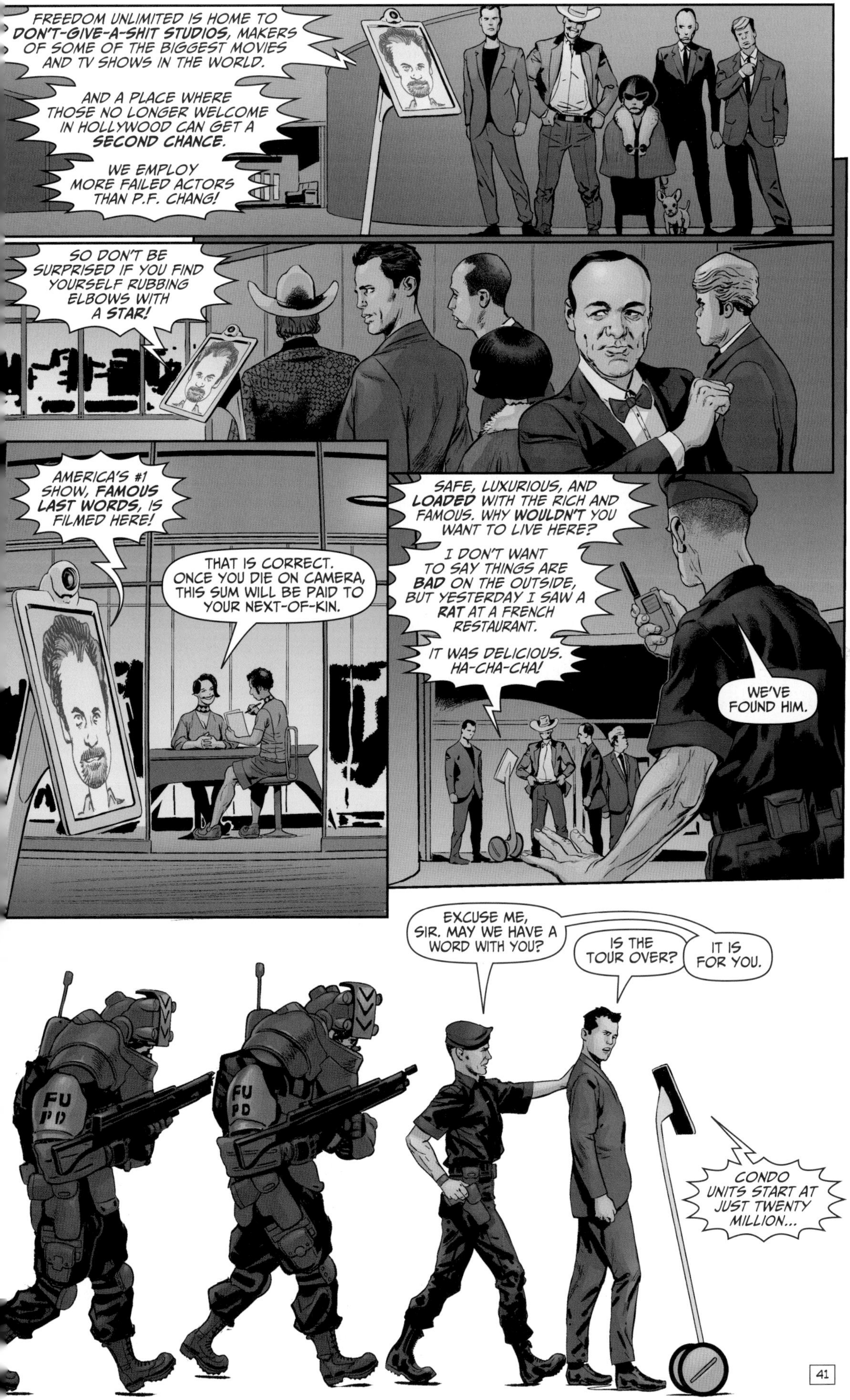
FREEDOM UNLIMITED IS HOME TO DON'T-GIVE-A-SHIT STUDIOS, MAKERS OF SOME OF THE BIGGEST MOVIES AND TV SHOWS IN THE WORLD.
AND A PLACE WHERE THOSE NO LONGER WELCOME IN HOLLYWOOD CAN GET A SECOND CHANCE.
WE EMPLOY MORE FAILED ACTORS THAN P.F. CHANG!
SO DON'T BE SURPRISED IF YOU FIND YOURSELF RUBBING ELBOWS WITH A STAR!
AMERICA'S #1 SHOW, FAMOUS LAST WORDS, IS FILMED HERE!
THAT IS CORRECT. ONCE YOU DIE ON CAMERA, THIS SUM WILL BE PAID TO YOUR NEXT-OF-KIN.
SAFE, LUXURIOUS, AND LOADED WITH THE RICH AND FAMOUS. WHY WOULDN'T YOU WANT TO LIVE HERE?
I DON'T WANT TO SAY THINGS ARE BAD ON THE OUTSIDE, BUT YESTERDAY I SAW A RAT AT A FRENCH RESTAURANT.
IT WAS DELICIOUS. HA-CHA-CHA!
WE'VE FOUND HIM.
EXCUSE ME, SIR. MAY WE HAVE A WORD WITH YOU?
IS THE TOUR OVER?
IT IS FOR YOU.
FU PD
FU PD
CONDO UNITS START AT JUST TWENTY MILLION...

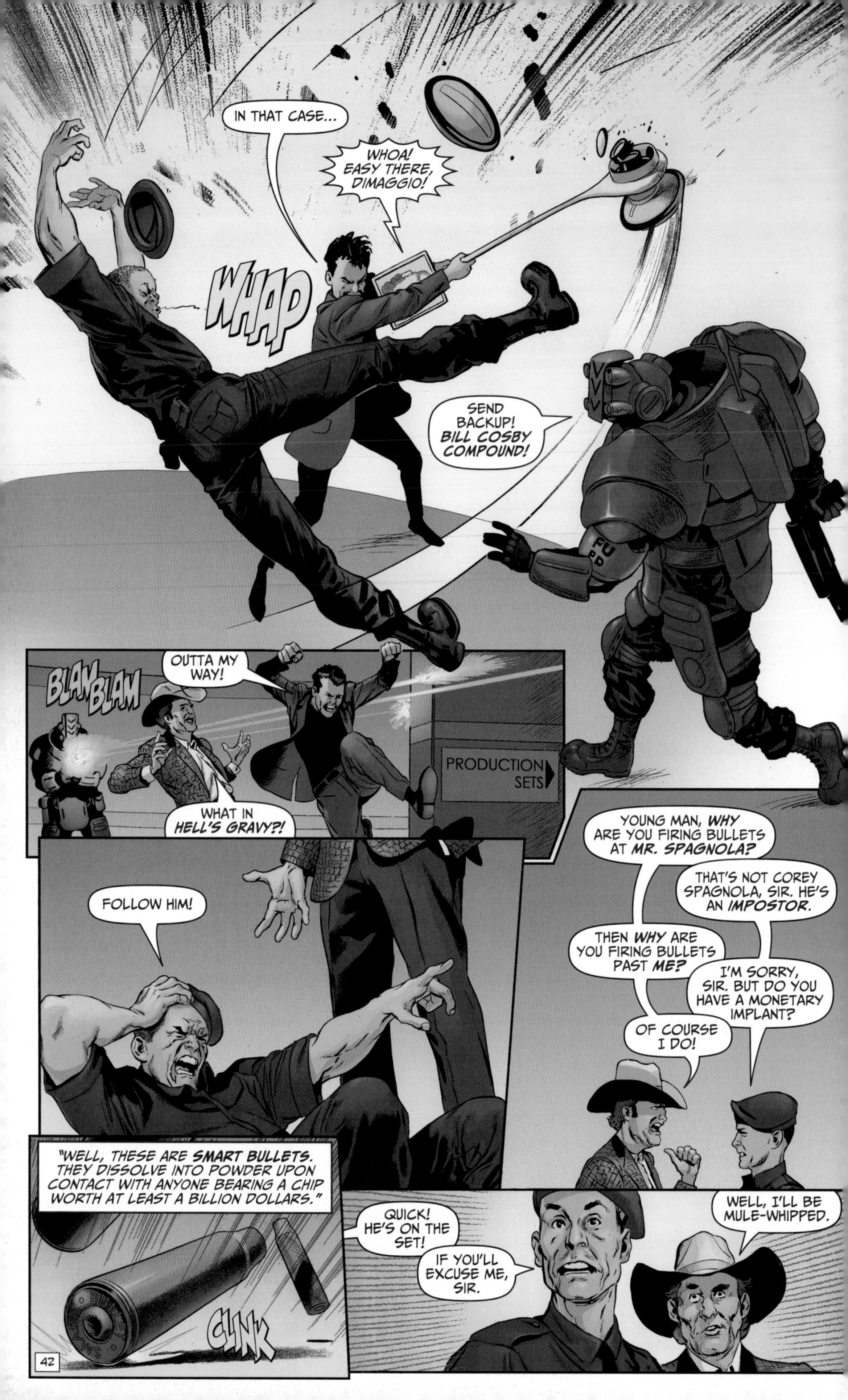

IN THAT CASE...
WHOA! EASY THERE, DIMAGGIO!
WHAP
SEND BACKUP! BILL COSBY COMPOUND!
FU PD
BLAM BLAM
OUTTA MY WAY!
PRODUCTION SETS
WHAT IN HELL'S GRAVY?!
YOUNG MAN, WHY ARE YOU FIRING BULLETS AT MR. SPAGNOLA?
THAT'S NOT COREY SPAGNOLA, SIR. HE'S AN IMPOSTOR.
THEN WHY ARE YOU FIRING BULLETS PAST ME?
I'M SORRY, SIR. BUT DO YOU HAVE A MONETARY IMPLANT?
OF COURSE I DO!
FOLLOW HIM!
"WELL, THESE ARE SMART BULLETS. THEY DISSOLVE INTO POWDER UPON CONTACT WITH ANYONE BEARING A CHIP WORTH AT LEAST A BILLION DOLLARS."
CLINK
QUICK! HE'S ON THE SET!
IF YOU'LL EXCUSE ME, SIR.
WELL, I'LL BE MULE-WHIPPED.

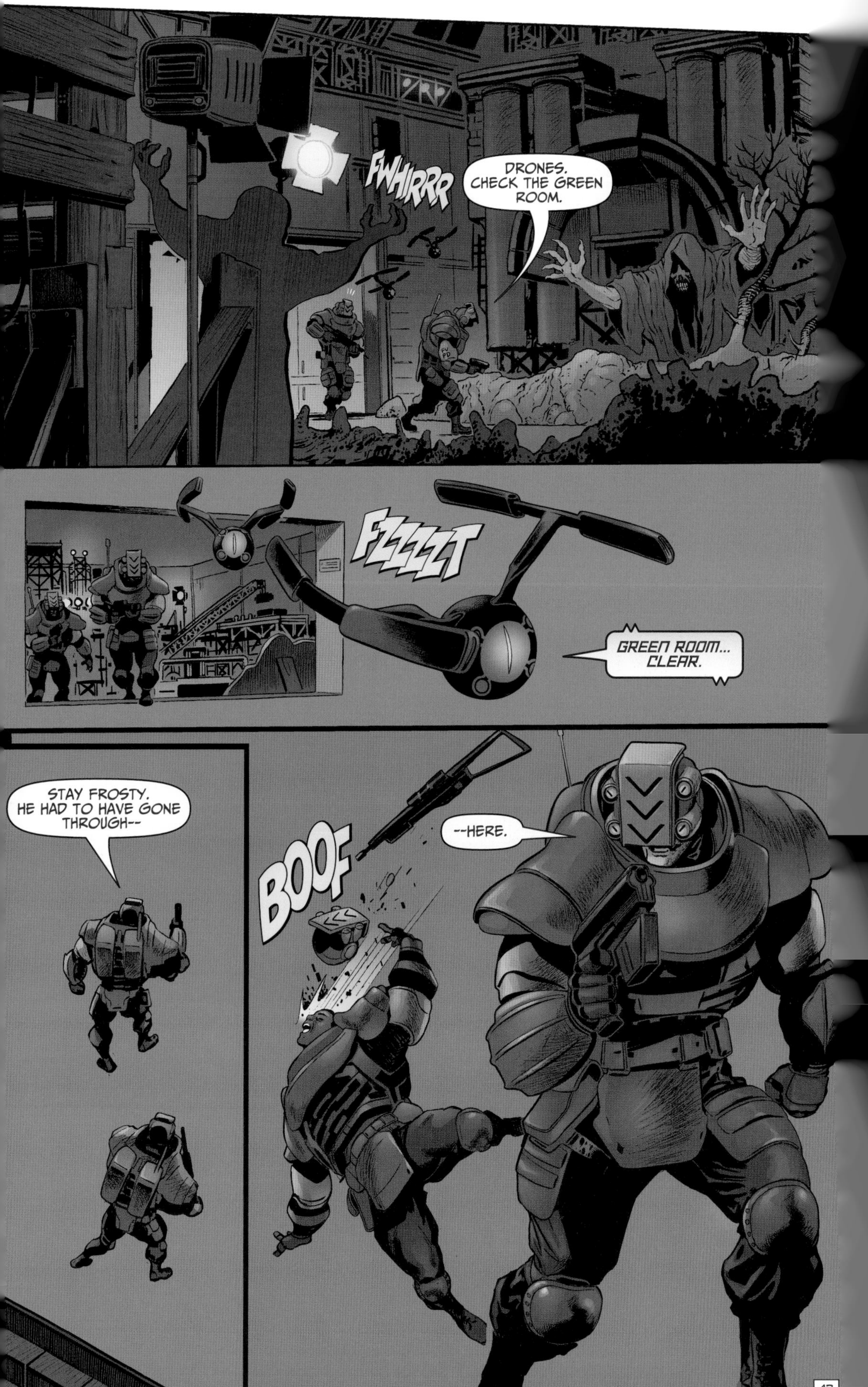
FWHIRRR
DRONES. CHECK THE GREEN ROOM.
FZZZZT
GREEN ROOM... CLEAR.
STAY FROSTY. HE HAD TO HAVE GONE THROUGH--
BOOF
--HERE.

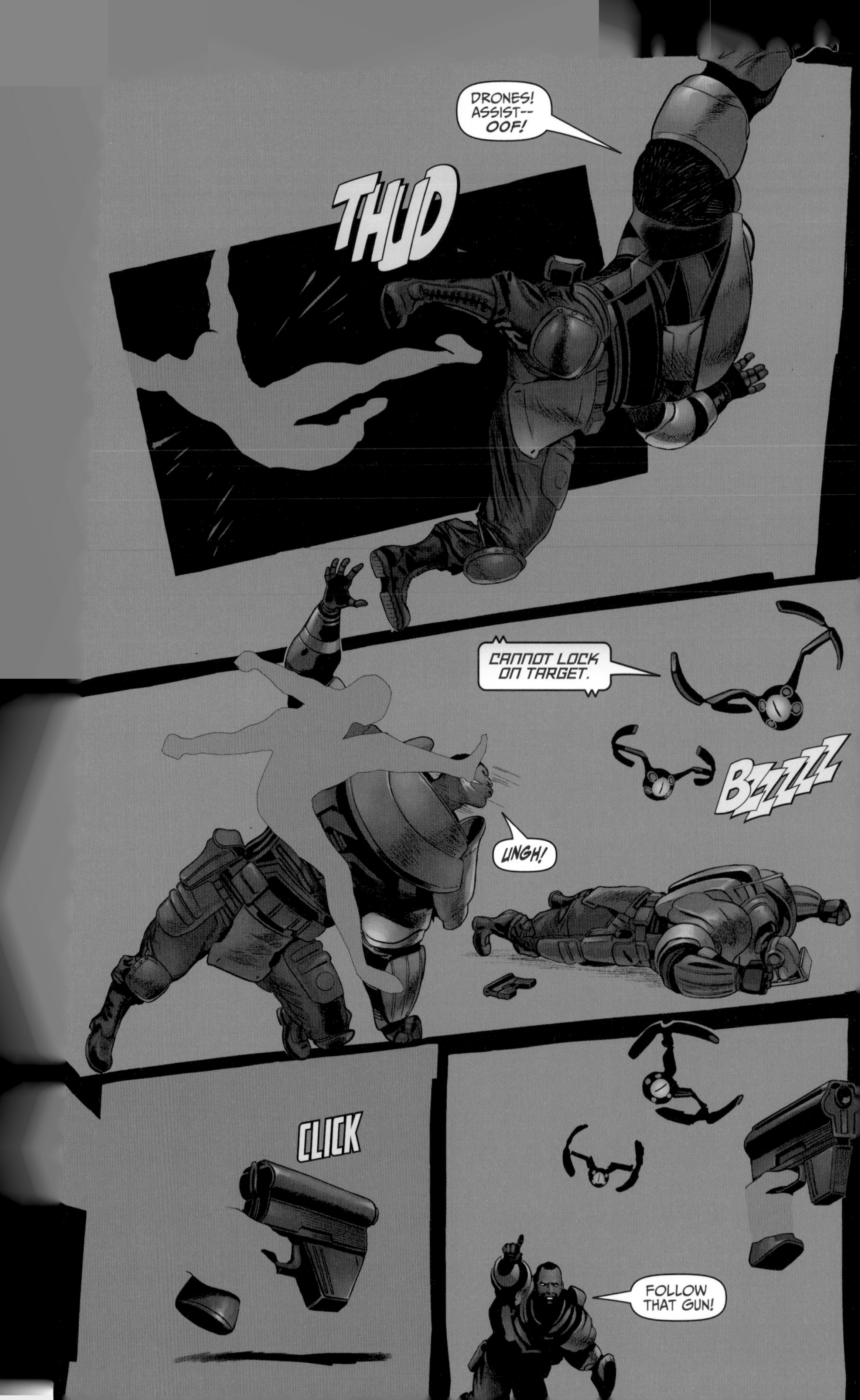
DRONES! ASSIST-- OOF!
THUD
CANNOT LOCK ON TARGET.
BZZZZZ
UNGH!
CLICK
FOLLOW THAT GUN!

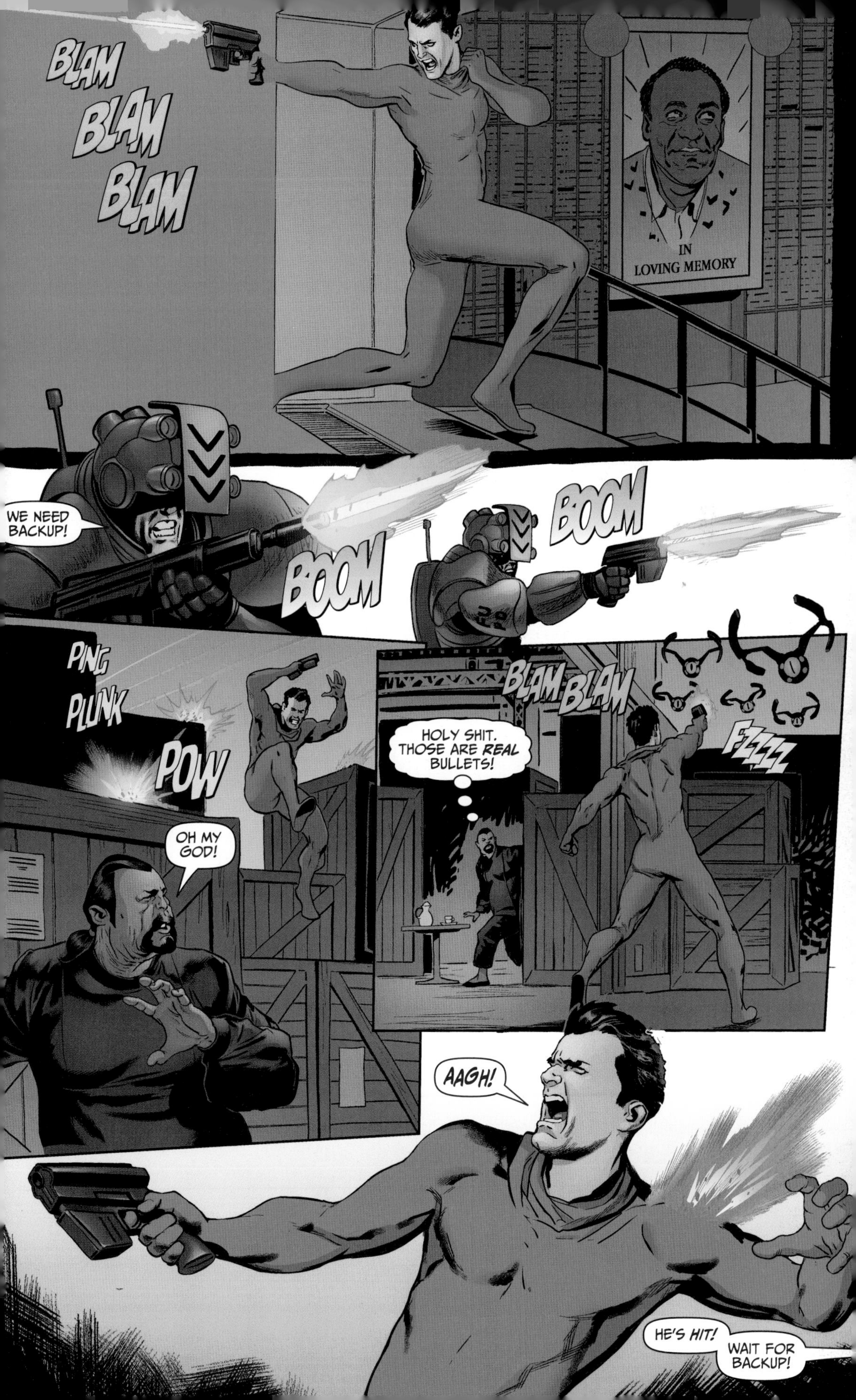
BLAM
BLAM
BLAM
IN LOVING MEMORY
WE NEED BACKUP!
BOOM
BOOM
PING
PLUNK
POW
OH MY GOD!
HOLY SHIT. THOSE ARE *REAL* BULLETS!
BLAM BLAM
FZZZZ
AAGH!
HE'S *HIT!*
WAIT FOR BACKUP!

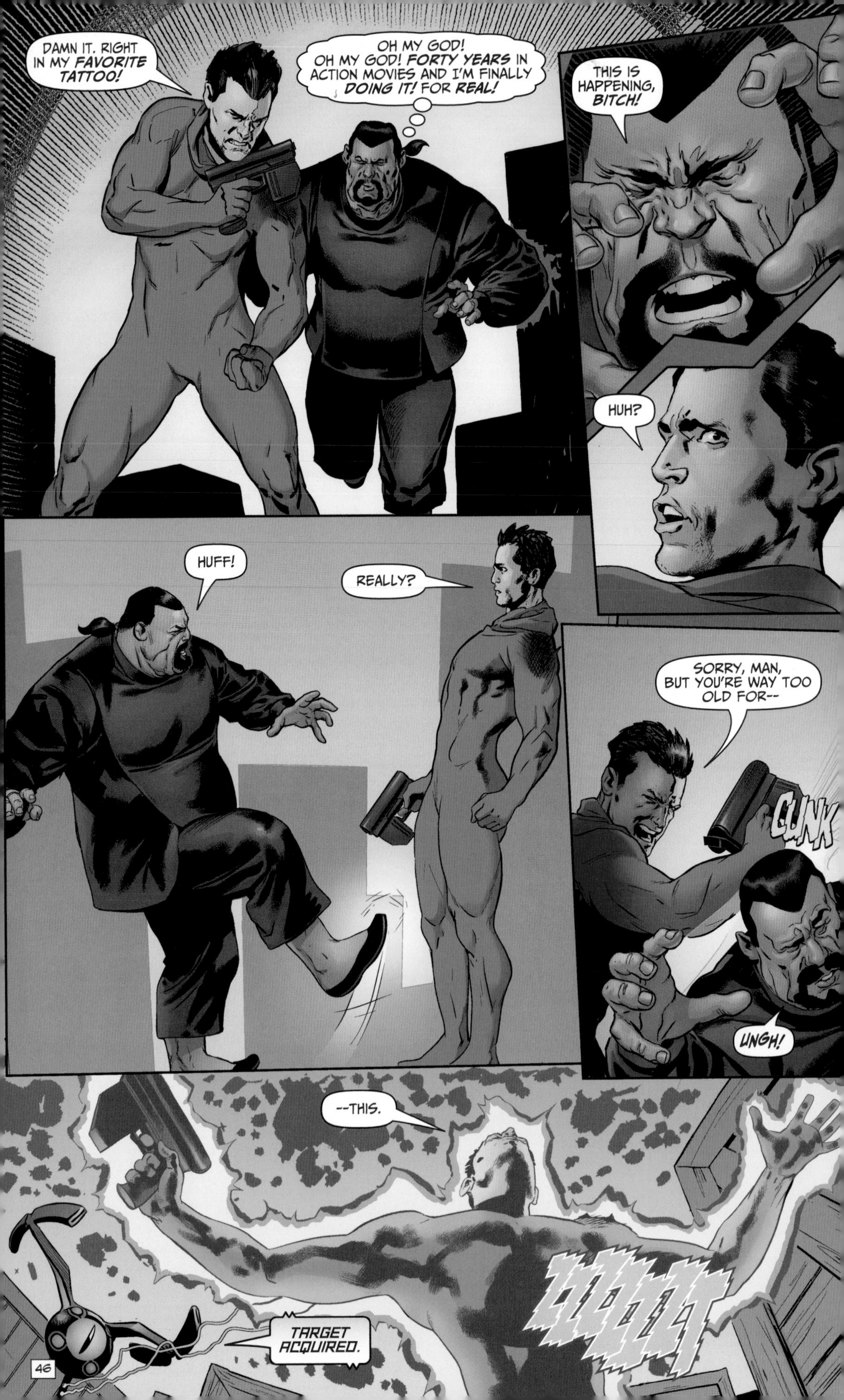
DAMN IT. RIGHT IN MY FAVORITE TATTOO!
OH MY GOD! OH MY GOD! FORTY YEARS IN ACTION MOVIES AND I'M FINALLY DOING IT! FOR REAL!
THIS IS HAPPENING, BITCH!
HUH?
HUFF!
REALLY?
SORRY, MAN, BUT YOU'RE WAY TOO OLD FOR--
CLUNK
UNGH!
--THIS.
TARGET ACQUIRED.

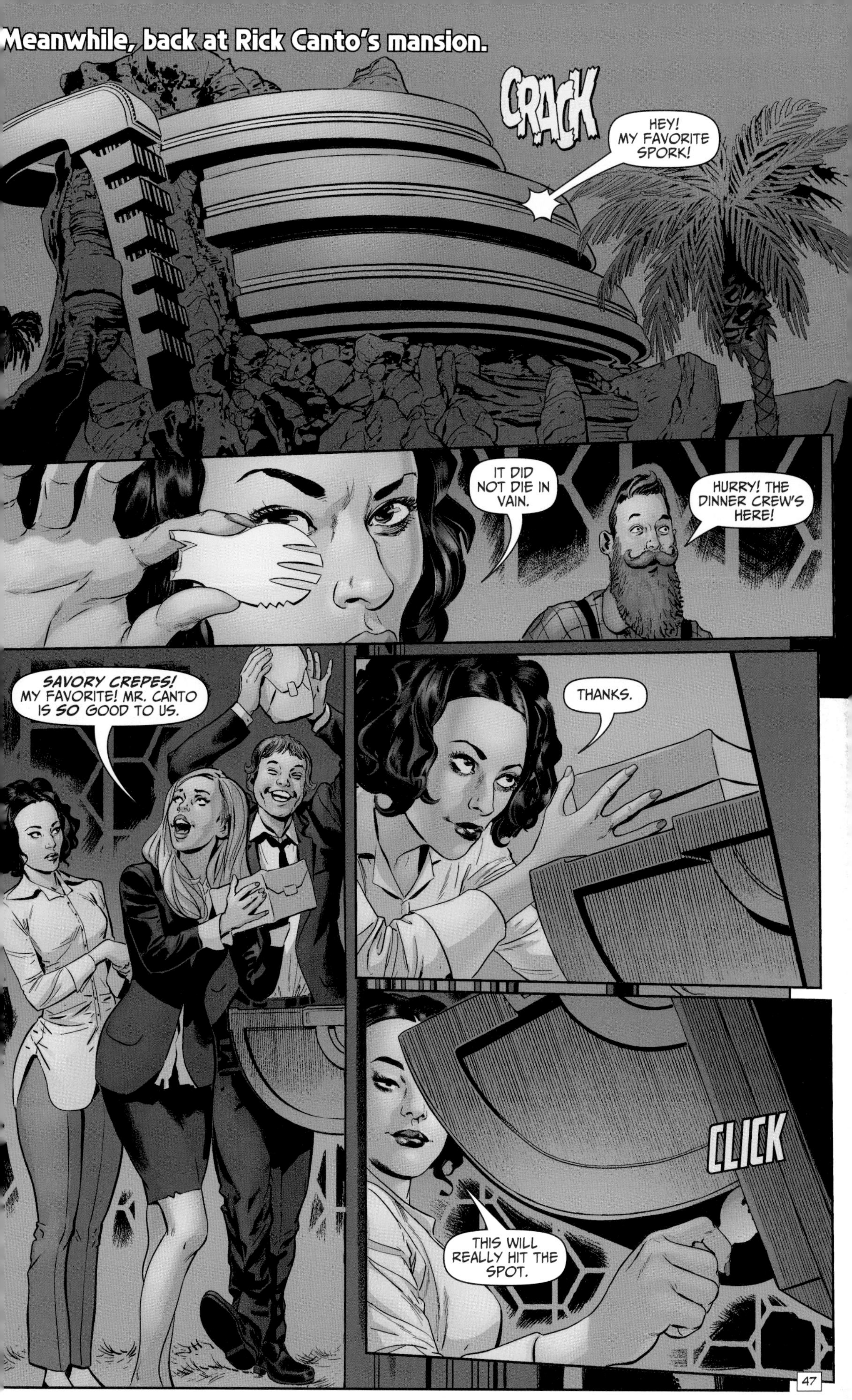
Meanwhile, back at Rick Canto's mansion.
CRACK
HEY! MY FAVORITE SPORK!
IT DID NOT DIE IN VAIN.
HURRY! THE DINNER CREW'S HERE!
SAVORY CREPES! MY FAVORITE! MR. CANTO IS SO GOOD TO US.
THANKS.
CLICK
THIS WILL REALLY HIT THE SPOT.

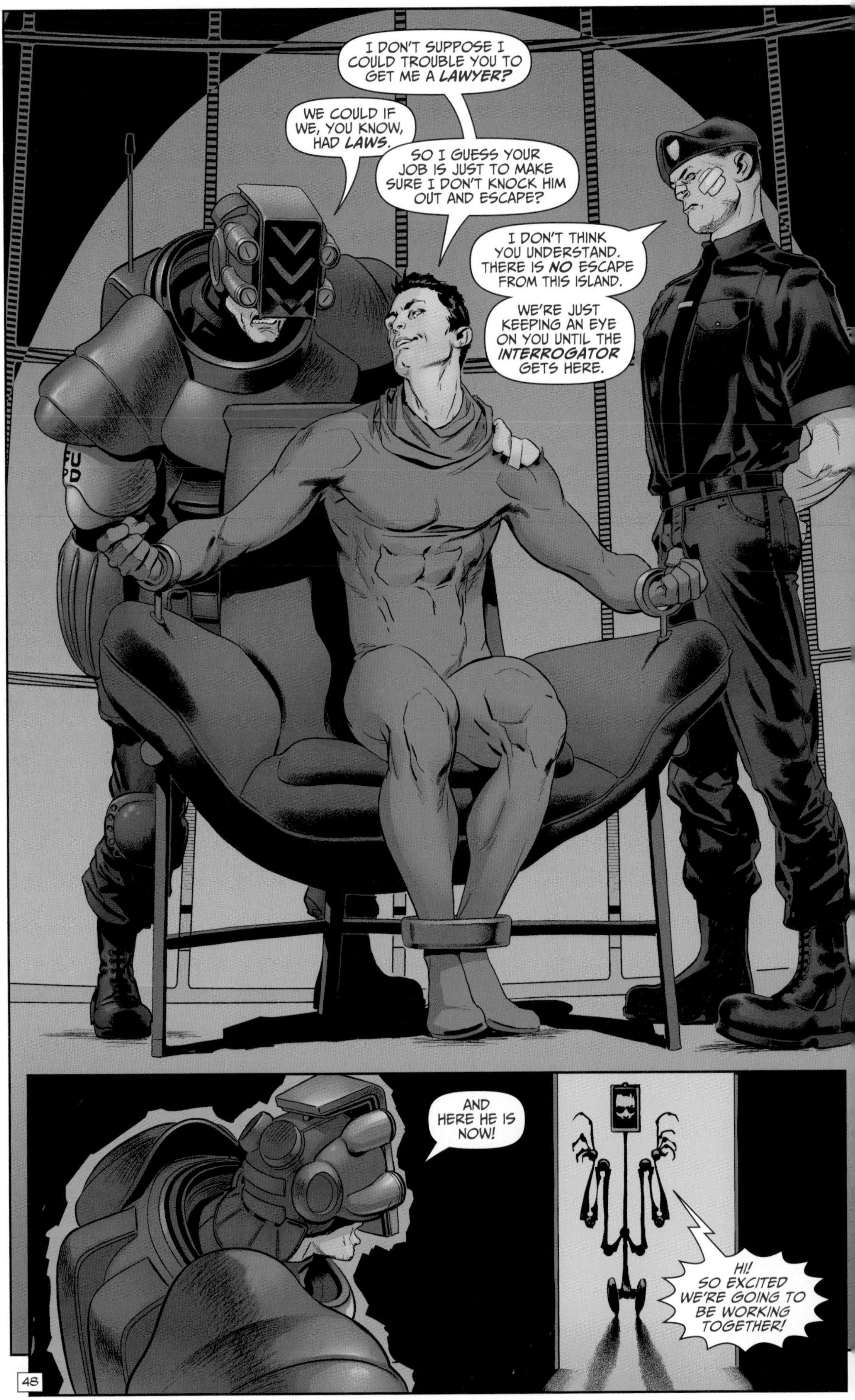
I DON'T SUPPOSE I COULD TROUBLE YOU TO GET ME A LAWYER?
WE COULD IF WE, YOU KNOW, HAD LAWS.
SO I GUESS YOUR JOB IS JUST TO MAKE SURE I DON'T KNOCK HIM OUT AND ESCAPE?
I DON'T THINK YOU UNDERSTAND. THERE IS NO ESCAPE FROM THIS ISLAND.
WE'RE JUST KEEPING AN EYE ON YOU UNTIL THE INTERROGATOR GETS HERE.
AND HERE HE IS NOW!
HI! SO EXCITED WE'RE GOING TO BE WORKING TOGETHER!

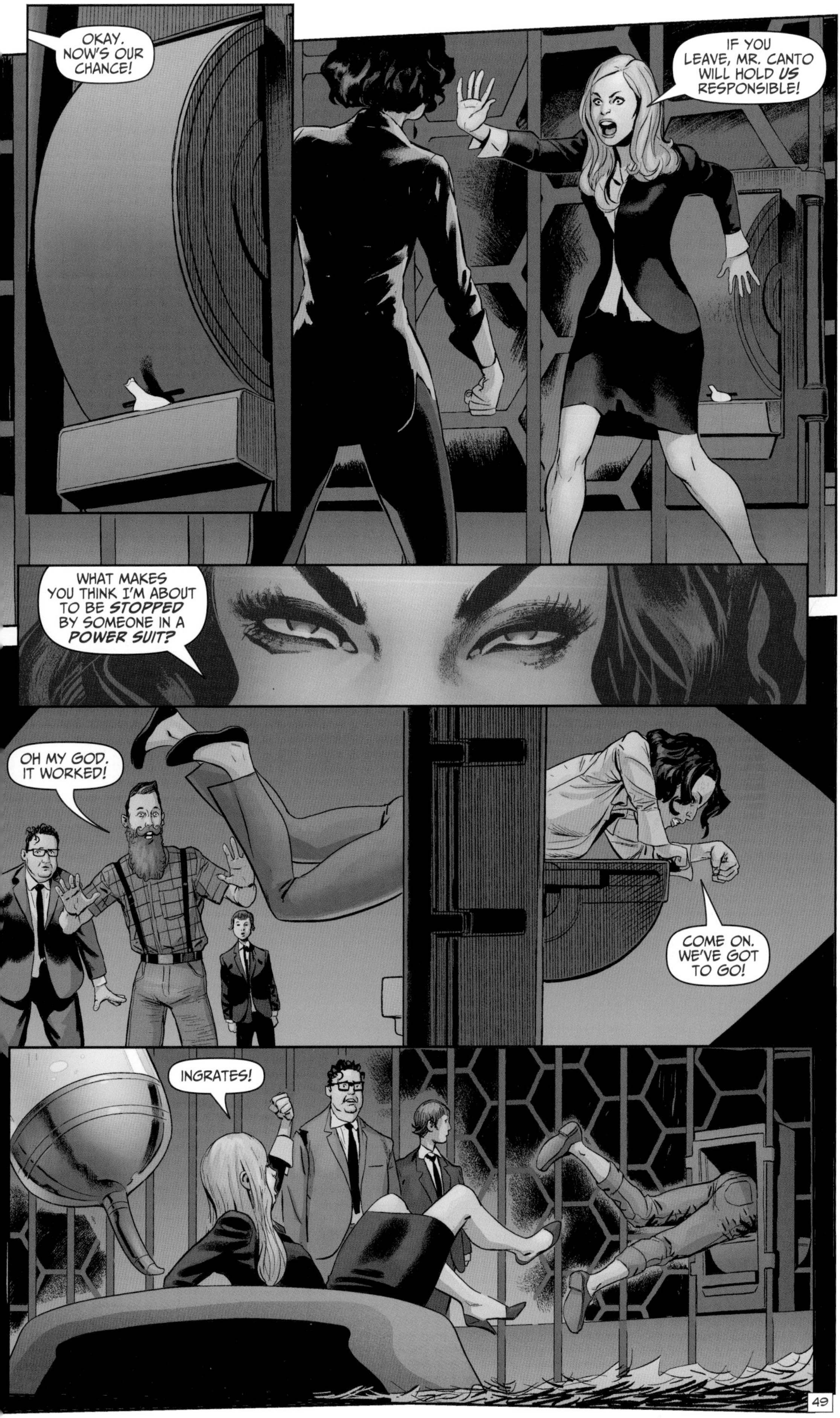

OKAY. NOW'S OUR CHANCE!
IF YOU LEAVE, MR. CANTO WILL HOLD *US* RESPONSIBLE!
WHAT MAKES YOU THINK I'M ABOUT TO BE ***STOPPED*** BY SOMEONE IN A ***POWER SUIT?***
OH MY GOD. IT WORKED!
COME ON. WE'VE GOT TO GO!
INGRATES!

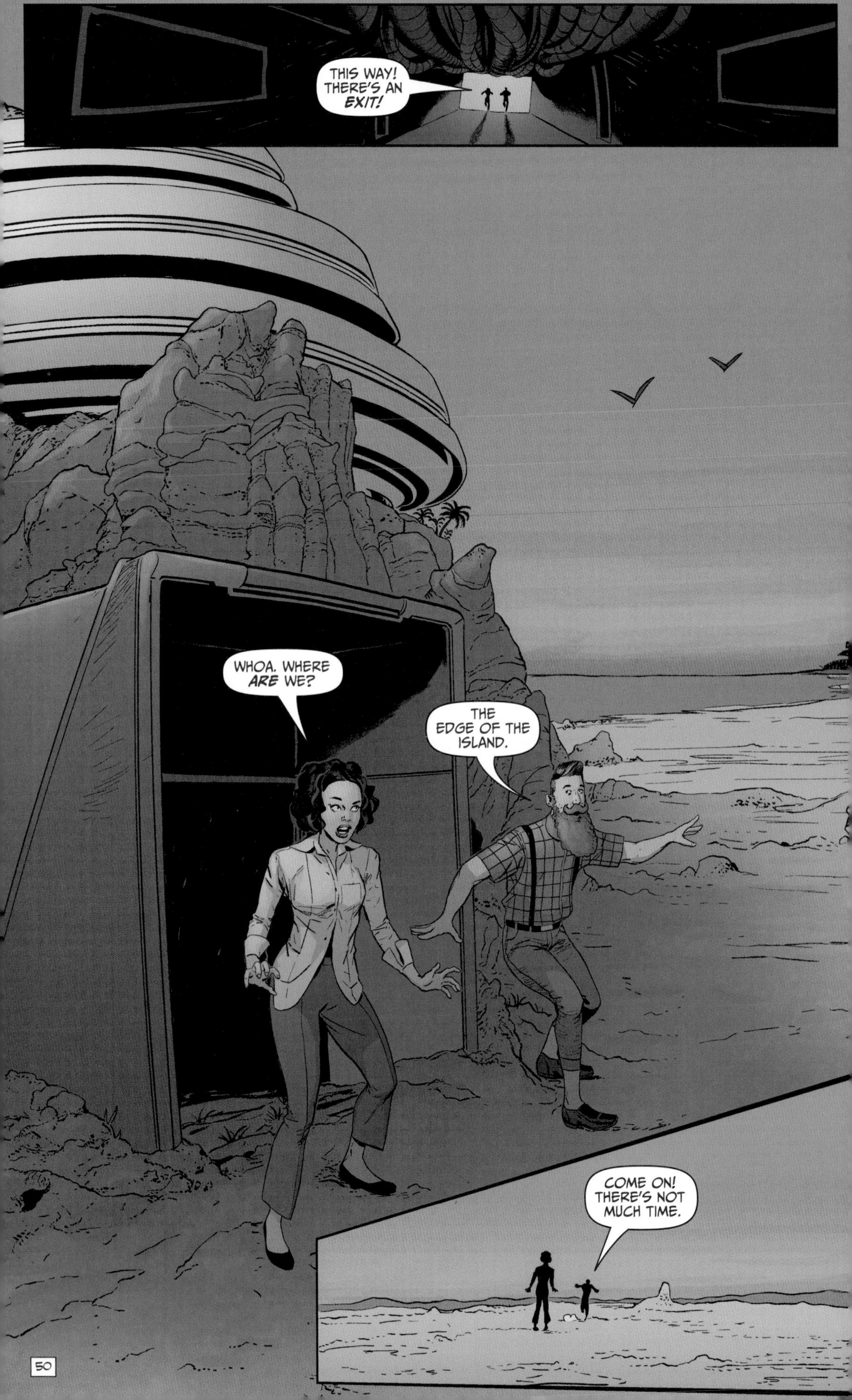

THIS WAY! THERE'S AN *EXIT!*
WHOA. WHERE *ARE* WE?
THE EDGE OF THE ISLAND.
COME ON! THERE'S NOT MUCH TIME.

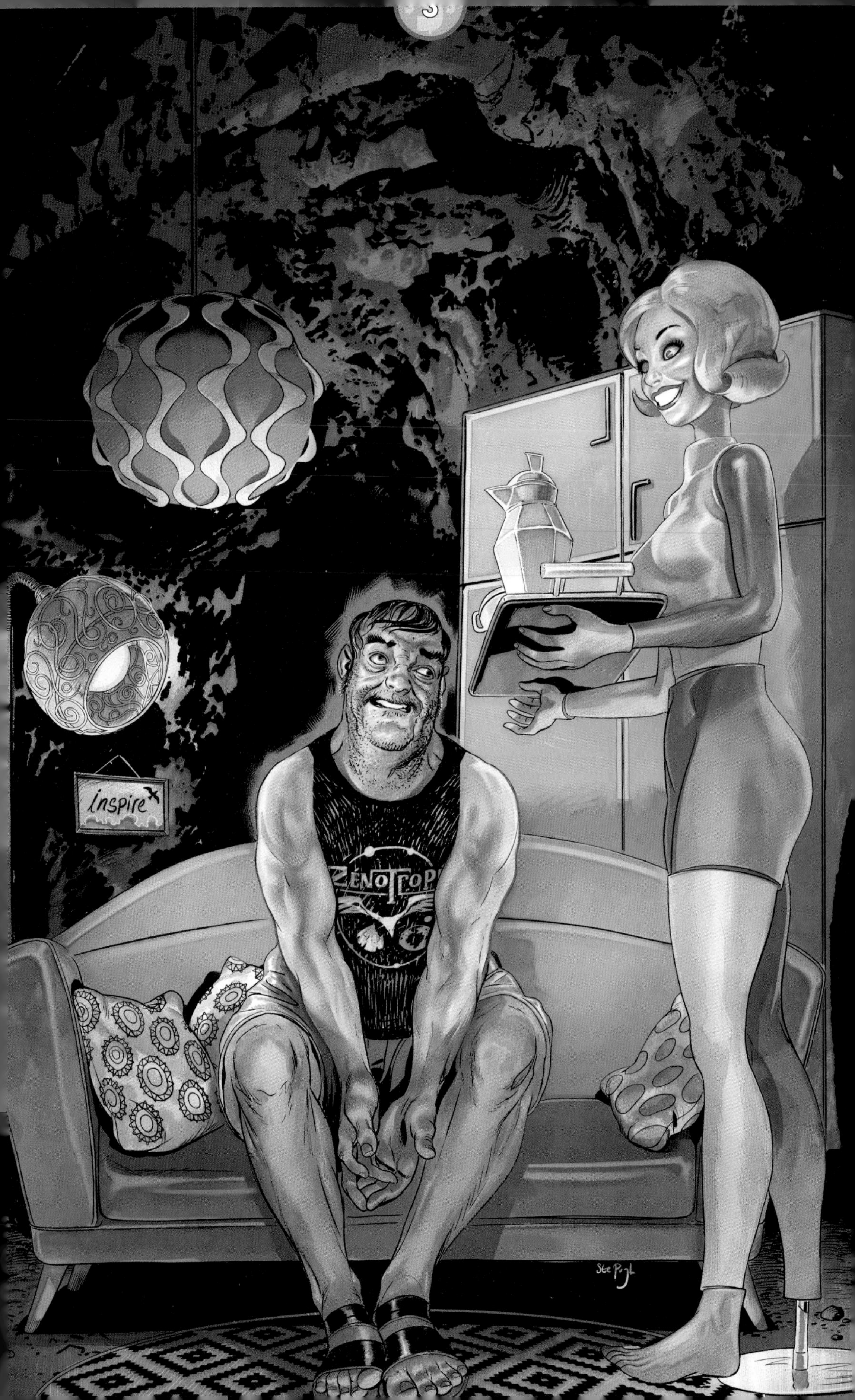
inspire

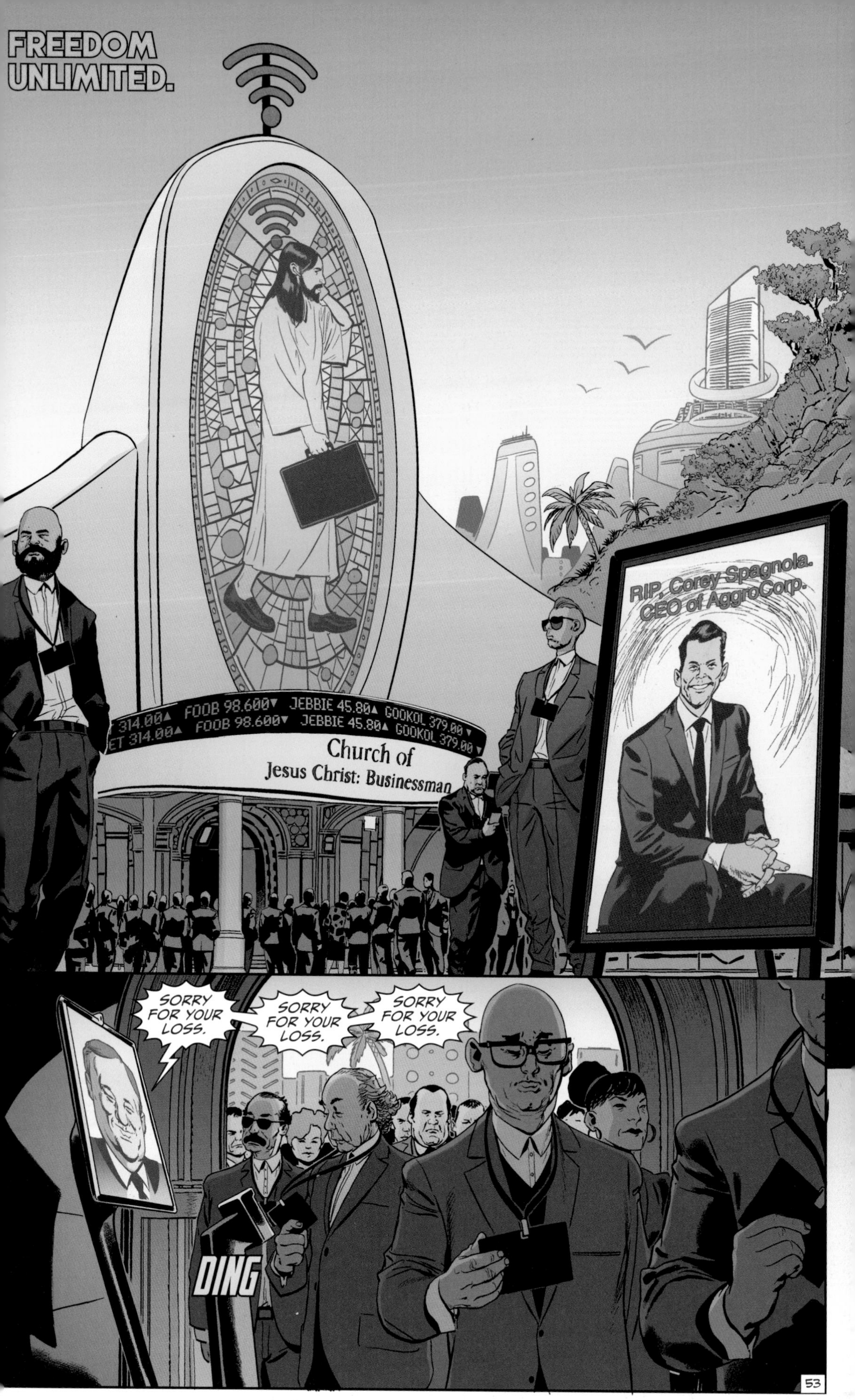
FREEDOM UNLIMITED.
314.00▲ FOOB 98.600▼ JEBBIE 45.80▲ GOKOL 379.00▼
ET 314.00▲ FOOB 98.600▼ JEBBIE 45.80▲ GOKOL 379.00▼
Church of Jesus Christ: Businessman
RIP, Corey Spagnola. CEO of AggroCorp.
SORRY FOR YOUR LOSS.
SORRY FOR YOUR LOSS.
SORRY FOR YOUR LOSS.
DING

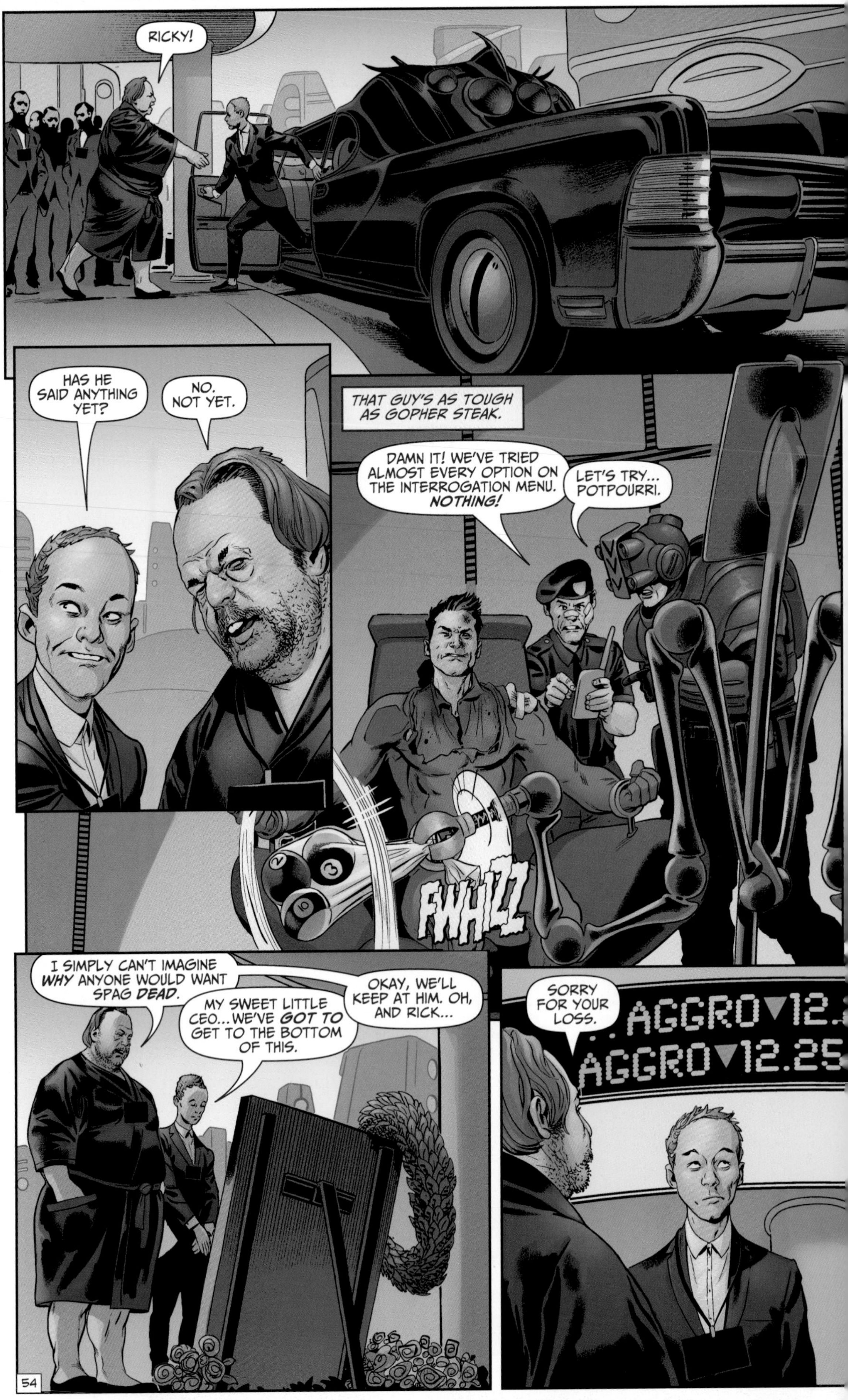
RICKY!
HAS HE SAID ANYTHING YET?
NO. NOT YET.
THAT GUY'S AS TOUGH AS GOPHER STEAK.
DAMN IT! WE'VE TRIED ALMOST EVERY OPTION ON THE INTERROGATION MENU. NOTHING!
LET'S TRY... POTPOURRI.
FWHIZZ
I SIMPLY CAN'T IMAGINE WHY ANYONE WOULD WANT SPAG DEAD.
MY SWEET LITTLE CEO...WE'VE GOT TO GET TO THE BOTTOM OF THIS.
OKAY, WE'LL KEEP AT HIM. OH, AND RICK...
SORRY FOR YOUR LOSS.
AGGRO▼12.25

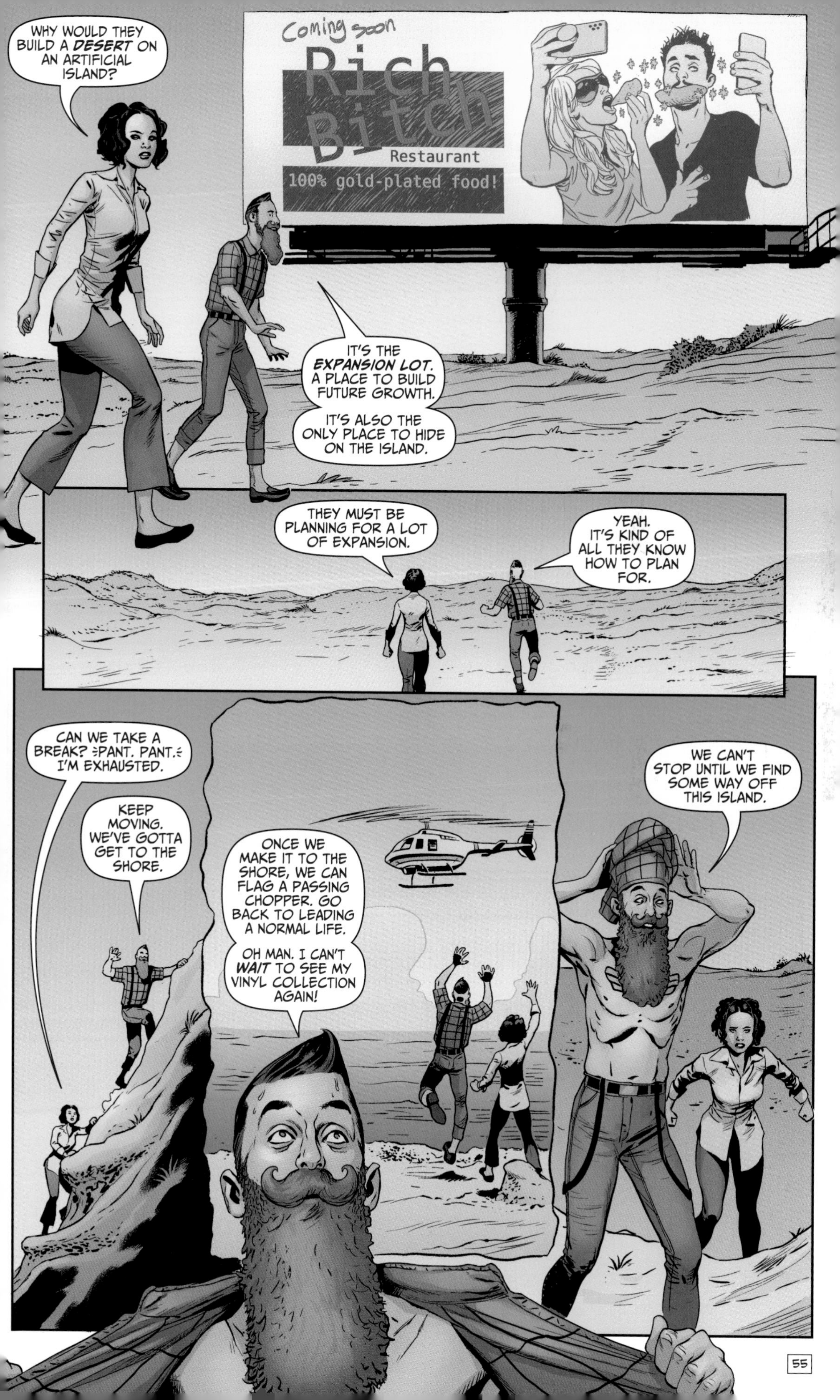

WHY WOULD THEY BUILD A DESERT ON AN ARTIFICIAL ISLAND?
Coming soon
Rich Bitch
Restaurant
100% gold-plated food!
IT'S THE EXPANSION LOT. A PLACE TO BUILD FUTURE GROWTH.
IT'S ALSO THE ONLY PLACE TO HIDE ON THE ISLAND.
THEY MUST BE PLANNING FOR A LOT OF EXPANSION.
YEAH. IT'S KIND OF ALL THEY KNOW HOW TO PLAN FOR.
CAN WE TAKE A BREAK? ⸗PANT. PANT.⸗ I'M EXHAUSTED.
KEEP MOVING. WE'VE GOTTA GET TO THE SHORE.
ONCE WE MAKE IT TO THE SHORE, WE CAN FLAG A PASSING CHOPPER. GO BACK TO LEADING A NORMAL LIFE.
OH MAN. I CAN'T WAIT TO SEE MY VINYL COLLECTION AGAIN!
WE CAN'T STOP UNTIL WE FIND SOME WAY OFF THIS ISLAND.

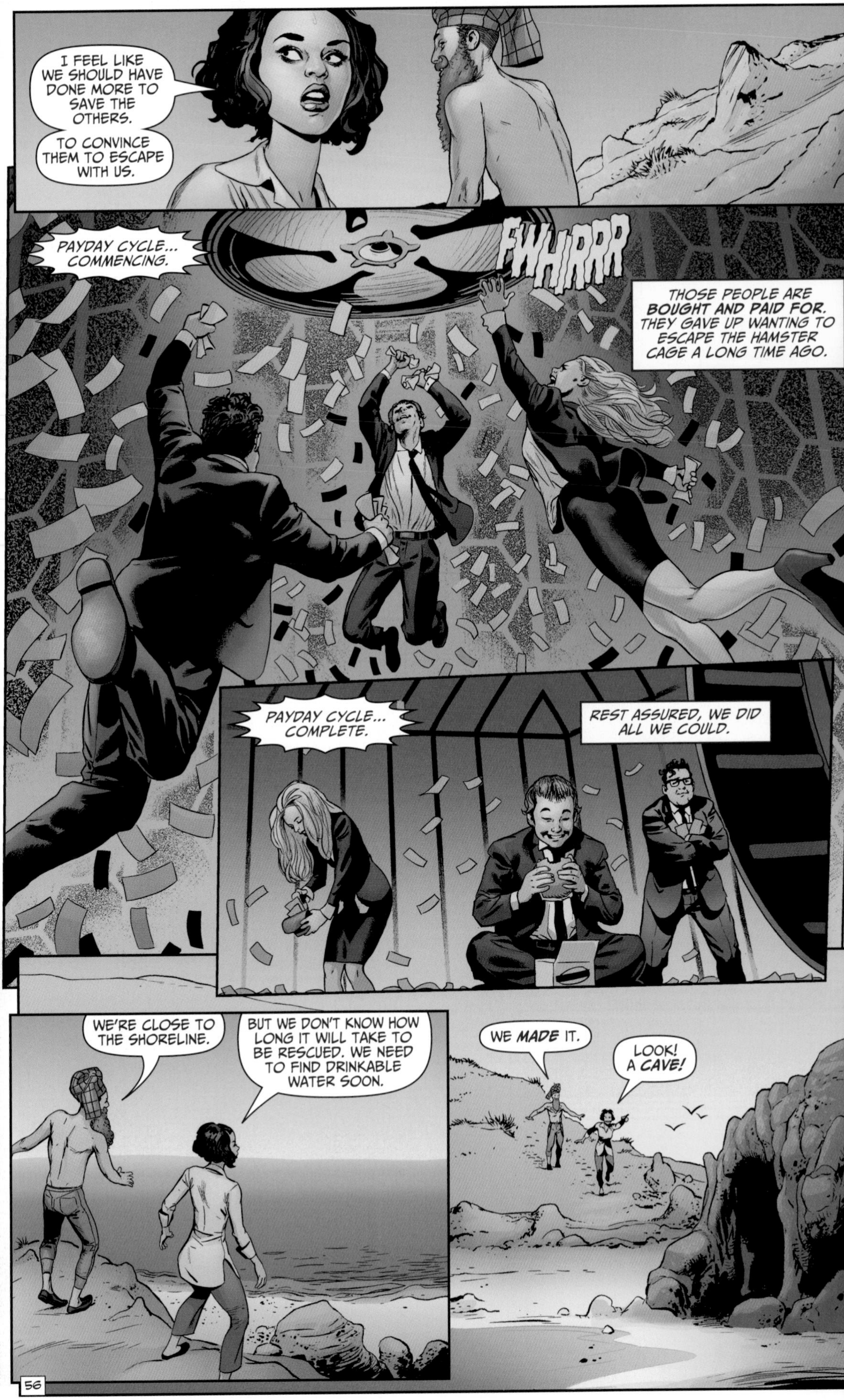
I FEEL LIKE WE SHOULD HAVE DONE MORE TO SAVE THE OTHERS.
TO CONVINCE THEM TO ESCAPE WITH US.
PAYDAY CYCLE... COMMENCING.
FWHIRRR
THOSE PEOPLE ARE BOUGHT AND PAID FOR. THEY GAVE UP WANTING TO ESCAPE THE HAMSTER CAGE A LONG TIME AGO.
PAYDAY CYCLE... COMPLETE.
REST ASSURED, WE DID ALL WE COULD.
WE'RE CLOSE TO THE SHORELINE.
BUT WE DON'T KNOW HOW LONG IT WILL TAKE TO BE RESCUED. WE NEED TO FIND DRINKABLE WATER SOON.
WE MADE IT.
LOOK! A CAVE!

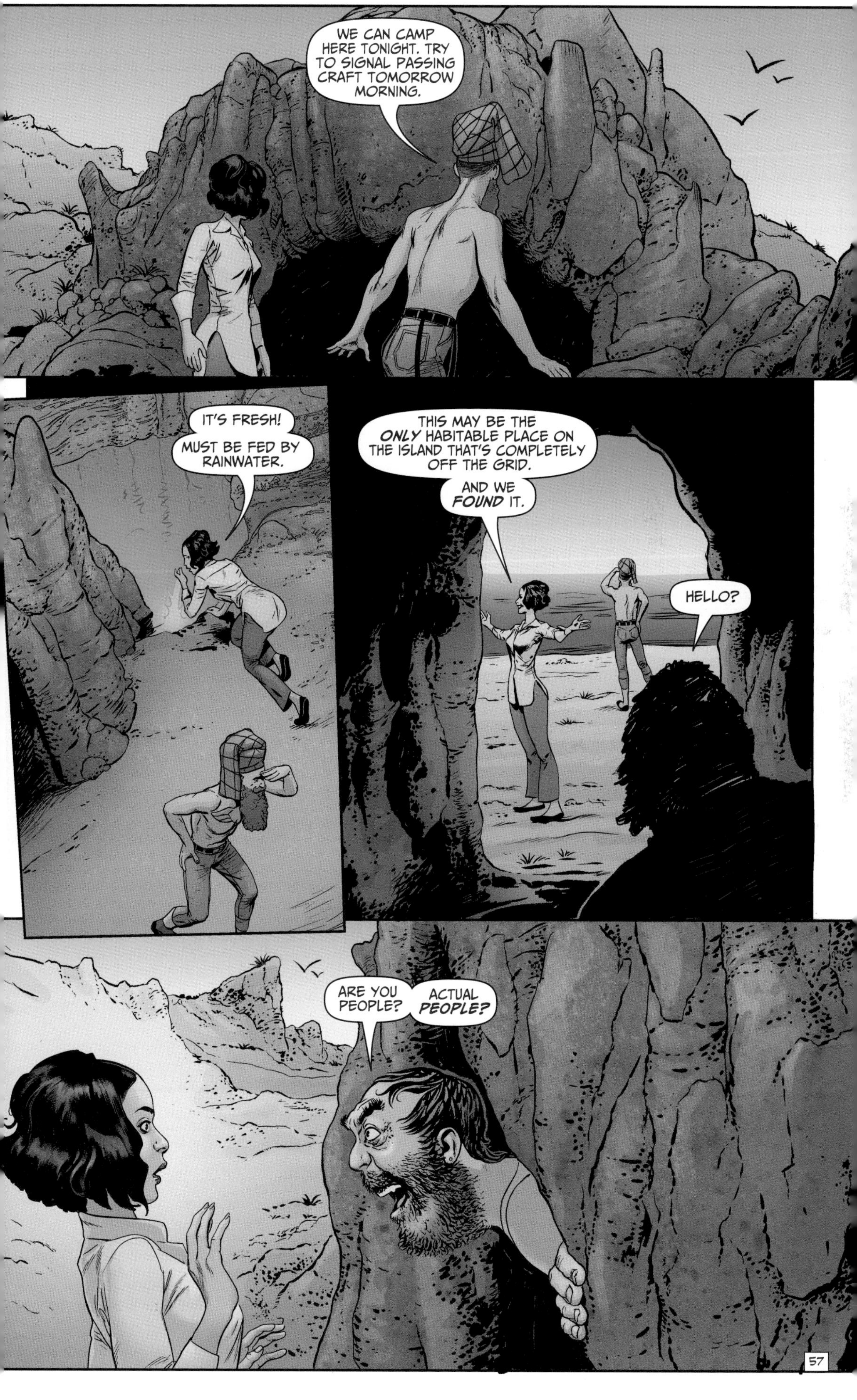
WE CAN CAMP HERE TONIGHT. TRY TO SIGNAL PASSING CRAFT TOMORROW MORNING.
IT'S FRESH!
MUST BE FED BY RAINWATER.
THIS MAY BE THE ONLY HABITABLE PLACE ON THE ISLAND THAT'S COMPLETELY OFF THE GRID.
AND WE FOUND IT.
HELLO?
ARE YOU PEOPLE?
ACTUAL PEOPLE?

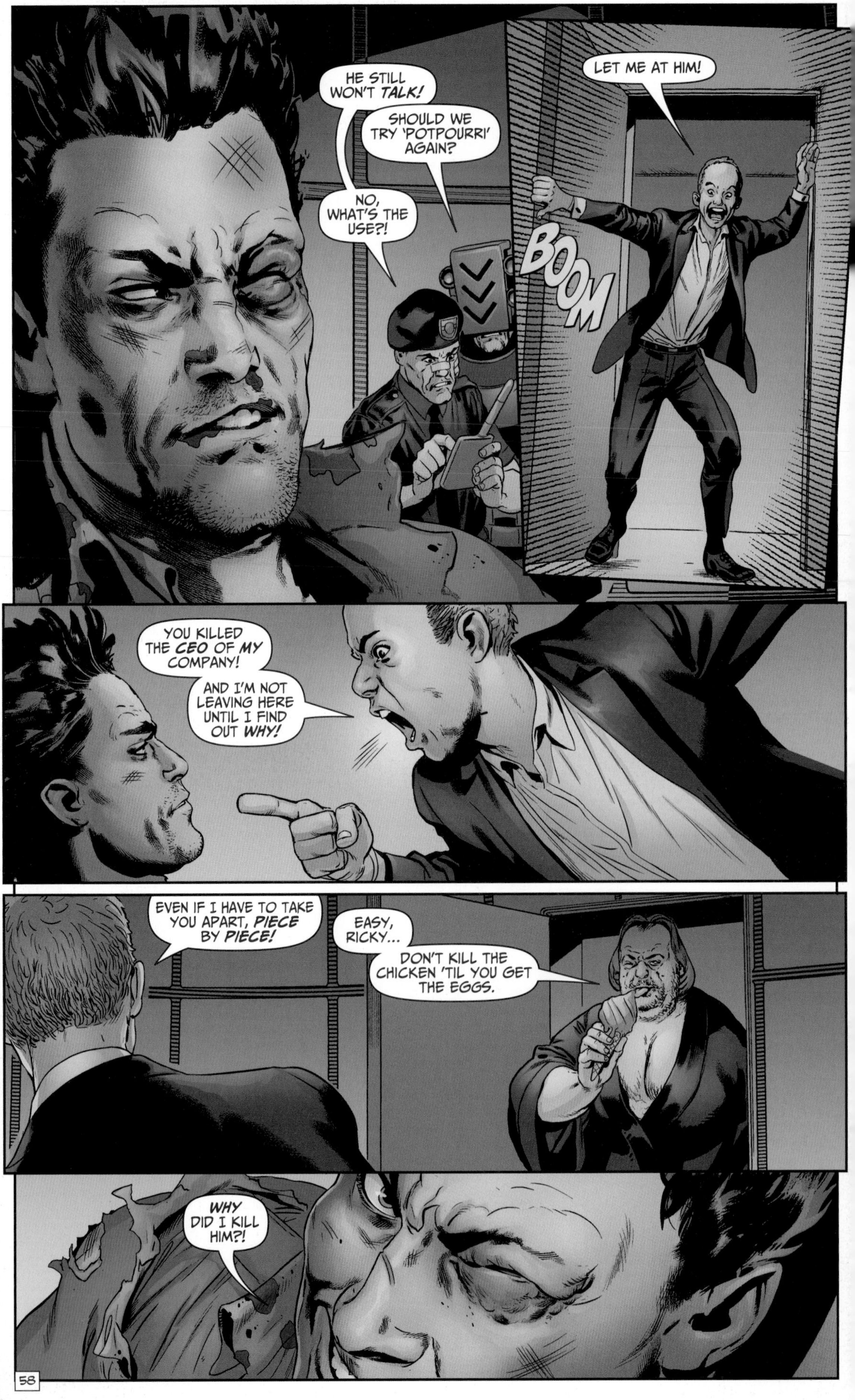
HE STILL WON'T TALK!
SHOULD WE TRY 'POTPOURRI' AGAIN?
NO, WHAT'S THE USE?!
LET ME AT HIM!
BOOM
YOU KILLED THE CEO OF MY COMPANY!
AND I'M NOT LEAVING HERE UNTIL I FIND OUT WHY!
EVEN IF I HAVE TO TAKE YOU APART, PIECE BY PIECE!
EASY, RICKY...
DON'T KILL THE CHICKEN 'TIL YOU GET THE EGGS.
WHY DID I KILL HIM?!

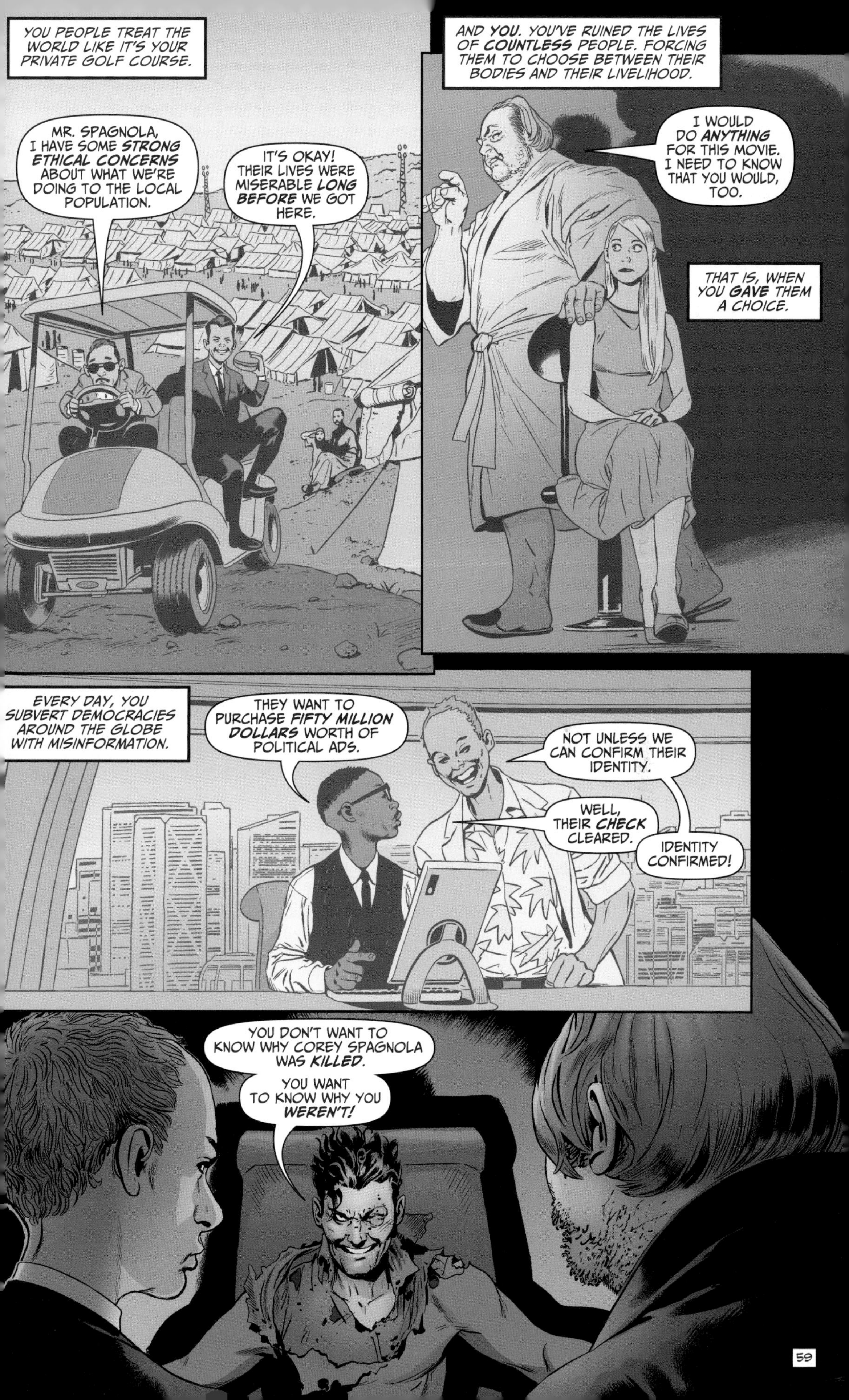
YOU PEOPLE TREAT THE WORLD LIKE IT'S YOUR PRIVATE GOLF COURSE.
MR. SPAGNOLA, I HAVE SOME STRONG ETHICAL CONCERNS ABOUT WHAT WE'RE DOING TO THE LOCAL POPULATION.
IT'S OKAY! THEIR LIVES WERE MISERABLE LONG BEFORE WE GOT HERE.
AND YOU. YOU'VE RUINED THE LIVES OF COUNTLESS PEOPLE. FORCING THEM TO CHOOSE BETWEEN THEIR BODIES AND THEIR LIVELIHOOD.
I WOULD DO ANYTHING FOR THIS MOVIE. I NEED TO KNOW THAT YOU WOULD, TOO.
THAT IS, WHEN YOU GAVE THEM A CHOICE.
EVERY DAY, YOU SUBVERT DEMOCRACIES AROUND THE GLOBE WITH MISINFORMATION.
THEY WANT TO PURCHASE FIFTY MILLION DOLLARS WORTH OF POLITICAL ADS.
NOT UNLESS WE CAN CONFIRM THEIR IDENTITY.
WELL, THEIR CHECK CLEARED.
IDENTITY CONFIRMED!
YOU DON'T WANT TO KNOW WHY COREY SPAGNOLA WAS KILLED.
YOU WANT TO KNOW WHY YOU WEREN'T!

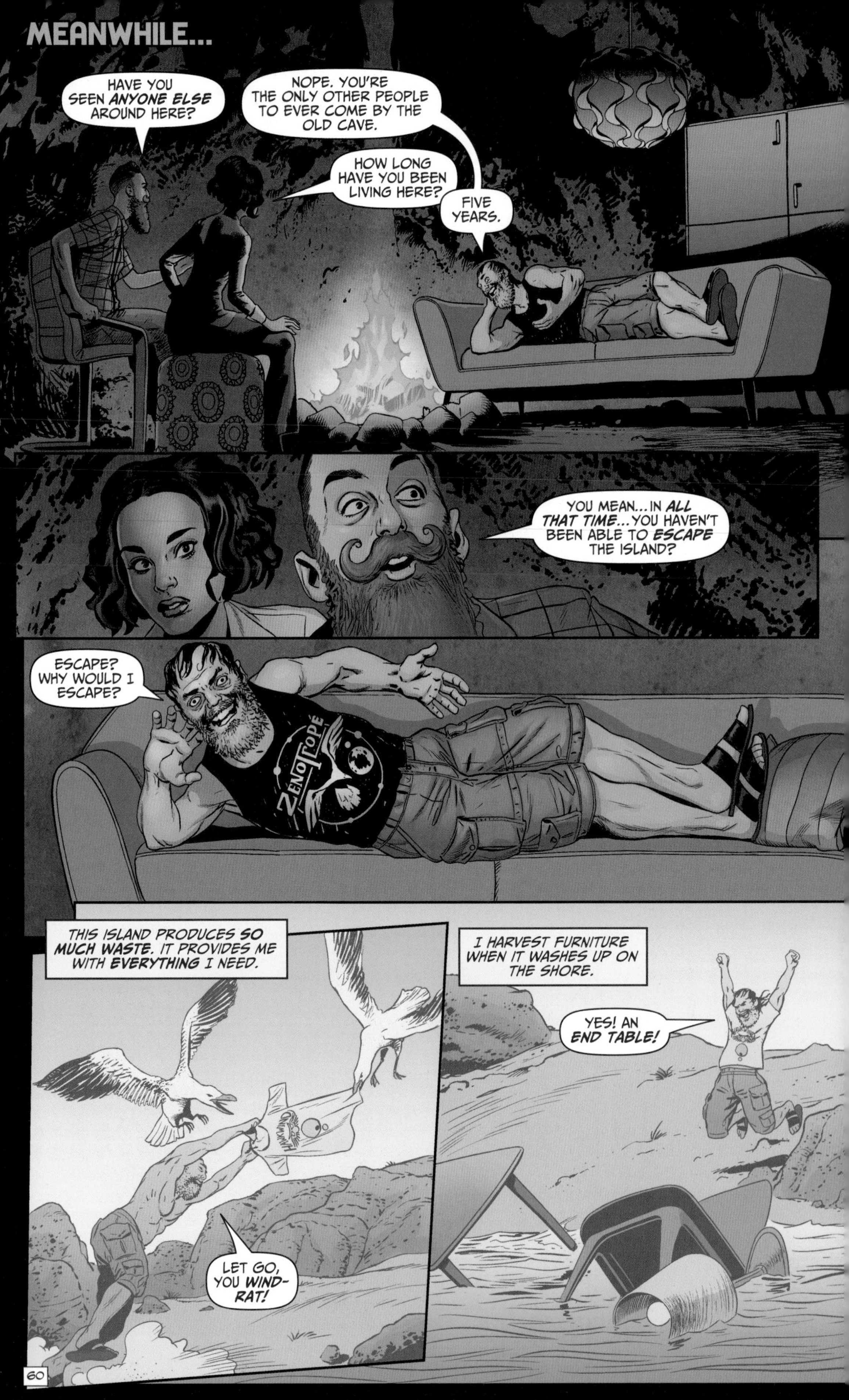
MEANWHILE...
HAVE YOU SEEN ANYONE ELSE AROUND HERE?
NOPE. YOU'RE THE ONLY OTHER PEOPLE TO EVER COME BY THE OLD CAVE.
HOW LONG HAVE YOU BEEN LIVING HERE?
FIVE YEARS.
YOU MEAN...IN ALL THAT TIME...YOU HAVEN'T BEEN ABLE TO ESCAPE THE ISLAND?
ESCAPE? WHY WOULD I ESCAPE?
ZENOSCOPE
THIS ISLAND PRODUCES SO MUCH WASTE. IT PROVIDES ME WITH EVERYTHING I NEED.
LET GO, YOU WIND-RAT!
I HARVEST FURNITURE WHEN IT WASHES UP ON THE SHORE.
YES! AN END TABLE!

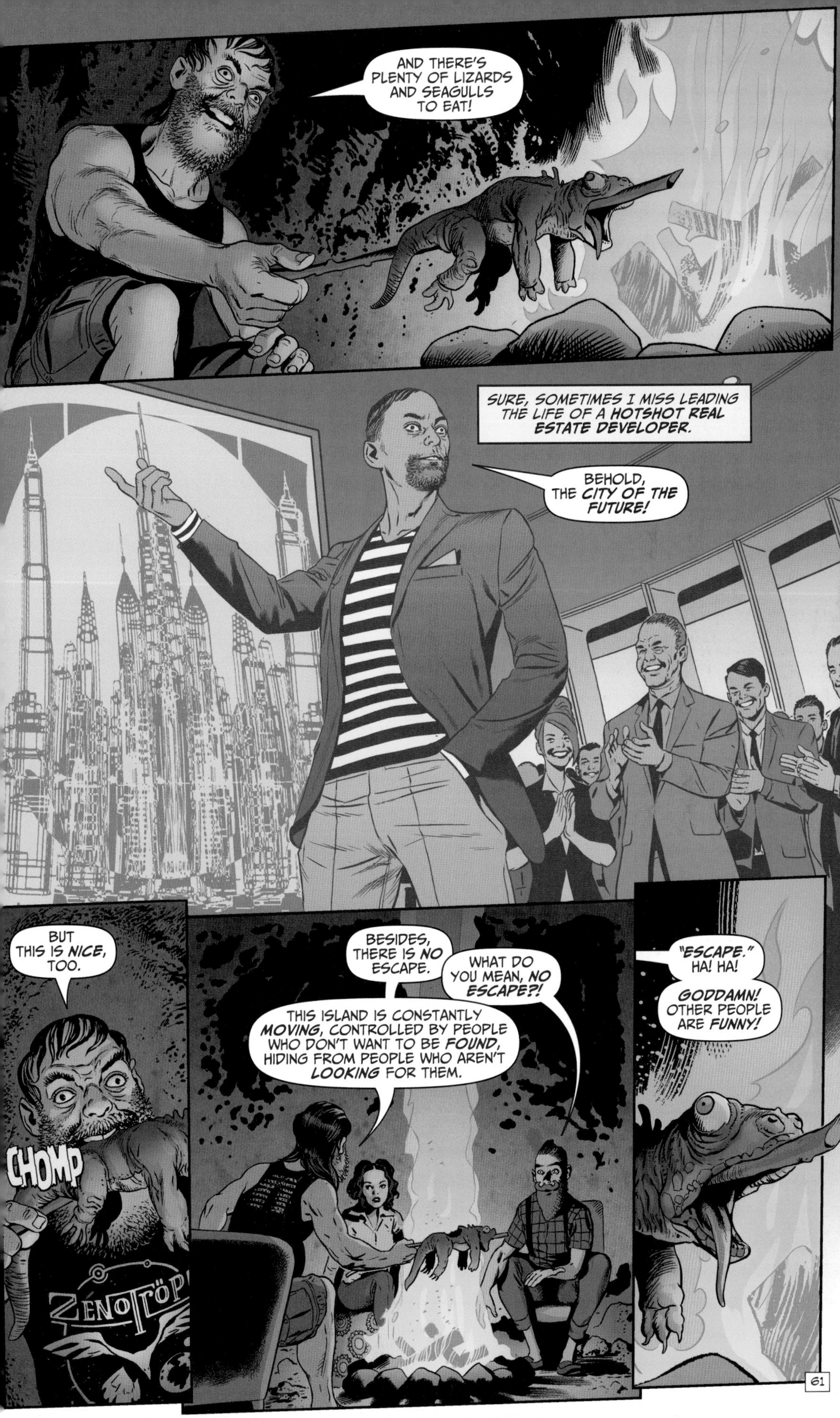
AND THERE'S PLENTY OF LIZARDS AND SEAGULLS TO EAT!
SURE, SOMETIMES I MISS LEADING THE LIFE OF A HOTSHOT REAL ESTATE DEVELOPER.
BEHOLD, THE CITY OF THE FUTURE!
BUT THIS IS NICE, TOO.
CHOMP
ZENOTRÖP
BESIDES, THERE IS NO ESCAPE.
WHAT DO YOU MEAN, NO ESCAPE?!
THIS ISLAND IS CONSTANTLY MOVING, CONTROLLED BY PEOPLE WHO DON'T WANT TO BE FOUND, HIDING FROM PEOPLE WHO AREN'T LOOKING FOR THEM.
"ESCAPE." HA! HA!
GODDAMN! OTHER PEOPLE ARE FUNNY!

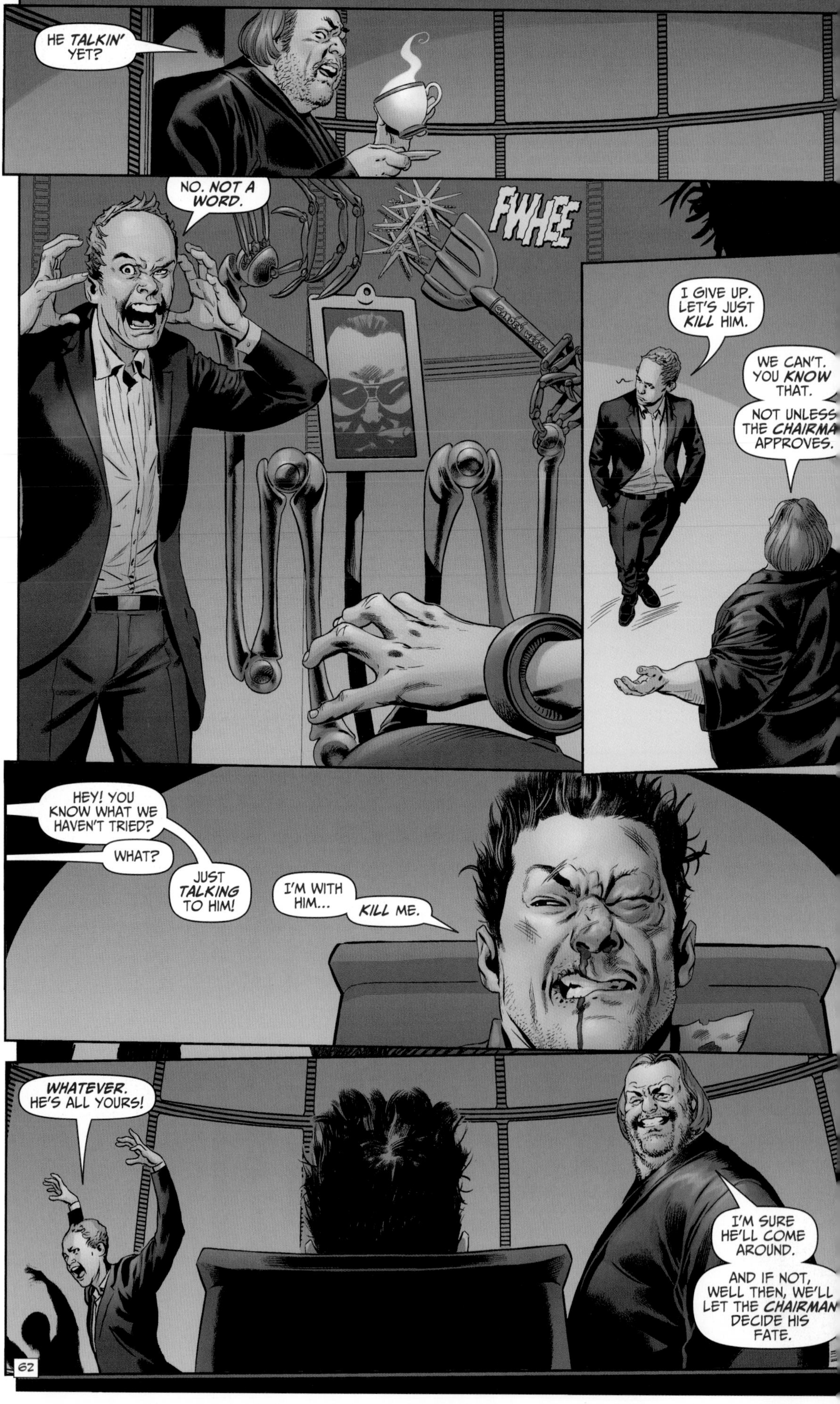
HE TALKIN' YET?
NO. NOT A WORD.
FWHEE
GARDEN WEEVIL
I GIVE UP. LET'S JUST KILL HIM.
WE CAN'T. YOU KNOW THAT.
NOT UNLESS THE CHAIRMAN APPROVES.
HEY! YOU KNOW WHAT WE HAVEN'T TRIED?
WHAT?
JUST TALKING TO HIM!
I'M WITH HIM...
KILL ME.
WHATEVER. HE'S ALL YOURS!
I'M SURE HE'LL COME AROUND.
AND IF NOT, WELL THEN, WE'LL LET THE CHAIRMAN DECIDE HIS FATE.

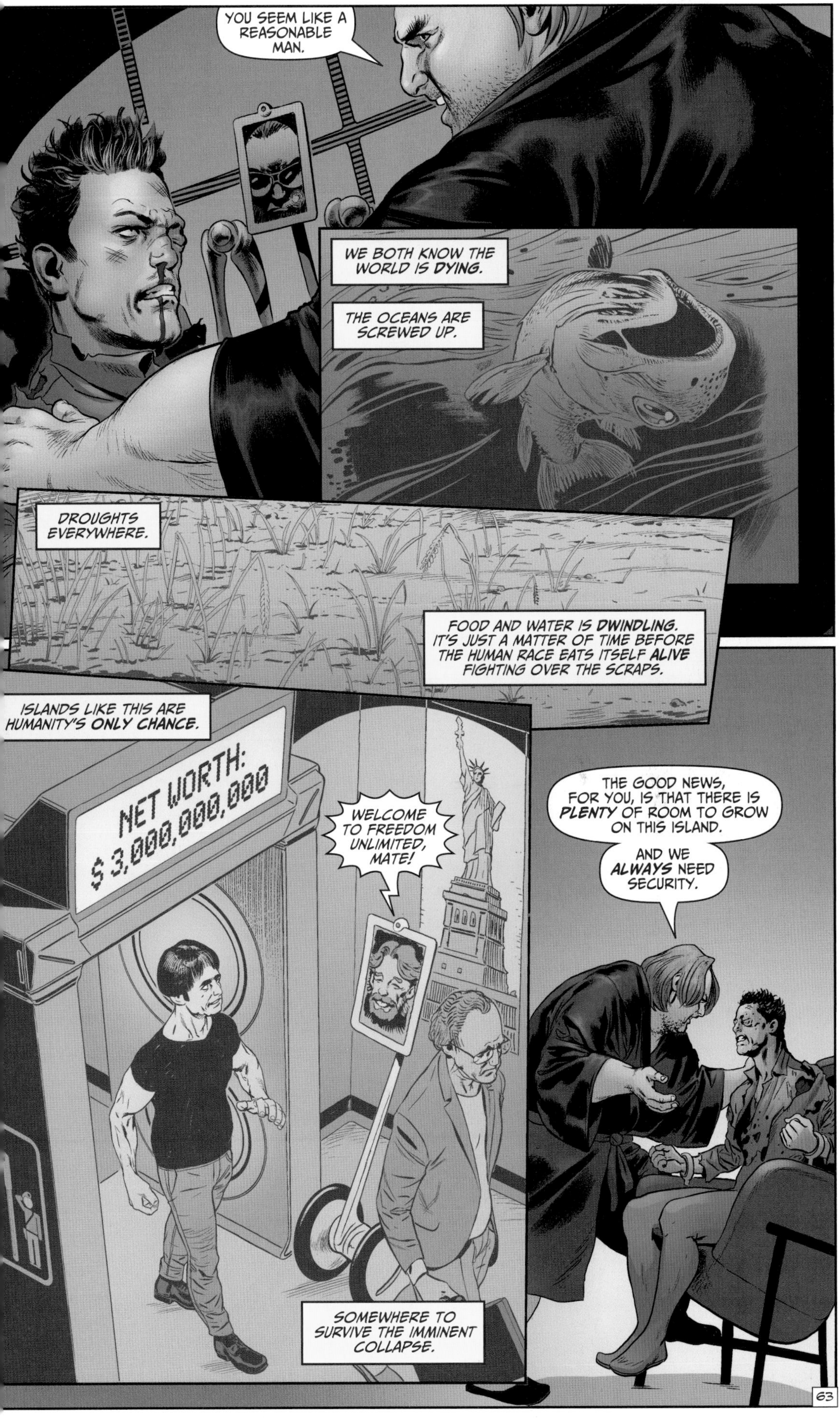
YOU SEEM LIKE A REASONABLE MAN.
WE BOTH KNOW THE WORLD IS DYING.
THE OCEANS ARE SCREWED UP.
DROUGHTS EVERYWHERE.
FOOD AND WATER IS DWINDLING. IT'S JUST A MATTER OF TIME BEFORE THE HUMAN RACE EATS ITSELF ALIVE FIGHTING OVER THE SCRAPS.
ISLANDS LIKE THIS ARE HUMANITY'S ONLY CHANCE.
NET WORTH: $ 3,000,000,000
WELCOME TO FREEDOM UNLIMITED, MATE!
SOMEWHERE TO SURVIVE THE IMMINENT COLLAPSE.
THE GOOD NEWS, FOR YOU, IS THAT THERE IS PLENTY OF ROOM TO GROW ON THIS ISLAND.
AND WE ALWAYS NEED SECURITY.

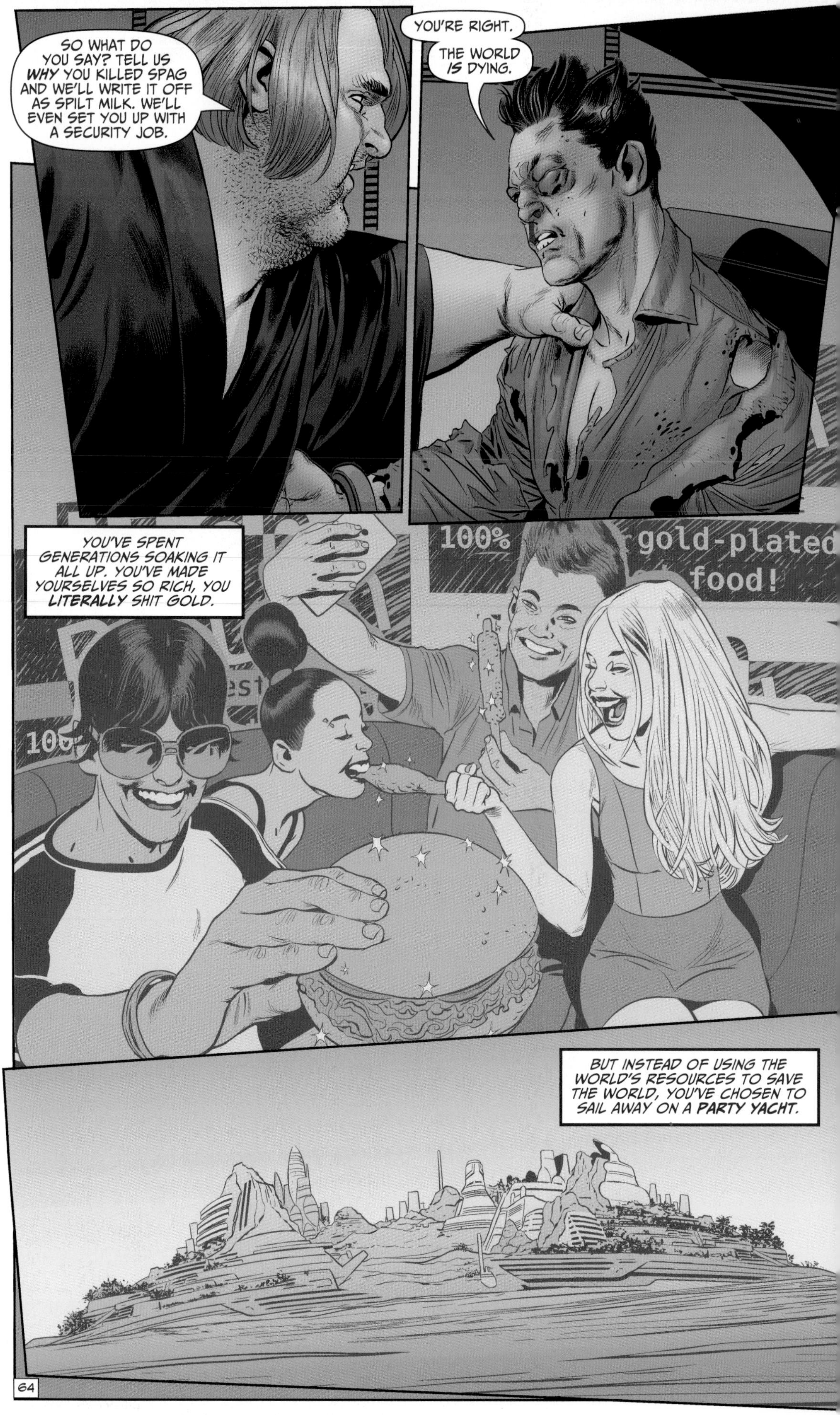

SO WHAT DO YOU SAY? TELL US *WHY* YOU KILLED SPAG AND WE'LL WRITE IT OFF AS SPILT MILK. WE'LL EVEN SET YOU UP WITH A SECURITY JOB.
YOU'RE RIGHT.
THE WORLD *IS* DYING.
YOU'VE SPENT GENERATIONS SOAKING IT ALL UP. YOU'VE MADE YOURSELVES SO RICH, YOU **LITERALLY** SHIT GOLD.
100%
gold-plated
food!
BUT INSTEAD OF USING THE WORLD'S RESOURCES TO SAVE THE WORLD, YOU'VE CHOSEN TO SAIL AWAY ON A **PARTY YACHT**.

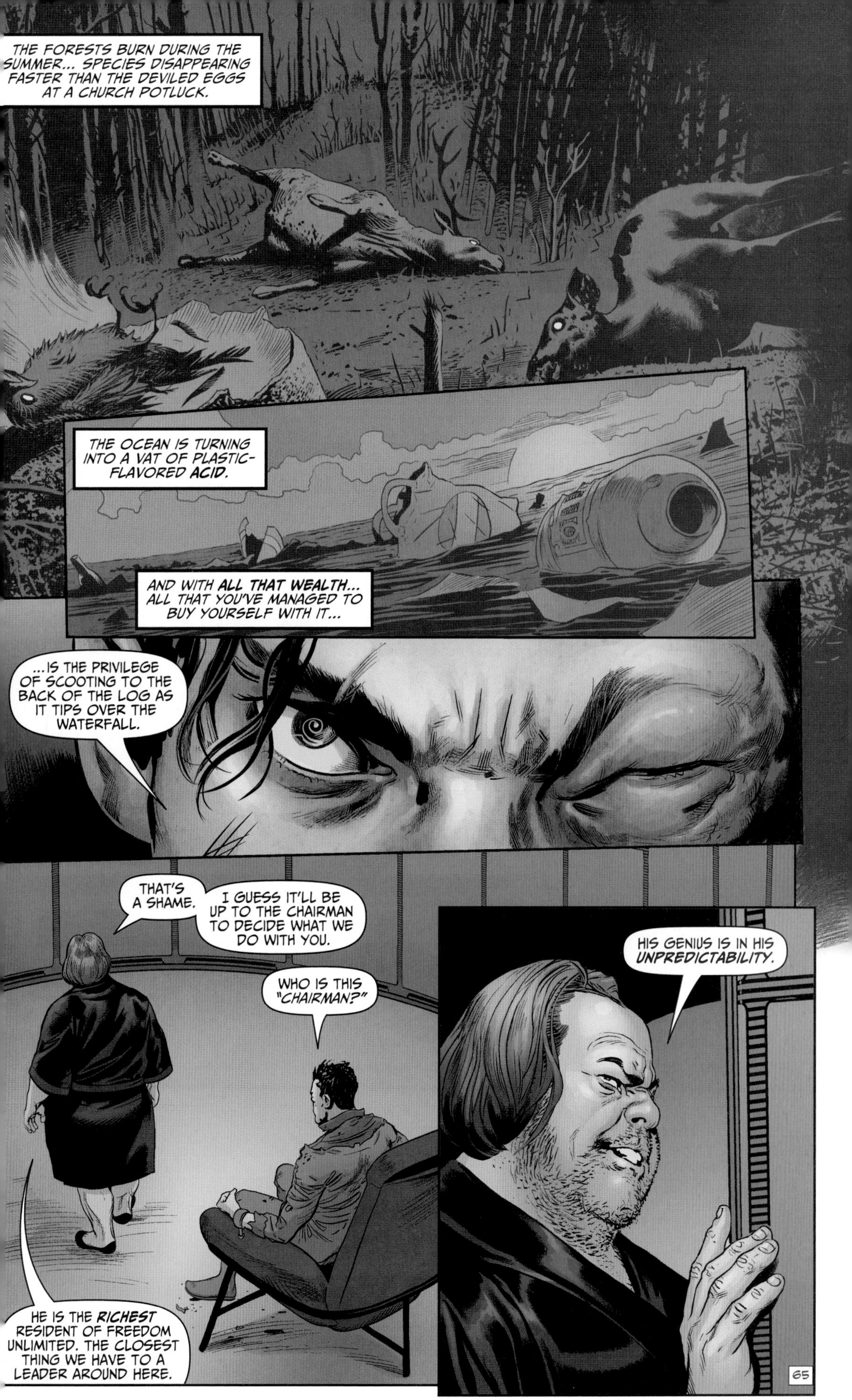
THE FORESTS BURN DURING THE SUMMER... SPECIES DISAPPEARING FASTER THAN THE DEVILED EGGS AT A CHURCH POTLUCK.
THE OCEAN IS TURNING INTO A VAT OF PLASTIC-FLAVORED ACID.
AND WITH ALL THAT WEALTH... ALL THAT YOU'VE MANAGED TO BUY YOURSELF WITH IT...
...IS THE PRIVILEGE OF SCOOTING TO THE BACK OF THE LOG AS IT TIPS OVER THE WATERFALL.
THAT'S A SHAME.
I GUESS IT'LL BE UP TO THE CHAIRMAN TO DECIDE WHAT WE DO WITH YOU.
WHO IS THIS "CHAIRMAN?"
HE IS THE RICHEST RESIDENT OF FREEDOM UNLIMITED. THE CLOSEST THING WE HAVE TO A LEADER AROUND HERE.
HIS GENIUS IS IN HIS UNPREDICTABILITY.

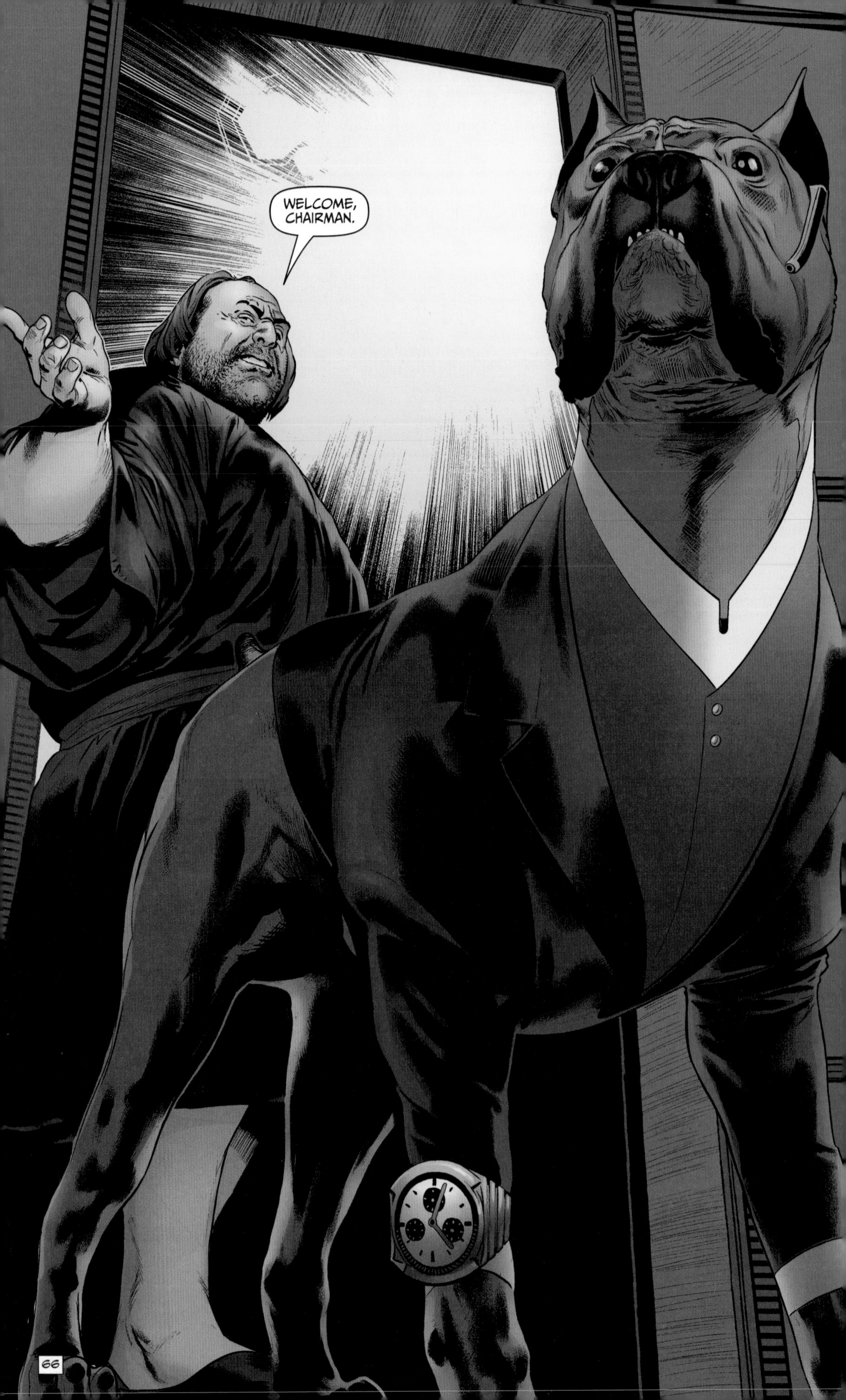
WELCOME, CHAIRMAN.

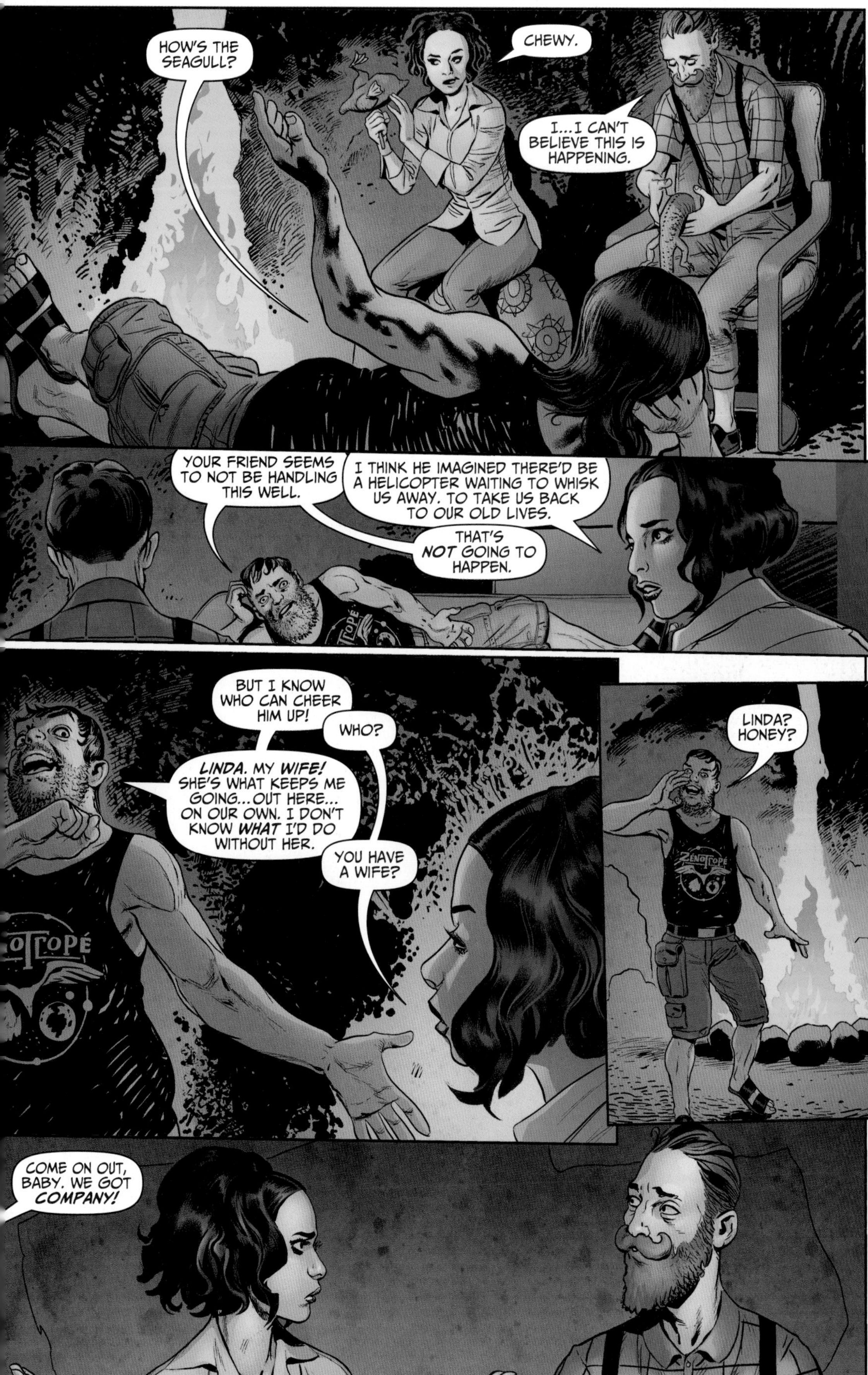
HOW'S THE SEAGULL?
CHEWY.
I...I CAN'T BELIEVE THIS IS HAPPENING.
YOUR FRIEND SEEMS TO NOT BE HANDLING THIS WELL.
I THINK HE IMAGINED THERE'D BE A HELICOPTER WAITING TO WHISK US AWAY. TO TAKE US BACK TO OUR OLD LIVES.
THAT'S NOT GOING TO HAPPEN.
BUT I KNOW WHO CAN CHEER HIM UP!
WHO?
LINDA. MY WIFE! SHE'S WHAT KEEPS ME GOING...OUT HERE... ON OUR OWN. I DON'T KNOW WHAT I'D DO WITHOUT HER.
YOU HAVE A WIFE?
LINDA? HONEY?
COME ON OUT, BABY. WE GOT COMPANY!
ZENOTROPÉ

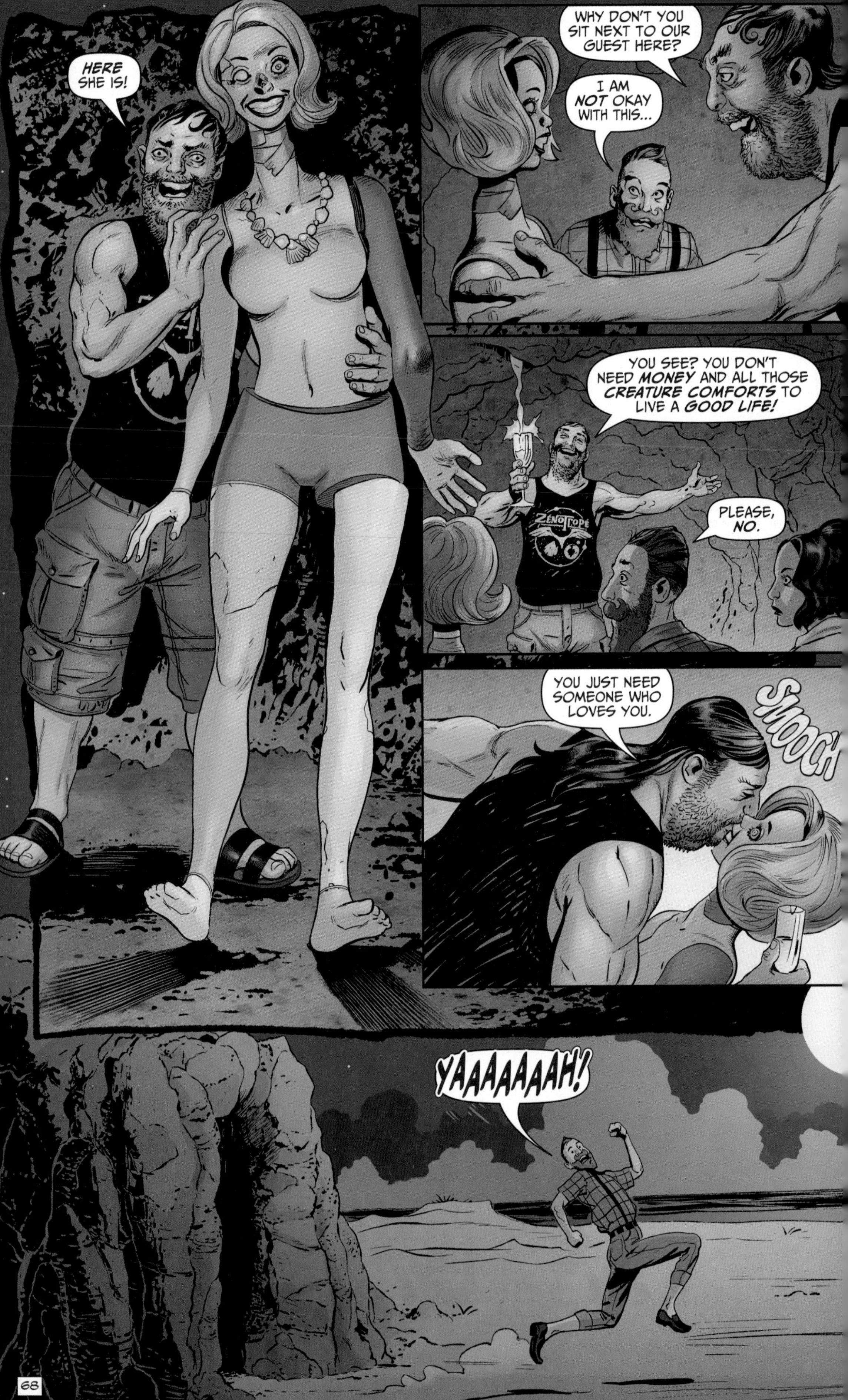
HERE SHE IS!
WHY DON'T YOU SIT NEXT TO OUR GUEST HERE?
I AM NOT OKAY WITH THIS...
YOU SEE? YOU DON'T NEED MONEY AND ALL THOSE CREATURE COMFORTS TO LIVE A GOOD LIFE!
ZÉNOTROPE
PLEASE, NO.
YOU JUST NEED SOMEONE WHO LOVES YOU.
SMOOCH
YAAAAAAAH!

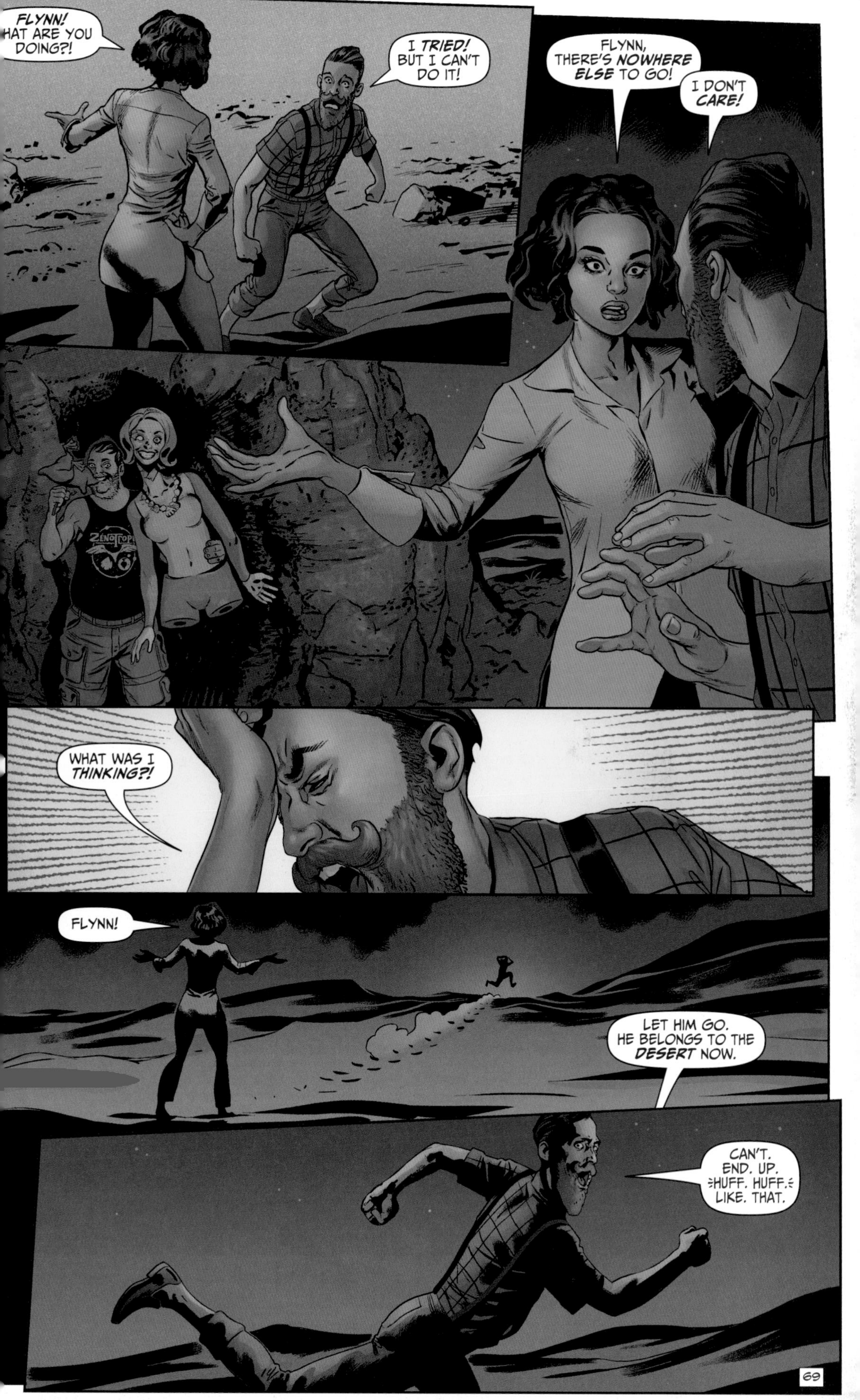
FLYNN! HAT ARE YOU DOING?!
I TRIED! BUT I CAN'T DO IT!
FLYNN, THERE'S NOWHERE ELSE TO GO!
I DON'T CARE!
WHAT WAS I THINKING?!
FLYNN!
LET HIM GO. HE BELONGS TO THE DESERT NOW.
CAN'T. END. UP. HUFF. HUFF. LIKE. THAT.

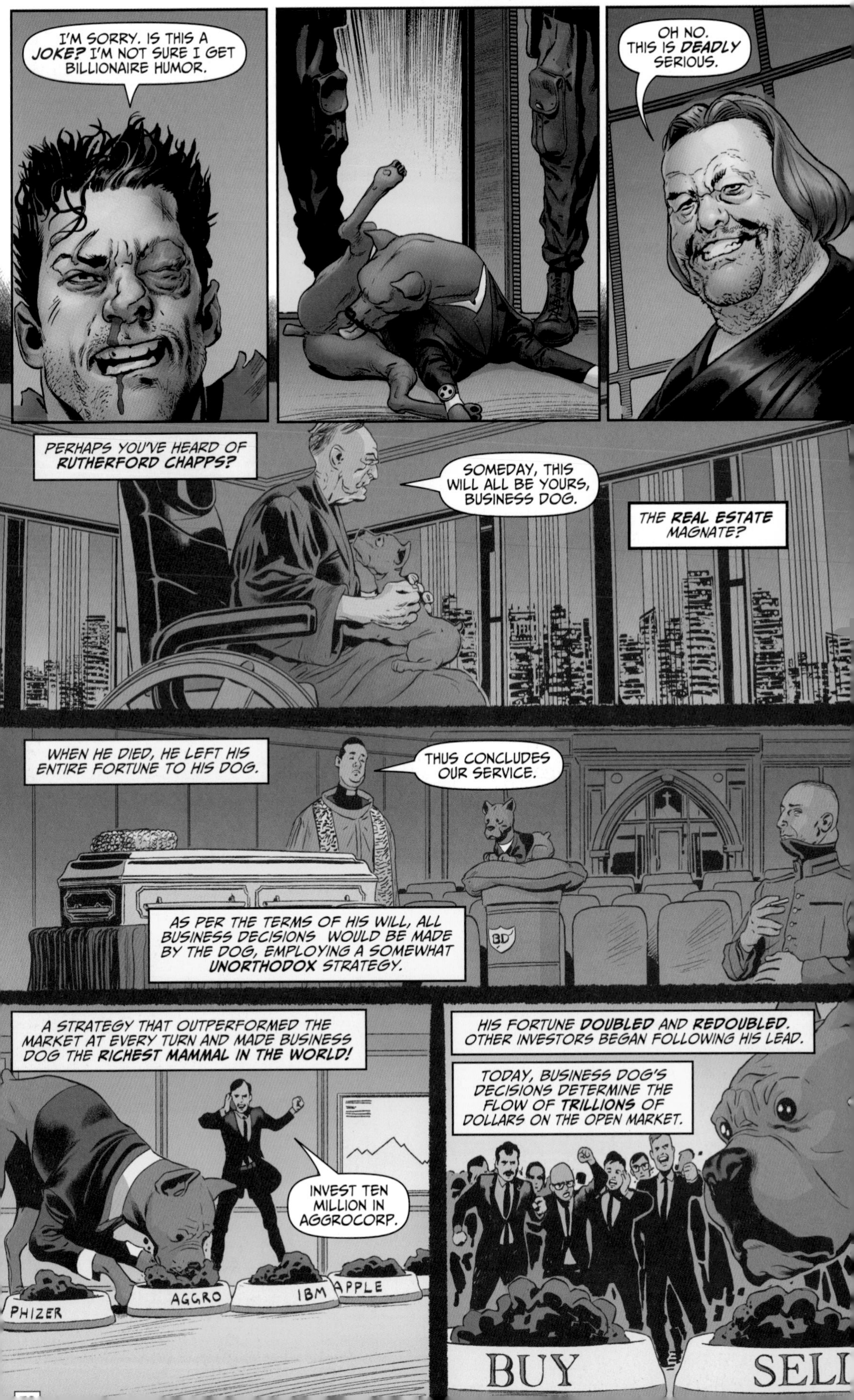

I'M SORRY. IS THIS A JOKE? I'M NOT SURE I GET BILLIONAIRE HUMOR.
OH NO. THIS IS DEADLY SERIOUS.
PERHAPS YOU'VE HEARD OF RUTHERFORD CHAPPS?
SOMEDAY, THIS WILL ALL BE YOURS, BUSINESS DOG.
THE REAL ESTATE MAGNATE?
WHEN HE DIED, HE LEFT HIS ENTIRE FORTUNE TO HIS DOG.
THUS CONCLUDES OUR SERVICE.
BD
AS PER THE TERMS OF HIS WILL, ALL BUSINESS DECISIONS WOULD BE MADE BY THE DOG, EMPLOYING A SOMEWHAT UNORTHODOX STRATEGY.
A STRATEGY THAT OUTPERFORMED THE MARKET AT EVERY TURN AND MADE BUSINESS DOG THE RICHEST MAMMAL IN THE WORLD!
INVEST TEN MILLION IN AGGROCORP.
PHIZER
AGGRO
IBM
APPLE
HIS FORTUNE DOUBLED AND REDOUBLED. OTHER INVESTORS BEGAN FOLLOWING HIS LEAD.
TODAY, BUSINESS DOG'S DECISIONS DETERMINE THE FLOW OF TRILLIONS OF DOLLARS ON THE OPEN MARKET.
BUY
SELL

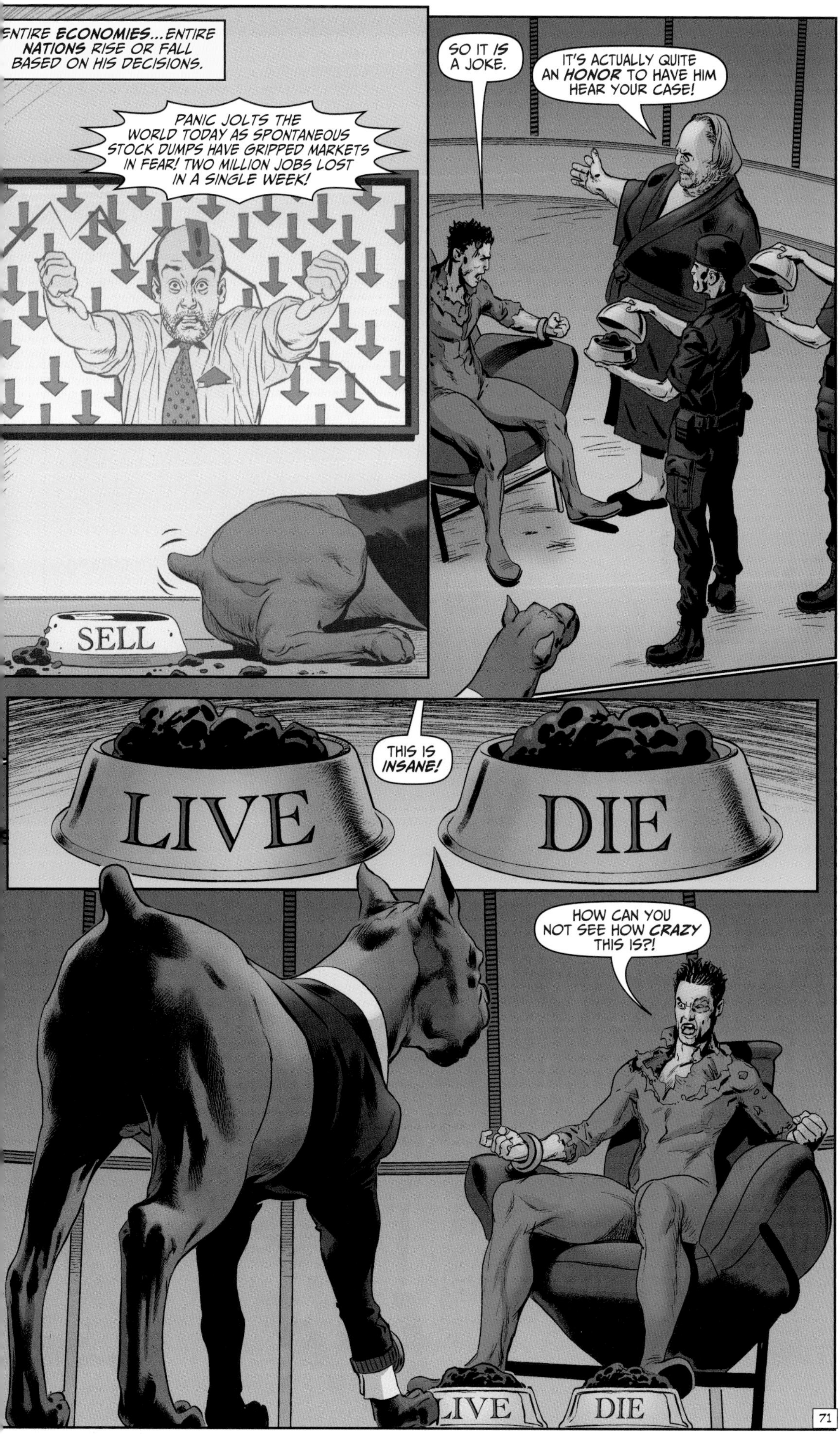
ENTIRE ECONOMIES...ENTIRE NATIONS RISE OR FALL BASED ON HIS DECISIONS.
PANIC JOLTS THE WORLD TODAY AS SPONTANEOUS STOCK DUMPS HAVE GRIPPED MARKETS IN FEAR! TWO MILLION JOBS LOST IN A SINGLE WEEK!
SELL
SO IT IS A JOKE.
IT'S ACTUALLY QUITE AN HONOR TO HAVE HIM HEAR YOUR CASE!
LIVE
THIS IS INSANE!
DIE
HOW CAN YOU NOT SEE HOW CRAZY THIS IS?!
LIVE
DIE

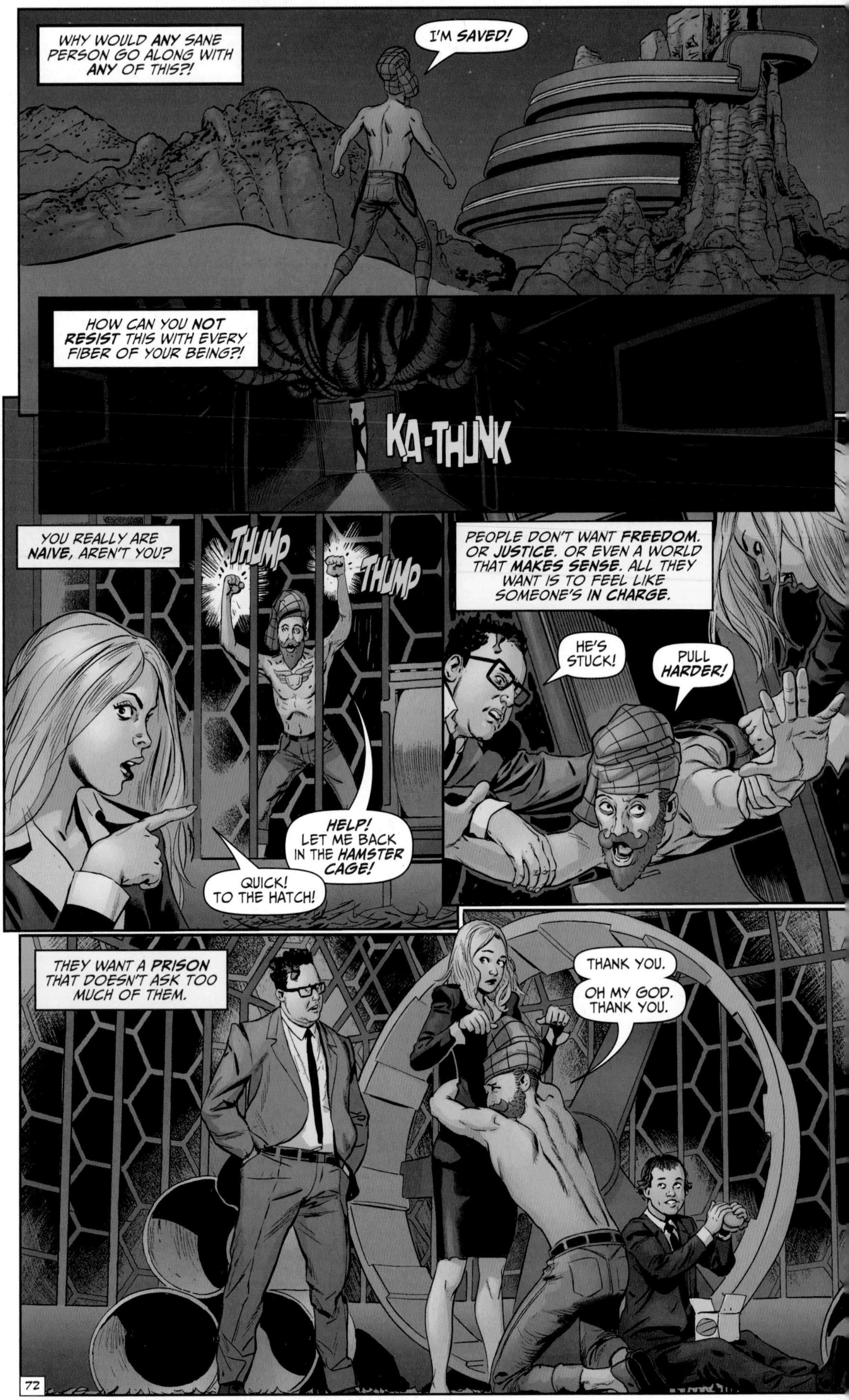
WHY WOULD ANY SANE PERSON GO ALONG WITH ANY OF THIS?!
I'M SAVED!
HOW CAN YOU NOT RESIST THIS WITH EVERY FIBER OF YOUR BEING?!
KA-THUNK
YOU REALLY ARE NAIVE, AREN'T YOU?
THUMP
THUMP
HELP! LET ME BACK IN THE HAMSTER CAGE!
QUICK! TO THE HATCH!
PEOPLE DON'T WANT FREEDOM. OR JUSTICE. OR EVEN A WORLD THAT MAKES SENSE. ALL THEY WANT IS TO FEEL LIKE SOMEONE'S IN CHARGE.
HE'S STUCK!
PULL HARDER!
THEY WANT A PRISON THAT DOESN'T ASK TOO MUCH OF THEM.
THANK YOU.
OH MY GOD. THANK YOU.

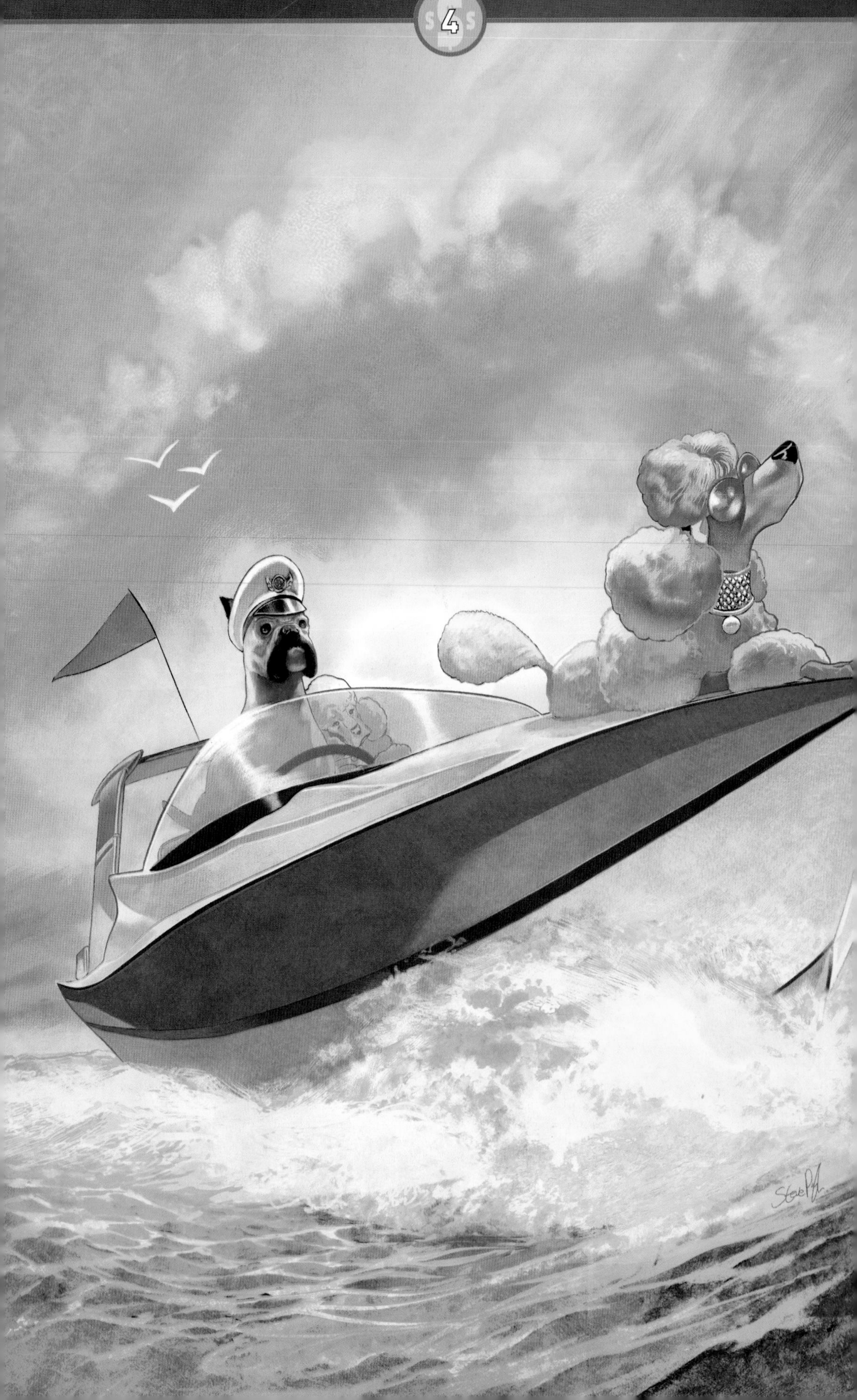

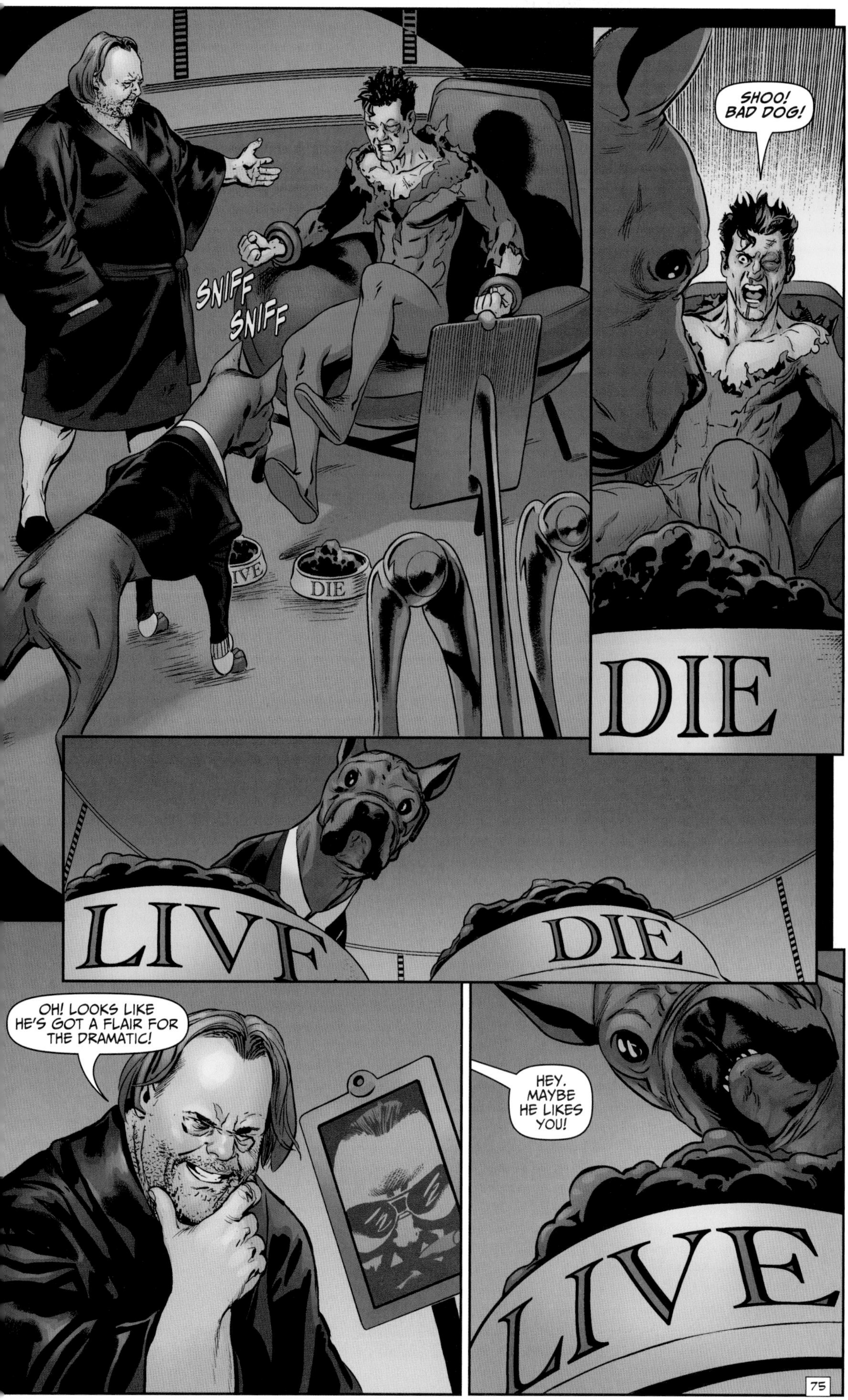
SNIFF
SNIFF
LIVE
DIE
SHOO! BAD DOG!
DIE
LIVE
DIE
OH! LOOKS LIKE HE'S GOT A FLAIR FOR THE DRAMATIC!
HEY. MAYBE HE LIKES YOU!
LIVE

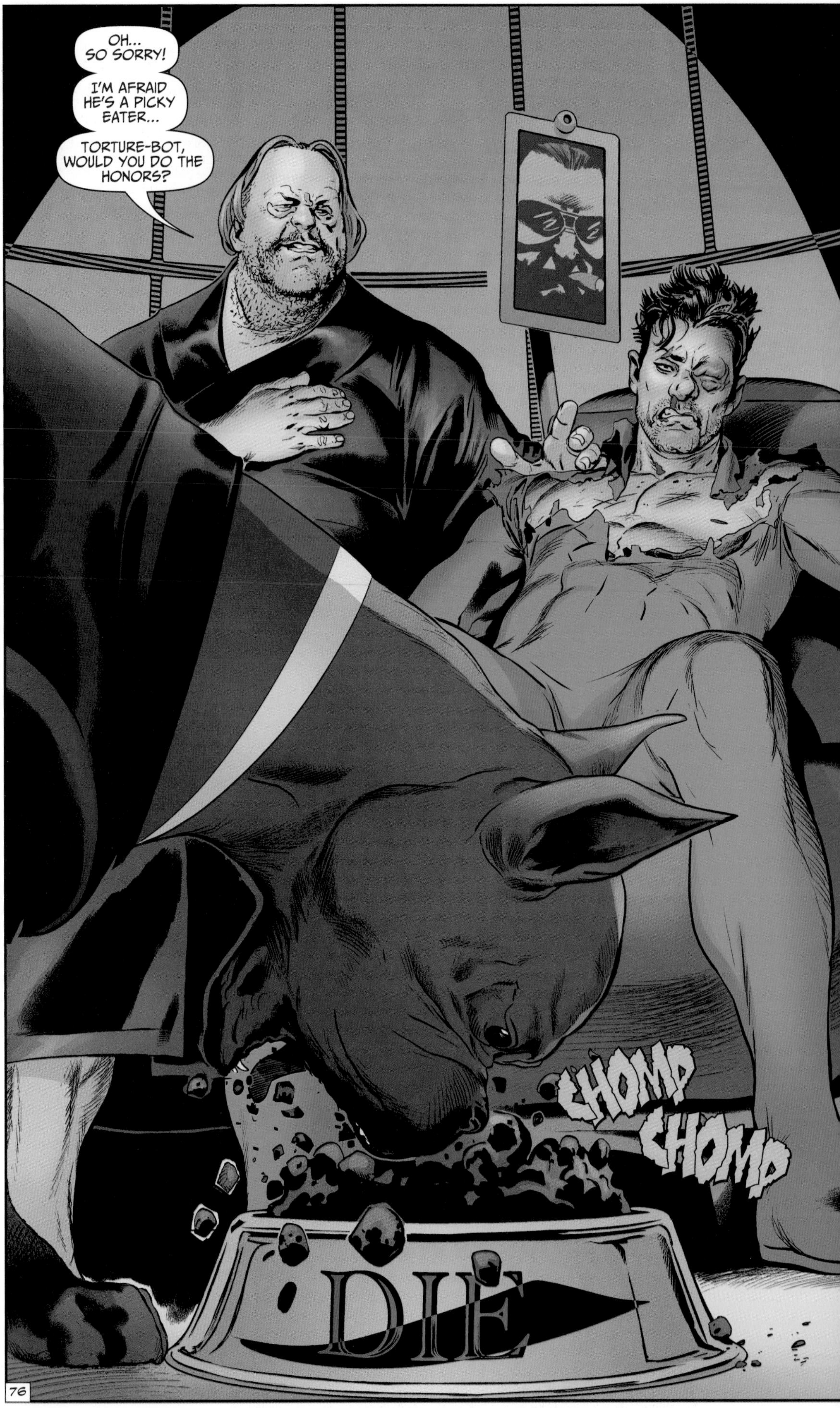
OH... SO SORRY!
I'M AFRAID HE'S A PICKY EATER...
TORTURE-BOT, WOULD YOU DO THE HONORS?
CHOMP
CHOMP
DIE

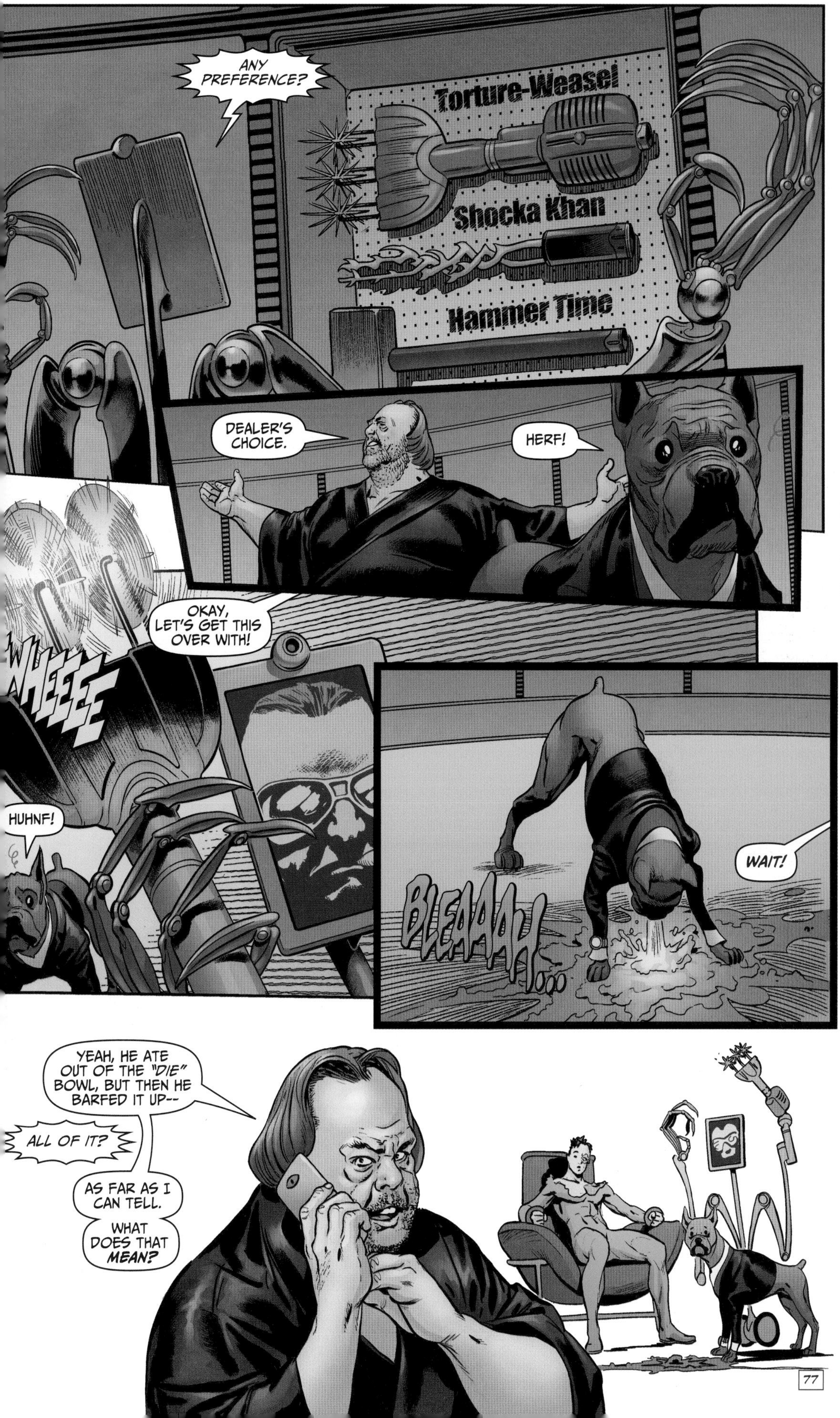
ANY PREFERENCE?
Torture-Weasel
Shocka Khan
Hammer Time
DEALER'S CHOICE.
HERF!
OKAY, LET'S GET THIS OVER WITH!
WHEEEE
HUHNF!
WAIT!
BLEAAAH...
YEAH, HE ATE OUT OF THE "DIE" BOWL, BUT THEN HE BARFED IT UP--
ALL OF IT?
AS FAR AS I CAN TELL.
WHAT DOES THAT MEAN?

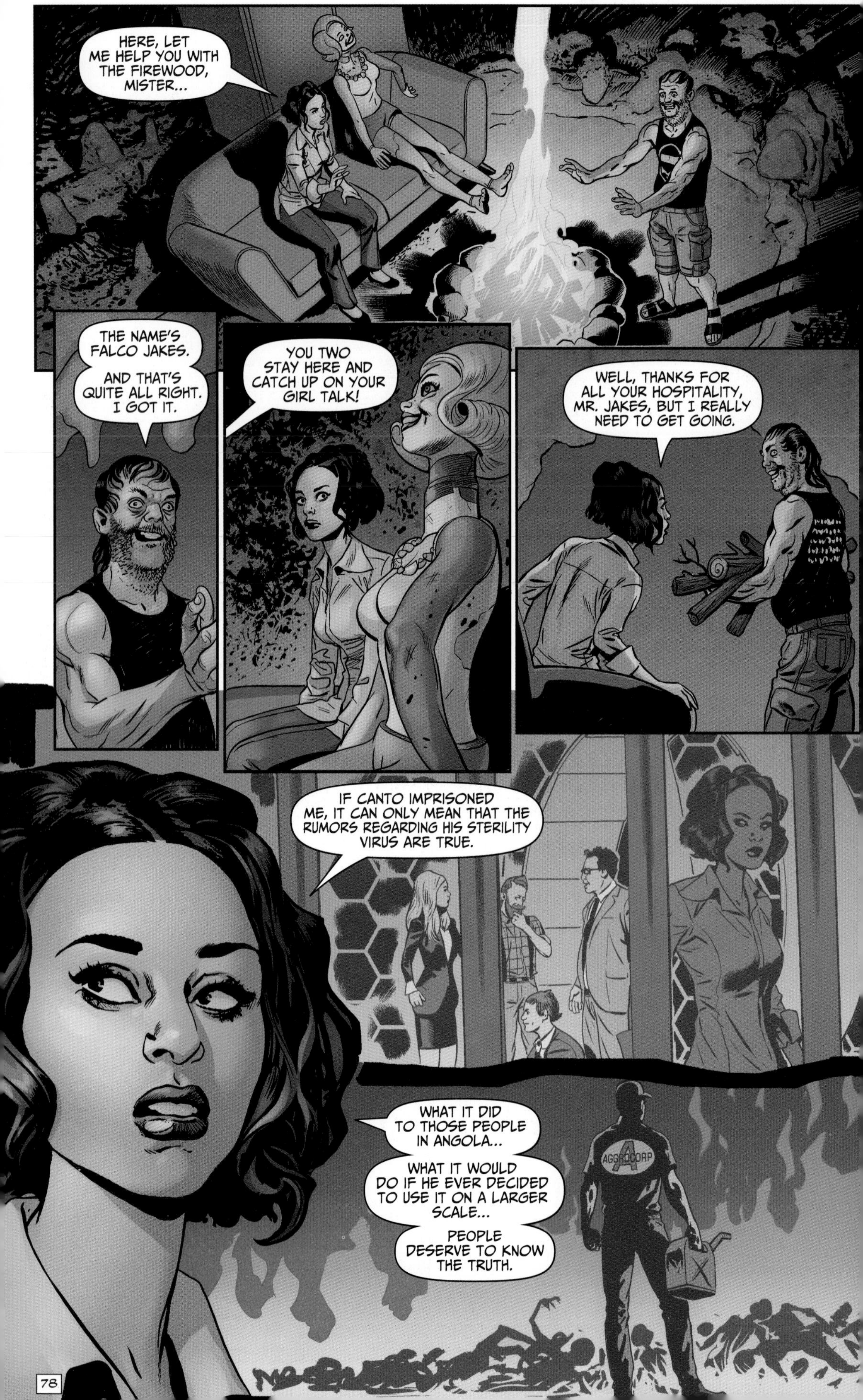
HERE, LET ME HELP YOU WITH THE FIREWOOD, MISTER...
THE NAME'S FALCO JAKES.
AND THAT'S QUITE ALL RIGHT. I GOT IT.
YOU TWO STAY HERE AND CATCH UP ON YOUR GIRL TALK!
WELL, THANKS FOR ALL YOUR HOSPITALITY, MR. JAKES, BUT I REALLY NEED TO GET GOING.
IF CANTO IMPRISONED ME, IT CAN ONLY MEAN THAT THE RUMORS REGARDING HIS STERILITY VIRUS ARE TRUE.
WHAT IT DID TO THOSE PEOPLE IN ANGOLA...
WHAT IT WOULD DO IF HE EVER DECIDED TO USE IT ON A LARGER SCALE...
PEOPLE DESERVE TO KNOW THE TRUTH.
AGGROCORP

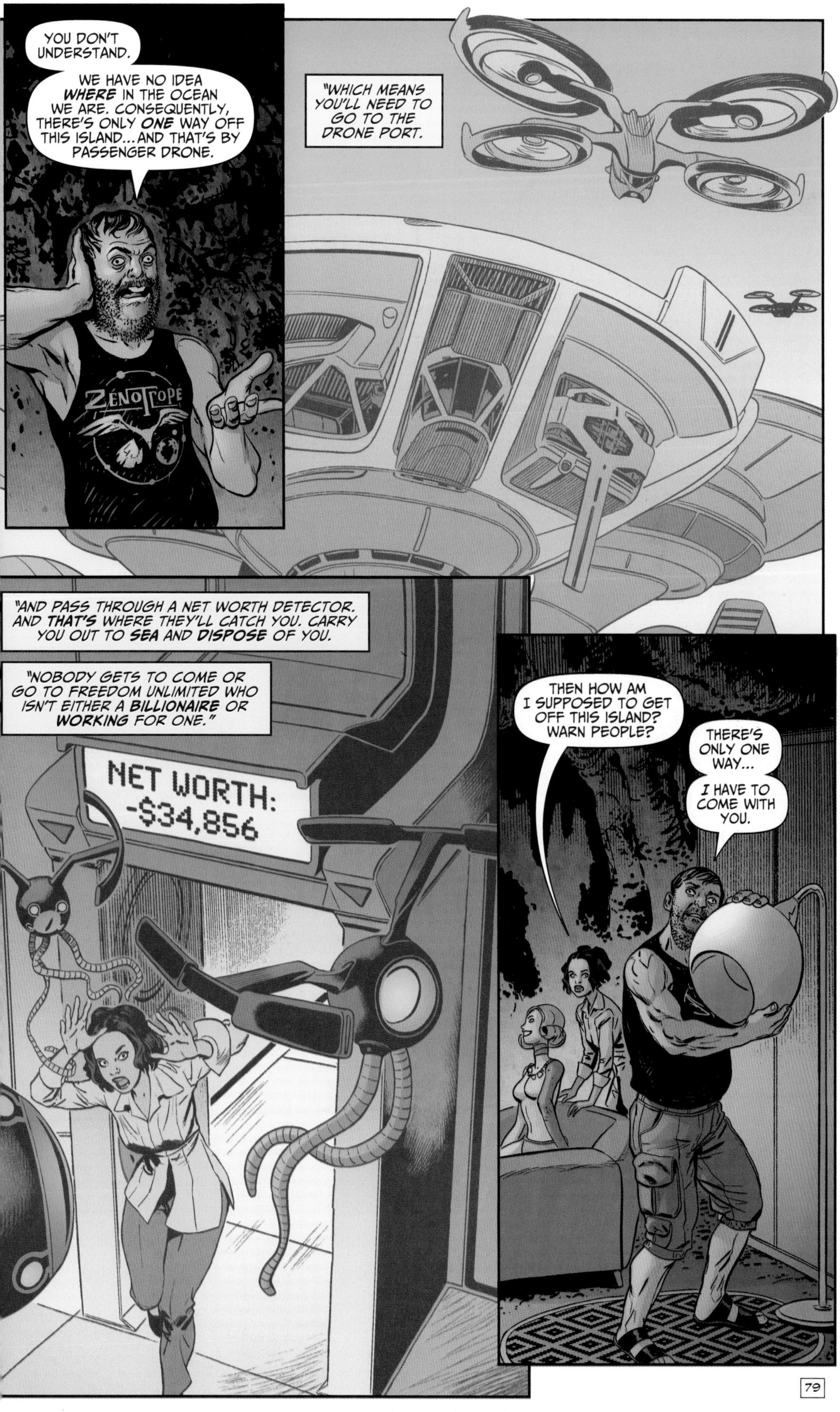
YOU DON'T UNDERSTAND.
WE HAVE NO IDEA **WHERE** IN THE OCEAN WE ARE. CONSEQUENTLY, THERE'S ONLY **ONE** WAY OFF THIS ISLAND...AND THAT'S BY PASSENGER DRONE.
"WHICH MEANS YOU'LL NEED TO GO TO THE DRONE PORT.
"AND PASS THROUGH A NET WORTH DETECTOR. AND **THAT'S** WHERE THEY'LL CATCH YOU. CARRY YOU OUT TO **SEA** AND **DISPOSE** OF YOU.
"NOBODY GETS TO COME OR GO TO FREEDOM UNLIMITED WHO ISN'T EITHER A **BILLIONAIRE** OR **WORKING** FOR ONE."
NET WORTH: -$34,856
THEN HOW AM I SUPPOSED TO GET OFF THIS ISLAND? WARN PEOPLE?
THERE'S ONLY ONE WAY...
I HAVE TO COME WITH YOU.

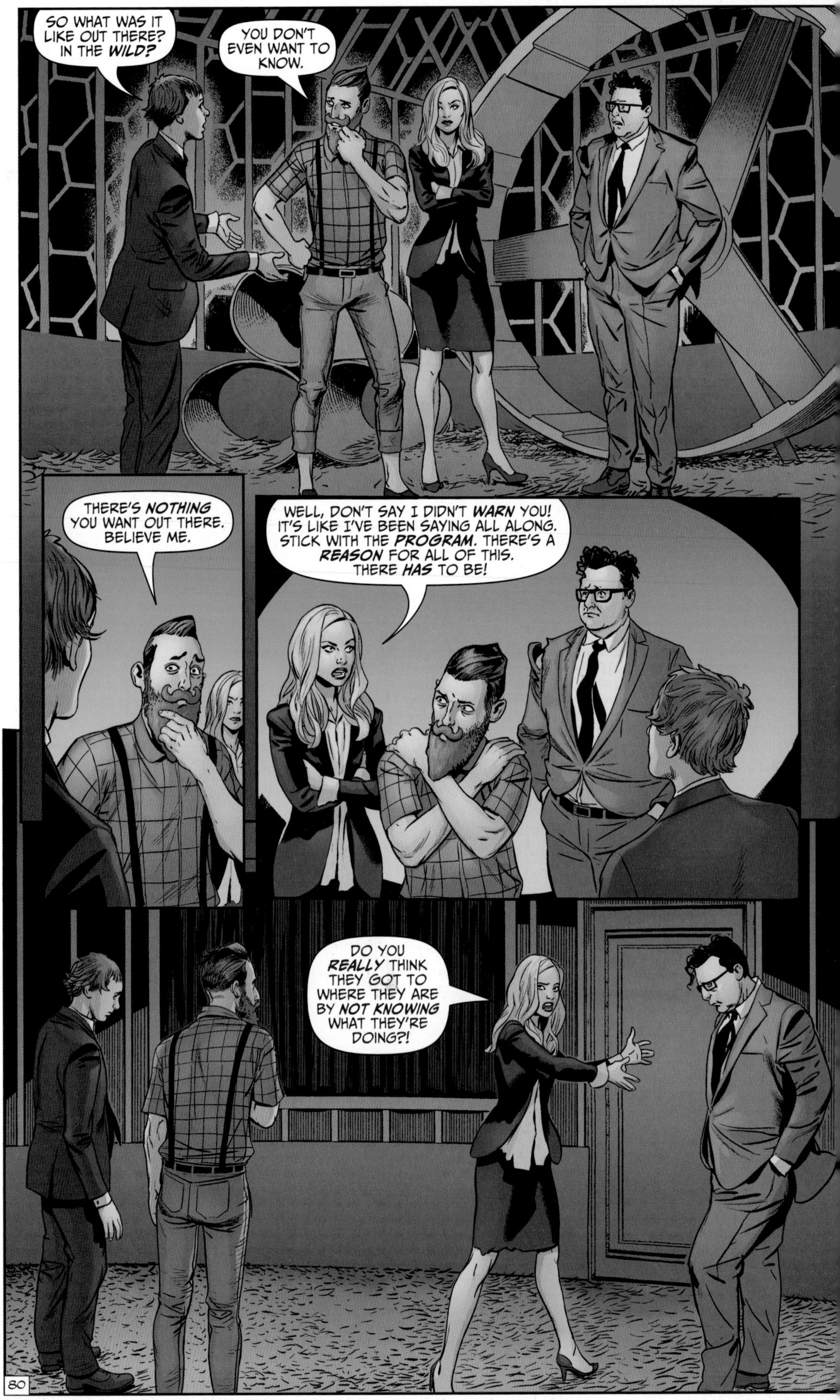
SO WHAT WAS IT LIKE OUT THERE? IN THE *WILD?*
YOU DON'T EVEN WANT TO KNOW.
THERE'S *NOTHING* YOU WANT OUT THERE. BELIEVE ME.
WELL, DON'T SAY I DIDN'T *WARN* YOU! IT'S LIKE I'VE BEEN SAYING ALL ALONG. STICK WITH THE *PROGRAM*. THERE'S A *REASON* FOR ALL OF THIS. THERE *HAS* TO BE!
DO YOU *REALLY* THINK THEY GOT TO WHERE THEY ARE BY *NOT KNOWING* WHAT THEY'RE DOING?!

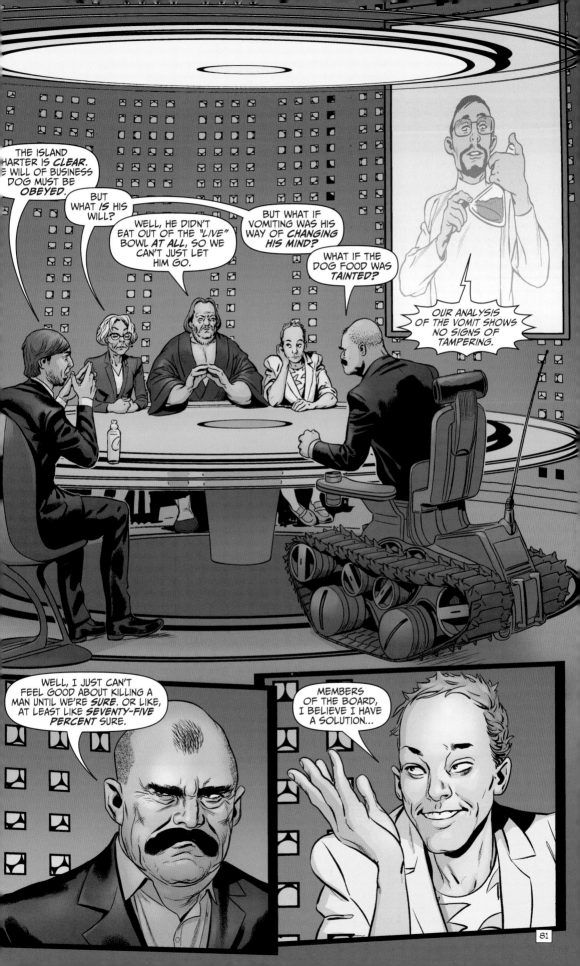

THE ISLAND CHARTER IS *CLEAR.* THE WILL OF BUSINESS DOG MUST BE *OBEYED.*

BUT WHAT *IS* HIS WILL?

WELL, HE DIDN'T EAT OUT OF THE *"LIVE"* BOWL *AT ALL,* SO WE CAN'T JUST LET HIM GO.

BUT WHAT IF VOMITING WAS HIS WAY OF *CHANGING HIS MIND?*

WHAT IF THE DOG FOOD WAS *TAINTED?*

OUR ANALYSIS OF THE VOMIT SHOWS NO SIGNS OF TAMPERING.

WELL, I JUST CAN'T FEEL GOOD ABOUT KILLING A MAN UNTIL WE'RE *SURE.* OR LIKE, AT LEAST LIKE *SEVENTY-FIVE PERCENT* SURE.

MEMBERS OF THE BOARD, I BELIEVE I HAVE A SOLUTION...

81

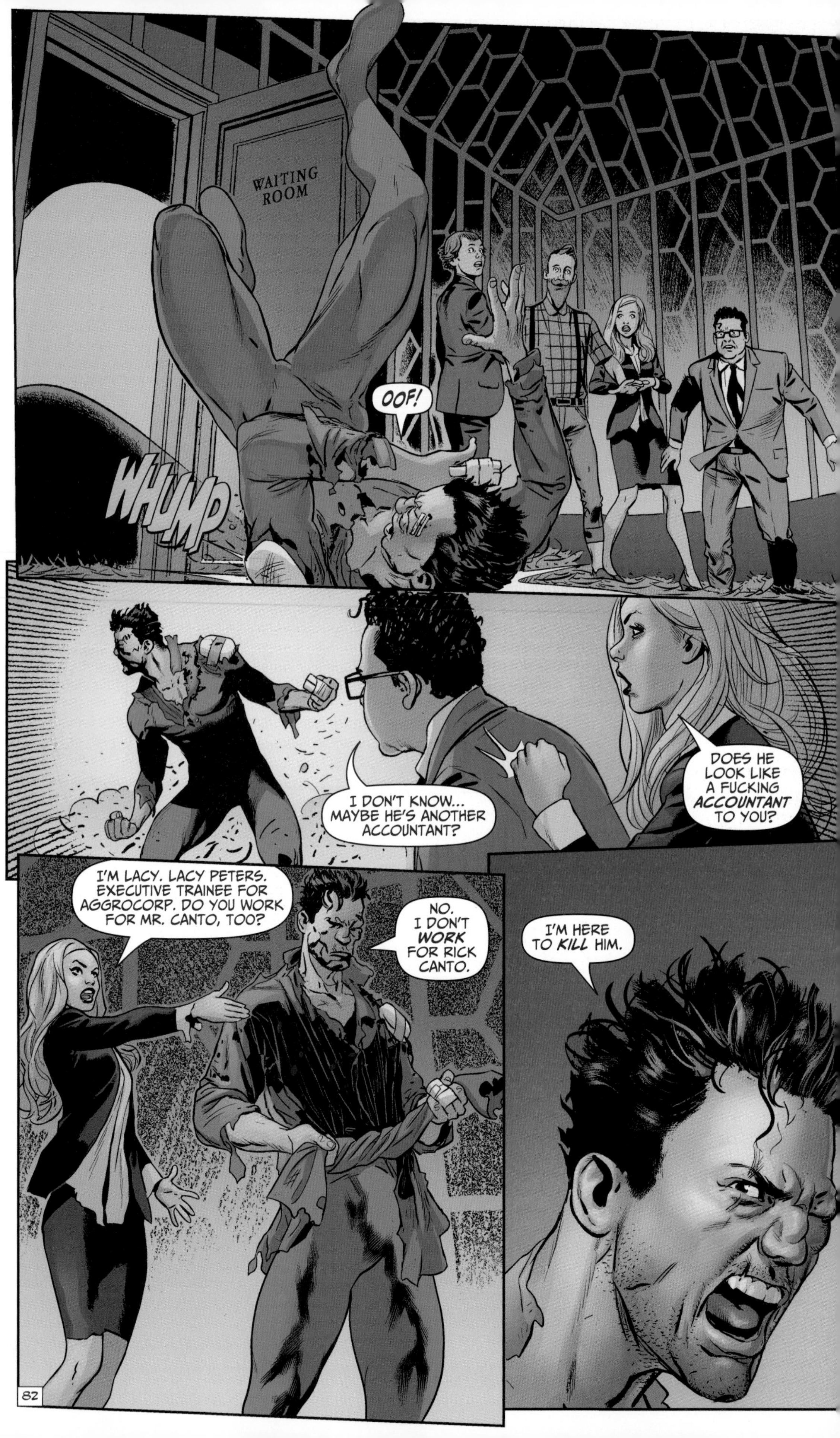

WAITING ROOM
OOF!
WHUMP
I DON'T KNOW... MAYBE HE'S ANOTHER ACCOUNTANT?
DOES HE LOOK LIKE A FUCKING ACCOUNTANT TO YOU?
I'M LACY. LACY PETERS. EXECUTIVE TRAINEE FOR AGGROCORP. DO YOU WORK FOR MR. CANTO, TOO?
NO. I DON'T WORK FOR RICK CANTO.
I'M HERE TO KILL HIM.

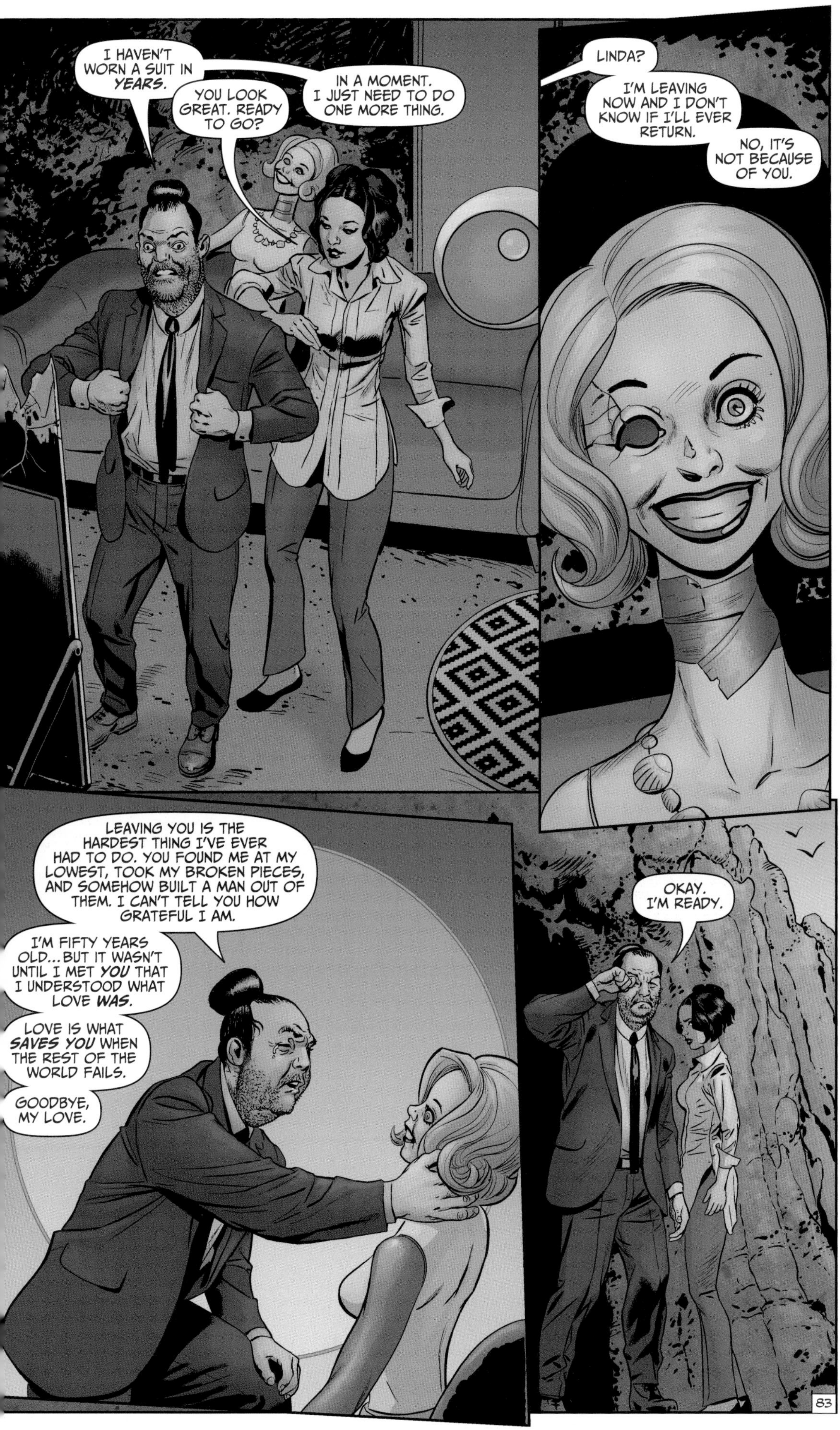

I HAVEN'T WORN A SUIT IN *YEARS*.
YOU LOOK GREAT. READY TO GO?
IN A MOMENT. I JUST NEED TO DO ONE MORE THING.
LINDA?
I'M LEAVING NOW AND I DON'T KNOW IF I'LL EVER RETURN.
NO, IT'S NOT BECAUSE OF YOU.
LEAVING YOU IS THE HARDEST THING I'VE EVER HAD TO DO. YOU FOUND ME AT MY LOWEST, TOOK MY BROKEN PIECES, AND SOMEHOW BUILT A MAN OUT OF THEM. I CAN'T TELL YOU HOW GRATEFUL I AM.
I'M FIFTY YEARS OLD...BUT IT WASN'T UNTIL I MET *YOU* THAT I UNDERSTOOD WHAT LOVE *WAS*.
LOVE IS WHAT *SAVES YOU* WHEN THE REST OF THE WORLD FAILS.
GOODBYE, MY LOVE.
OKAY. I'M READY.

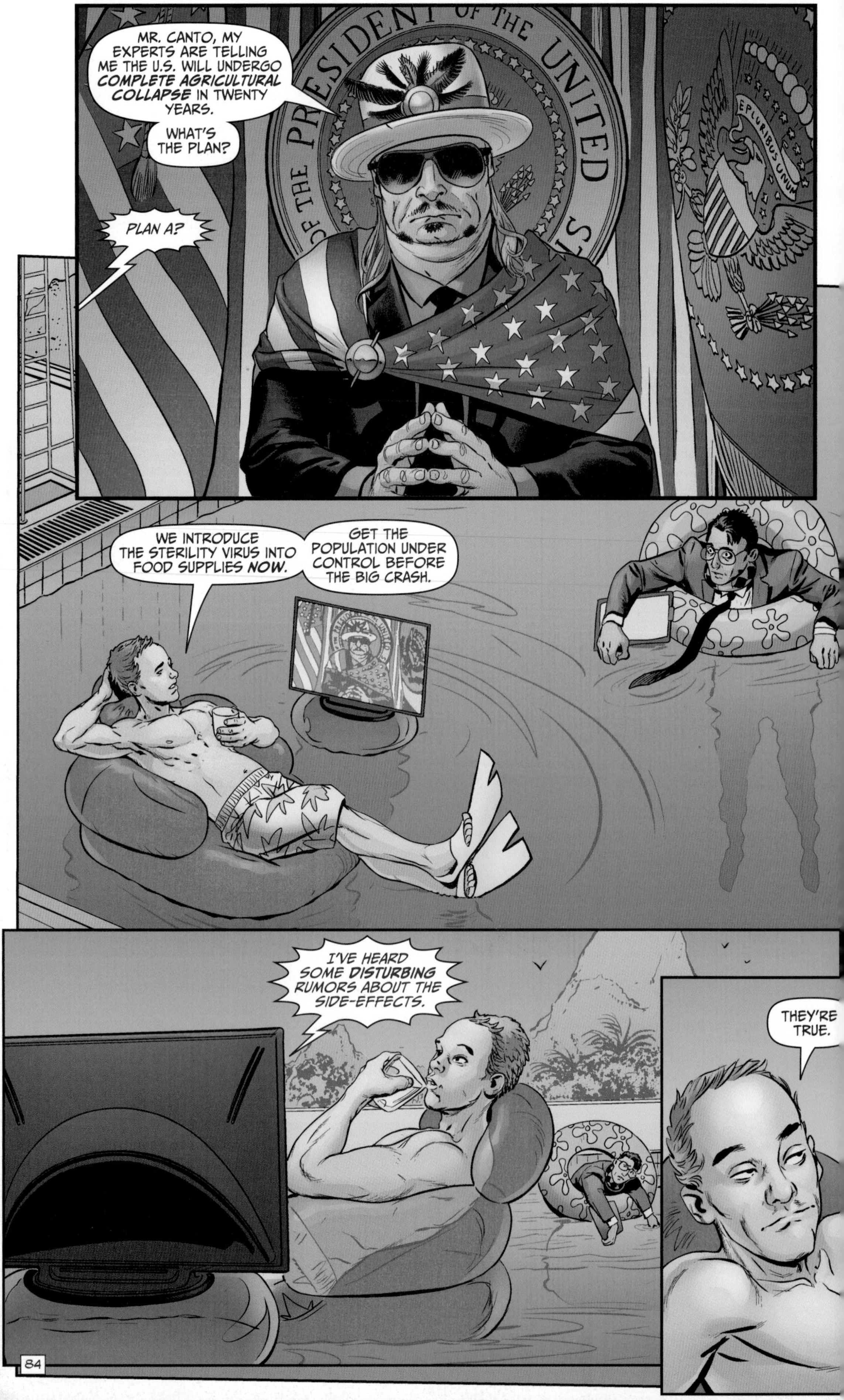

MR. CANTO, MY EXPERTS ARE TELLING ME THE U.S. WILL UNDERGO **COMPLETE AGRICULTURAL COLLAPSE** IN TWENTY YEARS.
WHAT'S THE PLAN?
PLAN A?
PRESIDENT OF THE UNITED STATES
E PLURIBUS UNUM
WE INTRODUCE THE STERILITY VIRUS INTO FOOD SUPPLIES **NOW.**
GET THE POPULATION UNDER CONTROL BEFORE THE BIG CRASH.
I'VE HEARD SOME ***DISTURBING*** *RUMORS ABOUT THE SIDE-EFFECTS.*
THEY'RE TRUE.

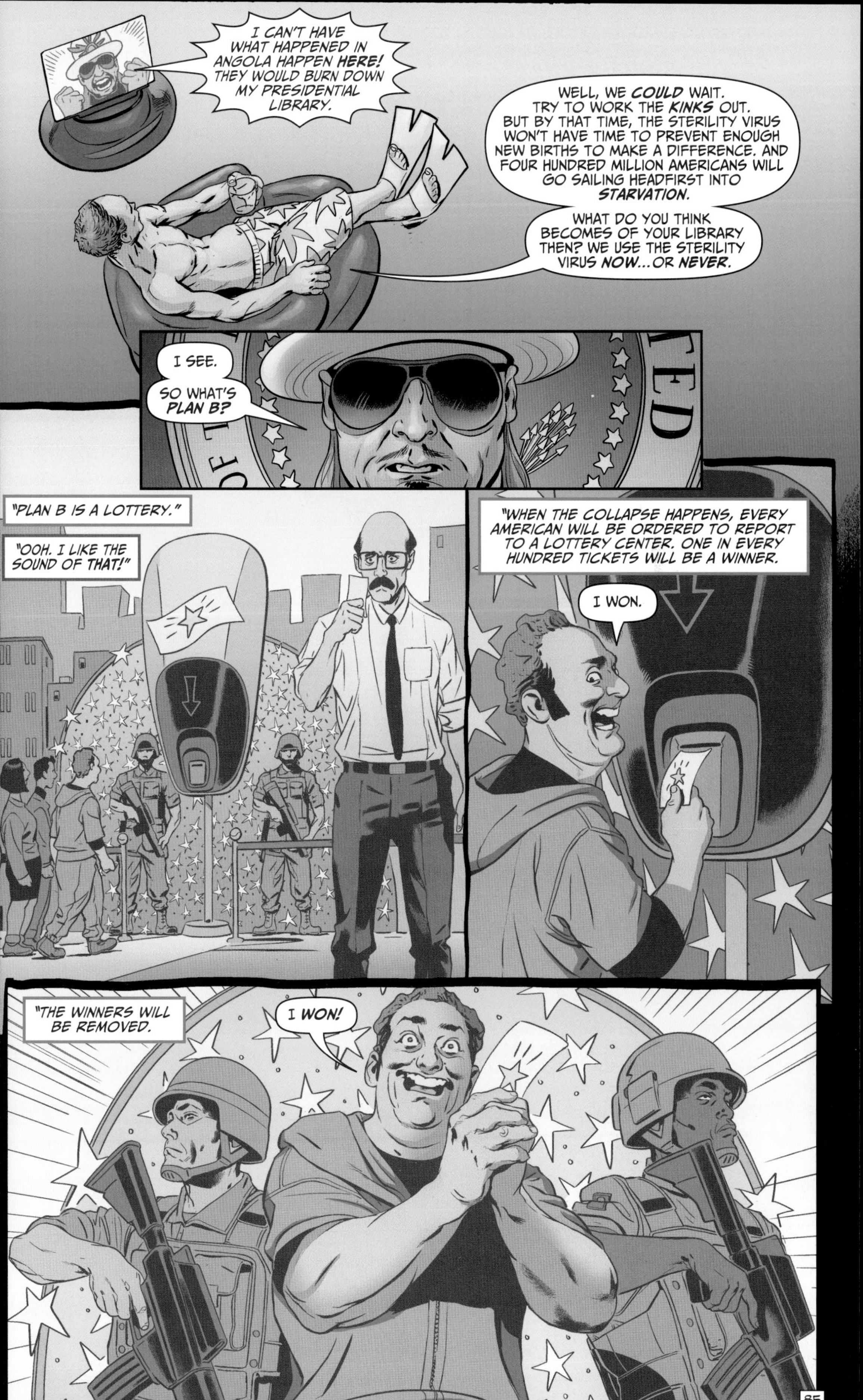
I CAN'T HAVE WHAT HAPPENED IN ANGOLA HAPPEN **HERE!** THEY WOULD BURN DOWN MY PRESIDENTIAL LIBRARY.
WELL, WE **COULD** WAIT. TRY TO WORK THE **KINKS** OUT. BUT BY THAT TIME, THE STERILITY VIRUS WON'T HAVE TIME TO PREVENT ENOUGH NEW BIRTHS TO MAKE A DIFFERENCE. AND FOUR HUNDRED MILLION AMERICANS WILL GO SAILING HEADFIRST INTO **STARVATION.**
WHAT DO YOU THINK BECOMES OF YOUR LIBRARY THEN? WE USE THE STERILITY VIRUS **NOW**...OR **NEVER.**
I SEE.
SO WHAT'S **PLAN B?**
"PLAN B IS A LOTTERY."
"OOH. I LIKE THE SOUND OF **THAT!**"
"WHEN THE COLLAPSE HAPPENS, EVERY AMERICAN WILL BE ORDERED TO REPORT TO A LOTTERY CENTER. ONE IN EVERY HUNDRED TICKETS WILL BE A WINNER.
I WON.
"THE WINNERS WILL BE REMOVED.
I **WON!**

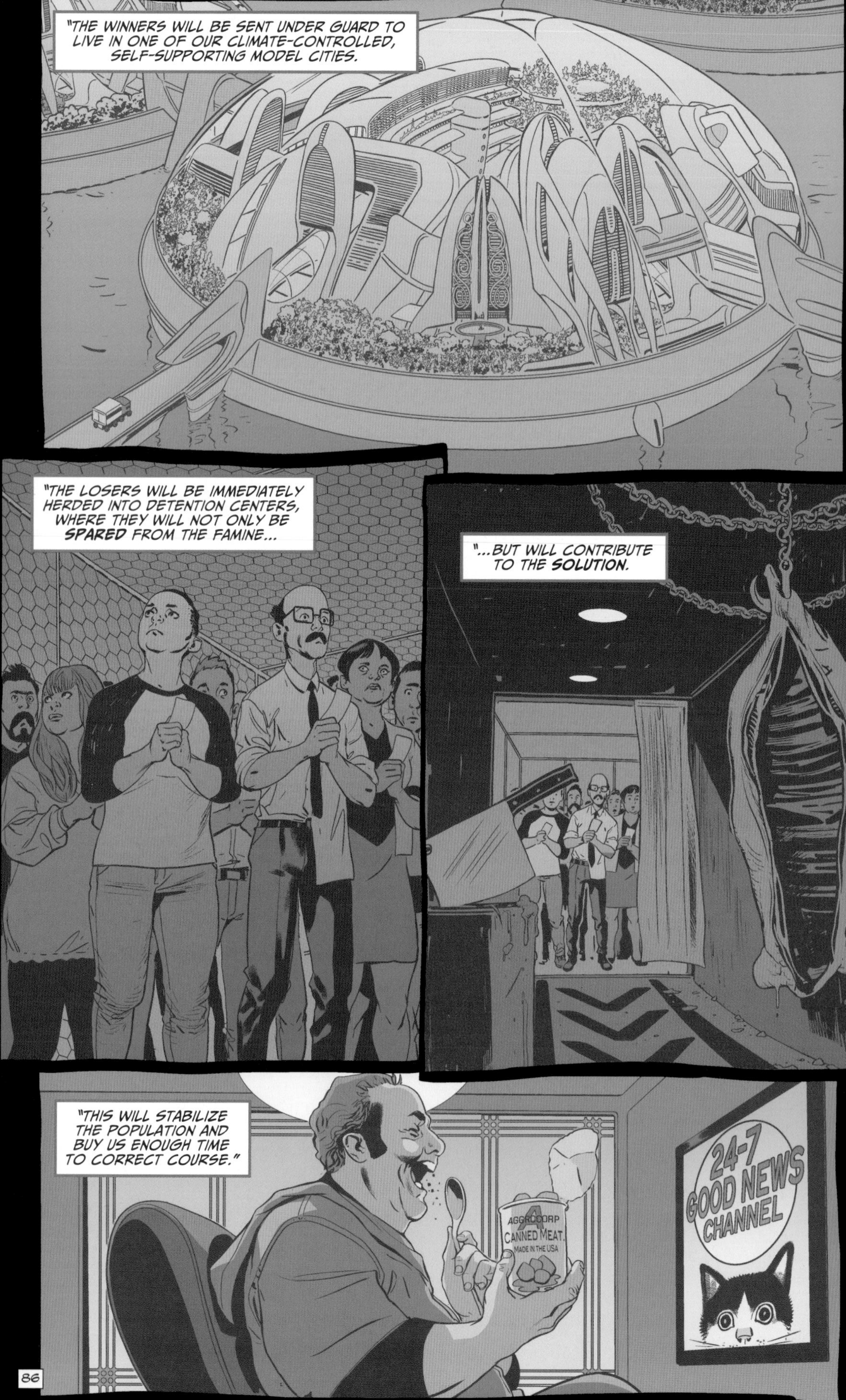
"THE WINNERS WILL BE SENT UNDER GUARD TO LIVE IN ONE OF OUR CLIMATE-CONTROLLED, SELF-SUPPORTING MODEL CITIES.
"THE LOSERS WILL BE IMMEDIATELY HERDED INTO DETENTION CENTERS, WHERE THEY WILL NOT ONLY BE SPARED FROM THE FAMINE...
"...BUT WILL CONTRIBUTE TO THE SOLUTION.
"THIS WILL STABILIZE THE POPULATION AND BUY US ENOUGH TIME TO CORRECT COURSE."
AGGROCORP
CANNED MEAT
MADE IN THE USA
24-7 GOOD NEWS CHANNEL

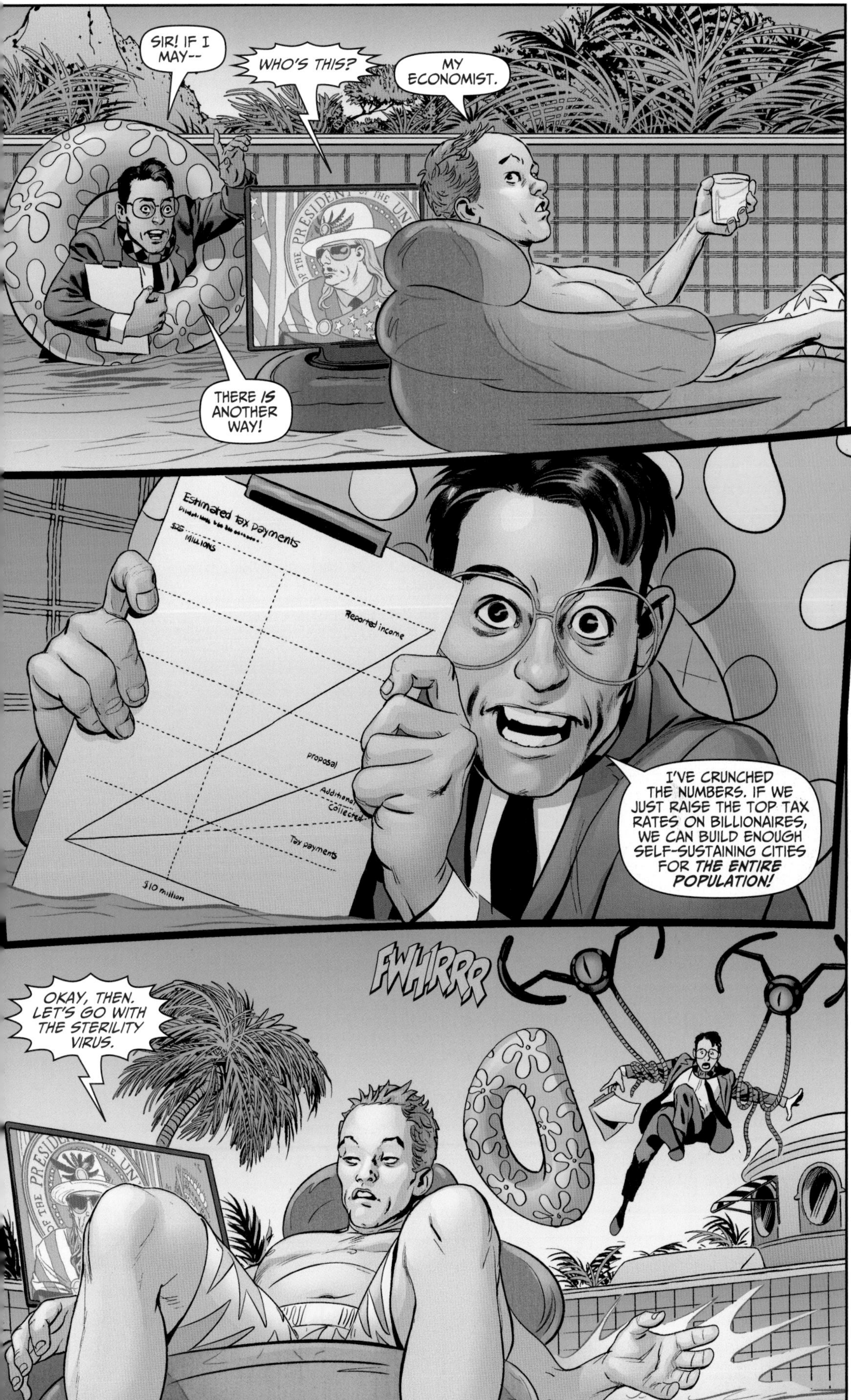
SIR! IF I MAY--
WHO'S THIS?
MY ECONOMIST.
THERE *IS* ANOTHER WAY!
Estimated tax payments
$25 Millions
Reported income
proposal
Additional collected
Tax payments
$10 million
I'VE CRUNCHED THE NUMBERS. IF WE JUST RAISE THE TOP TAX RATES ON BILLIONAIRES, WE CAN BUILD ENOUGH SELF-SUSTAINING CITIES FOR ***THE ENTIRE POPULATION!***
FWHIRRR
OKAY, THEN. LET'S GO WITH THE STERILITY VIRUS.

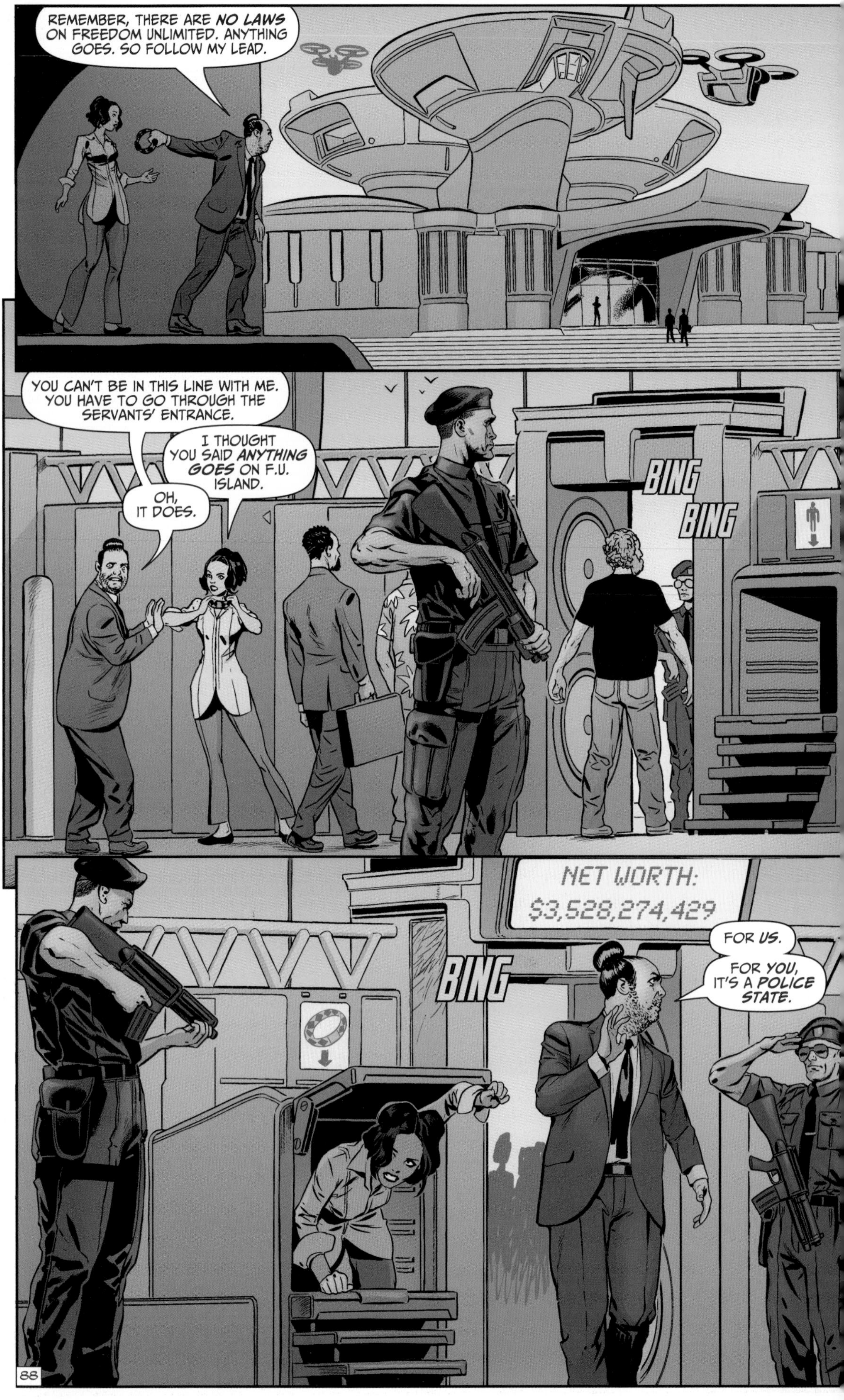
REMEMBER, THERE ARE NO LAWS ON FREEDOM UNLIMITED. ANYTHING GOES. SO FOLLOW MY LEAD.
YOU CAN'T BE IN THIS LINE WITH ME. YOU HAVE TO GO THROUGH THE SERVANTS' ENTRANCE.
I THOUGHT YOU SAID ANYTHING GOES ON F.U. ISLAND.
OH, IT DOES.
BING
BING
NET WORTH:
$3,528,274,429
BING
FOR US.
FOR YOU, IT'S A POLICE STATE.

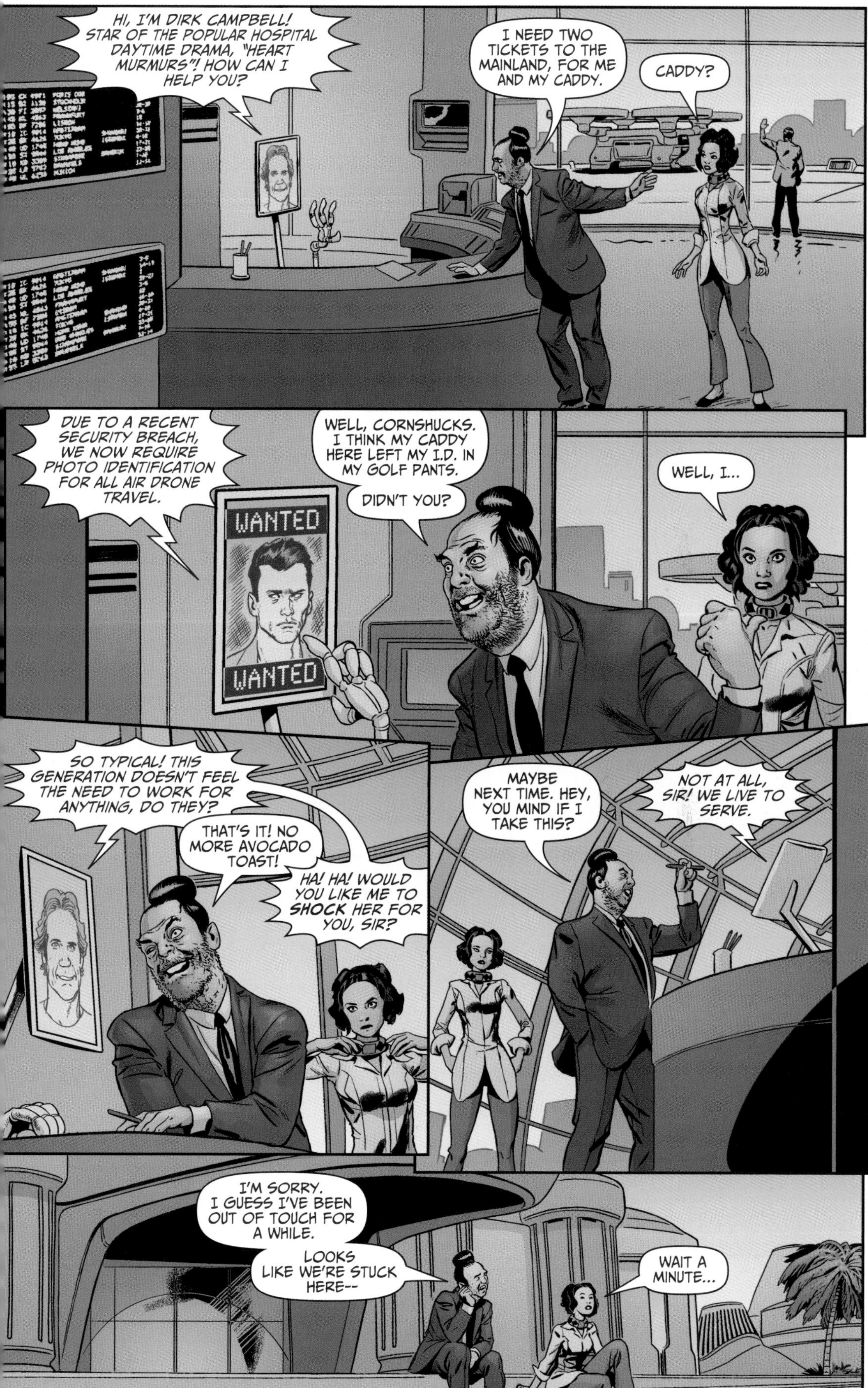
HI, I'M DIRK CAMPBELL! STAR OF THE POPULAR HOSPITAL DAYTIME DRAMA, "HEART MURMURS"! HOW CAN I HELP YOU?
I NEED TWO TICKETS TO THE MAINLAND, FOR ME AND MY CADDY.
CADDY?
DUE TO A RECENT SECURITY BREACH, WE NOW REQUIRE PHOTO IDENTIFICATION FOR ALL AIR DRONE TRAVEL.
WELL, CORNSHUCKS. I THINK MY CADDY HERE LEFT MY I.D. IN MY GOLF PANTS.
DIDN'T YOU?
WELL, I...
WANTED
WANTED
SO TYPICAL! THIS GENERATION DOESN'T FEEL THE NEED TO WORK FOR ANYTHING, DO THEY?
THAT'S IT! NO MORE AVOCADO TOAST!
HA! HA! WOULD YOU LIKE ME TO SHOCK HER FOR YOU, SIR?
MAYBE NEXT TIME. HEY, YOU MIND IF I TAKE THIS?
NOT AT ALL, SIR! WE LIVE TO SERVE.
I'M SORRY. I GUESS I'VE BEEN OUT OF TOUCH FOR A WHILE.
LOOKS LIKE WE'RE STUCK HERE--
WAIT A MINUTE...

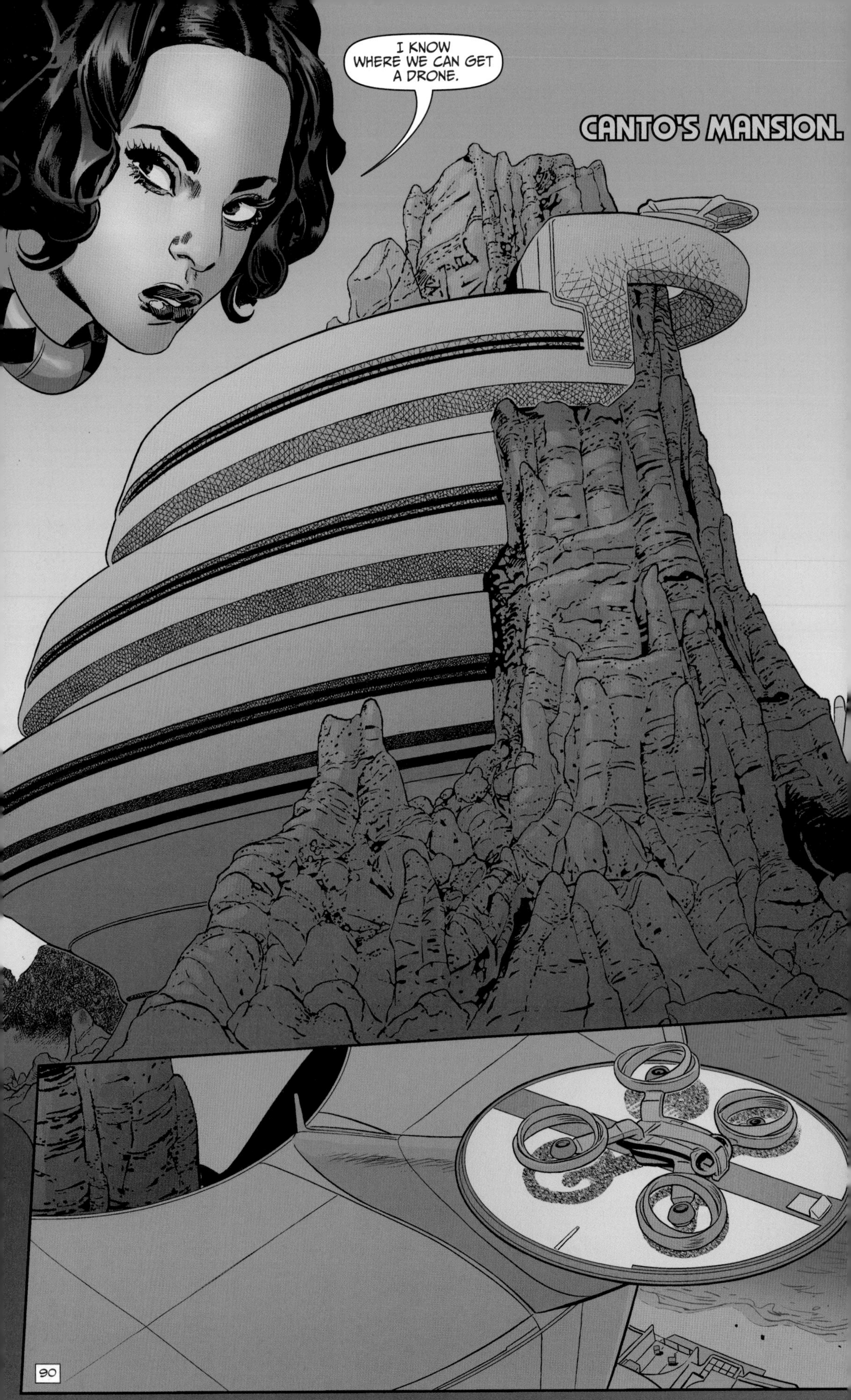
I KNOW WHERE WE CAN GET A DRONE.
CANTO'S MANSION.

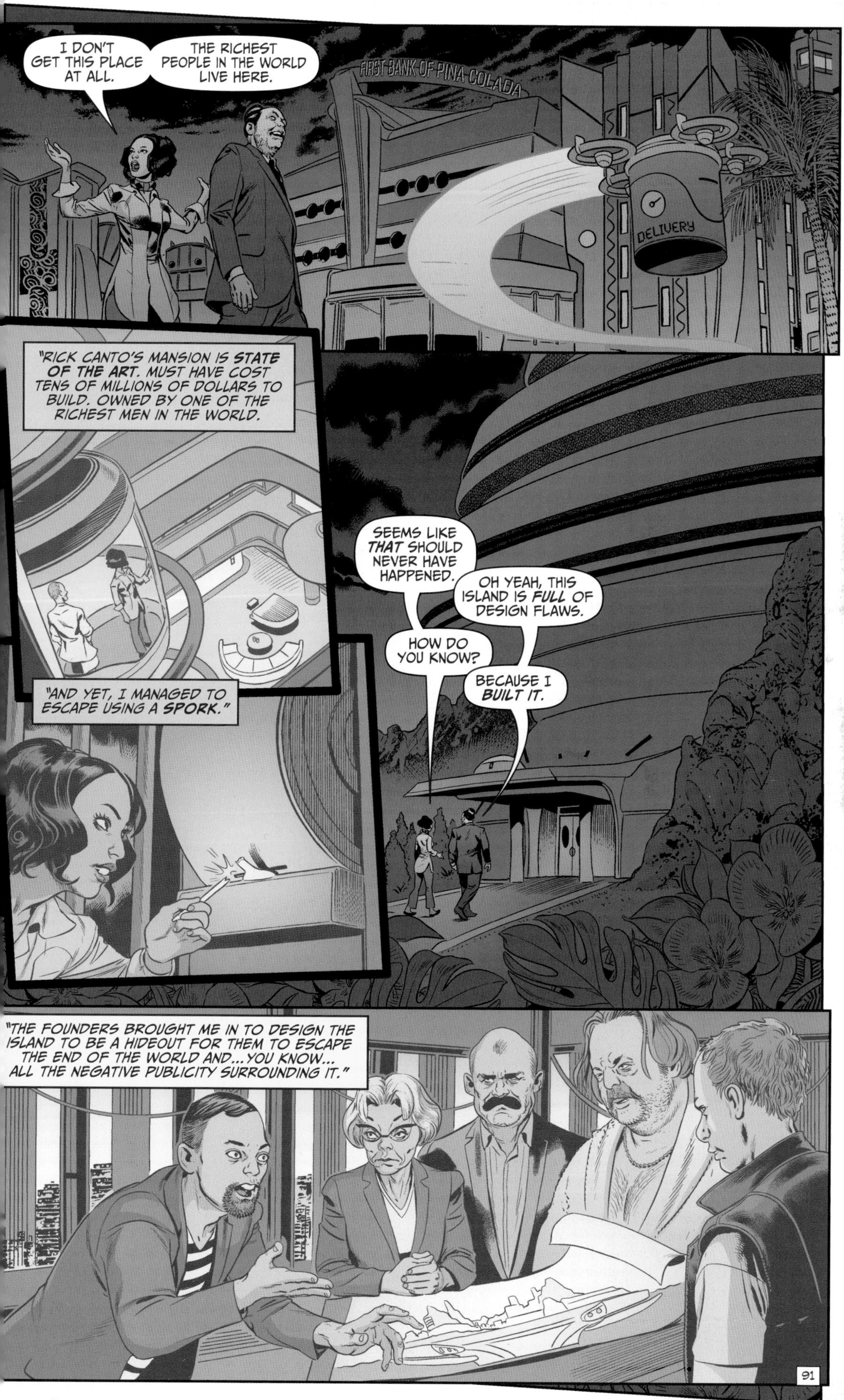
I DON'T GET THIS PLACE AT ALL.
THE RICHEST PEOPLE IN THE WORLD LIVE HERE.
FIRST BANK OF PINA COLADA
DELIVERY
"RICK CANTO'S MANSION IS STATE OF THE ART. MUST HAVE COST TENS OF MILLIONS OF DOLLARS TO BUILD. OWNED BY ONE OF THE RICHEST MEN IN THE WORLD.
"AND YET, I MANAGED TO ESCAPE USING A SPORK."
SEEMS LIKE THAT SHOULD NEVER HAVE HAPPENED.
OH YEAH, THIS ISLAND IS FULL OF DESIGN FLAWS.
HOW DO YOU KNOW?
BECAUSE I BUILT IT.
"THE FOUNDERS BROUGHT ME IN TO DESIGN THE ISLAND TO BE A HIDEOUT FOR THEM TO ESCAPE THE END OF THE WORLD AND...YOU KNOW... ALL THE NEGATIVE PUBLICITY SURROUNDING IT."

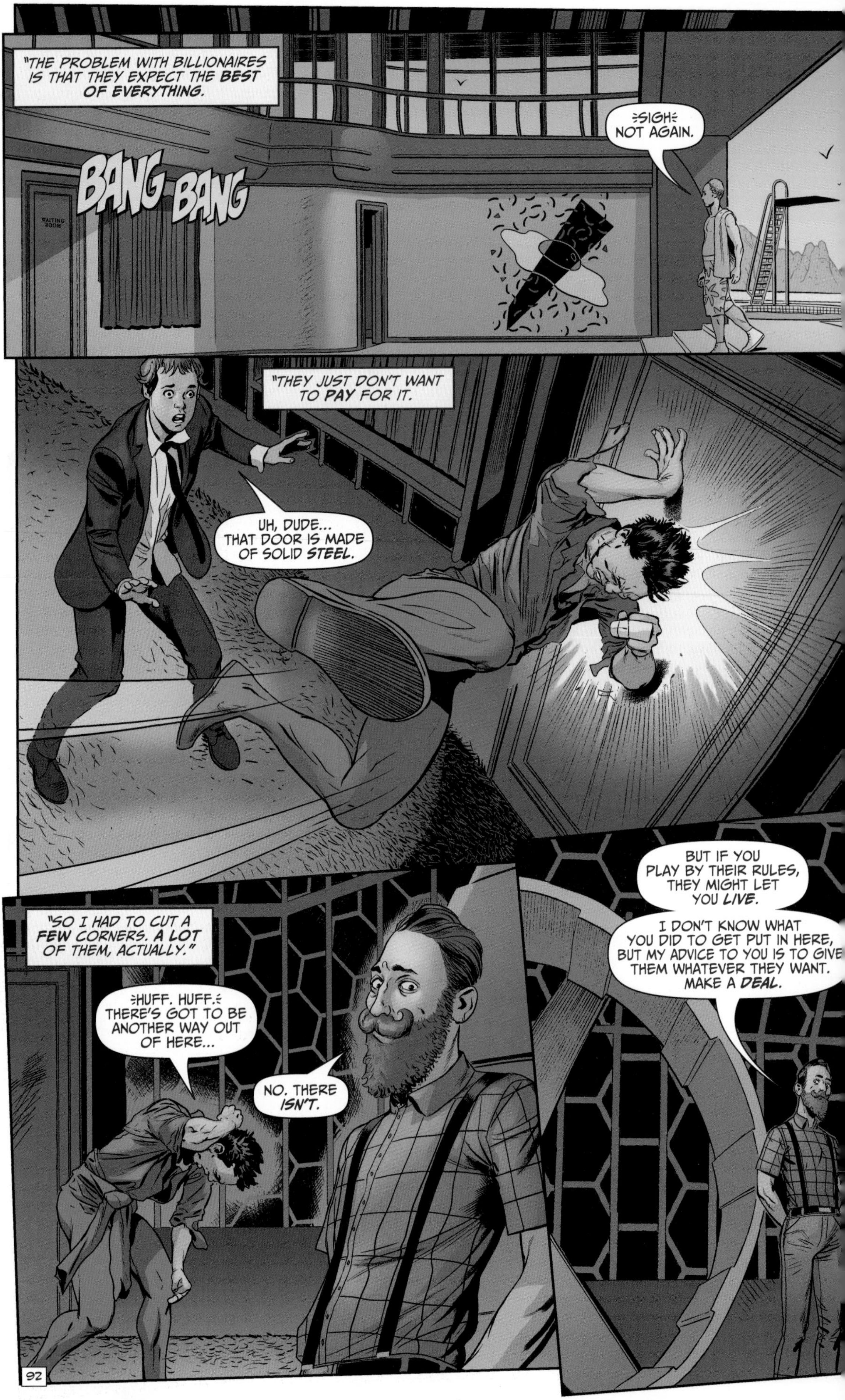
"THE PROBLEM WITH BILLIONAIRES IS THAT THEY EXPECT THE BEST OF EVERYTHING.
≡SIGH≡ NOT AGAIN.
BANG BANG
WAITING ROOM
"THEY JUST DON'T WANT TO PAY FOR IT.
UH, DUDE... THAT DOOR IS MADE OF SOLID STEEL.
"SO I HAD TO CUT A FEW CORNERS. A LOT OF THEM, ACTUALLY."
≡HUFF. HUFF.≡ THERE'S GOT TO BE ANOTHER WAY OUT OF HERE...
NO. THERE ISN'T.
BUT IF YOU PLAY BY THEIR RULES, THEY MIGHT LET YOU LIVE.
I DON'T KNOW WHAT YOU DID TO GET PUT IN HERE, BUT MY ADVICE TO YOU IS TO GIVE THEM WHATEVER THEY WANT. MAKE A DEAL.

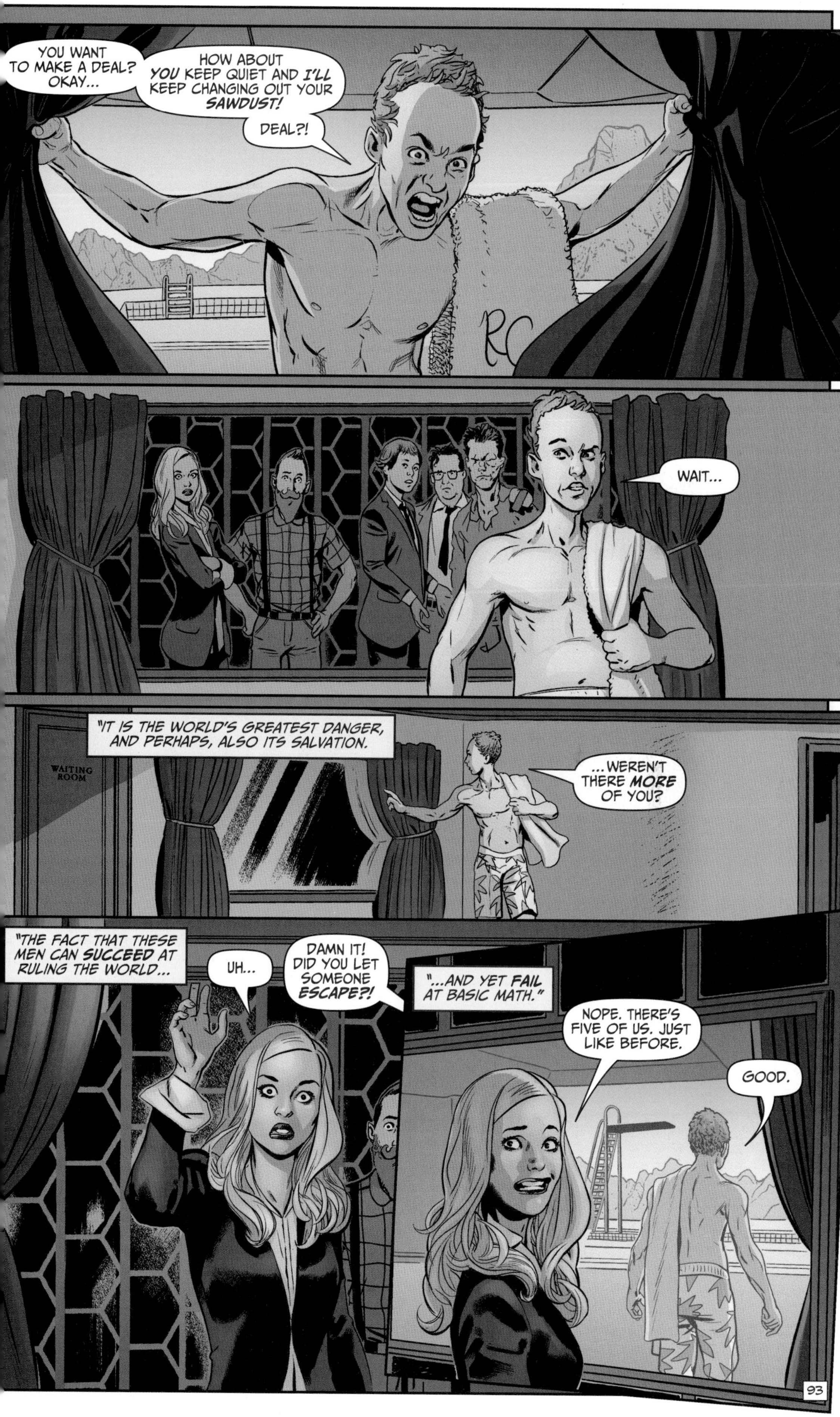

YOU WANT TO MAKE A DEAL? OKAY...
HOW ABOUT *YOU* KEEP QUIET AND *I'LL* KEEP CHANGING OUT YOUR *SAWDUST!*
DEAL?!
WAIT...
"IT IS THE WORLD'S GREATEST DANGER, AND PERHAPS, ALSO ITS SALVATION.
WAITING ROOM
...WEREN'T THERE *MORE* OF YOU?
"THE FACT THAT THESE MEN CAN *SUCCEED* AT RULING THE WORLD...
UH...
DAMN IT! DID YOU LET SOMEONE *ESCAPE?!*
"...AND YET *FAIL* AT BASIC MATH."
NOPE. THERE'S FIVE OF US. JUST LIKE BEFORE.
GOOD.

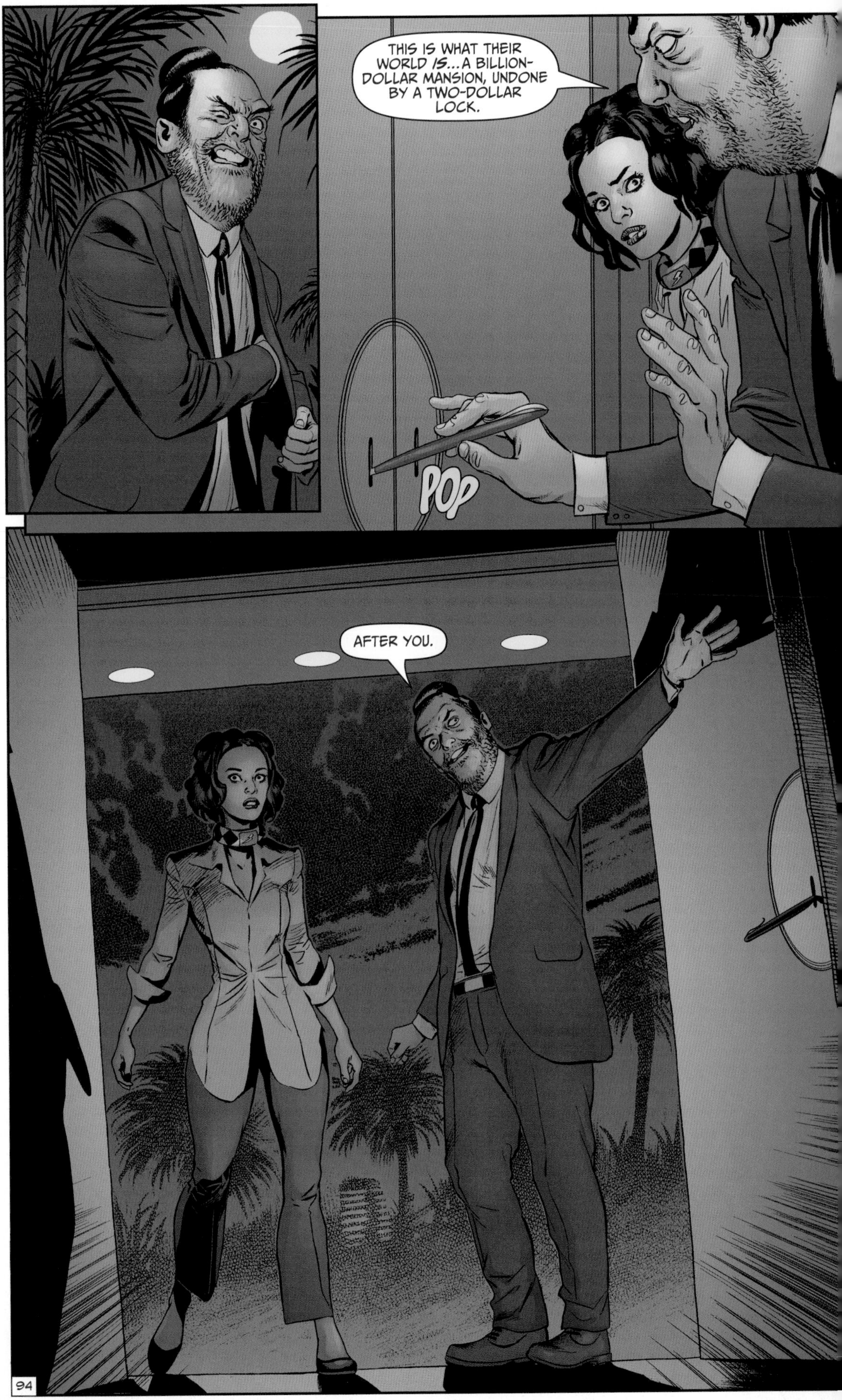
THIS IS WHAT THEIR WORLD *IS*...A BILLION-DOLLAR MANSION, UNDONE BY A TWO-DOLLAR LOCK.
POP
AFTER YOU.

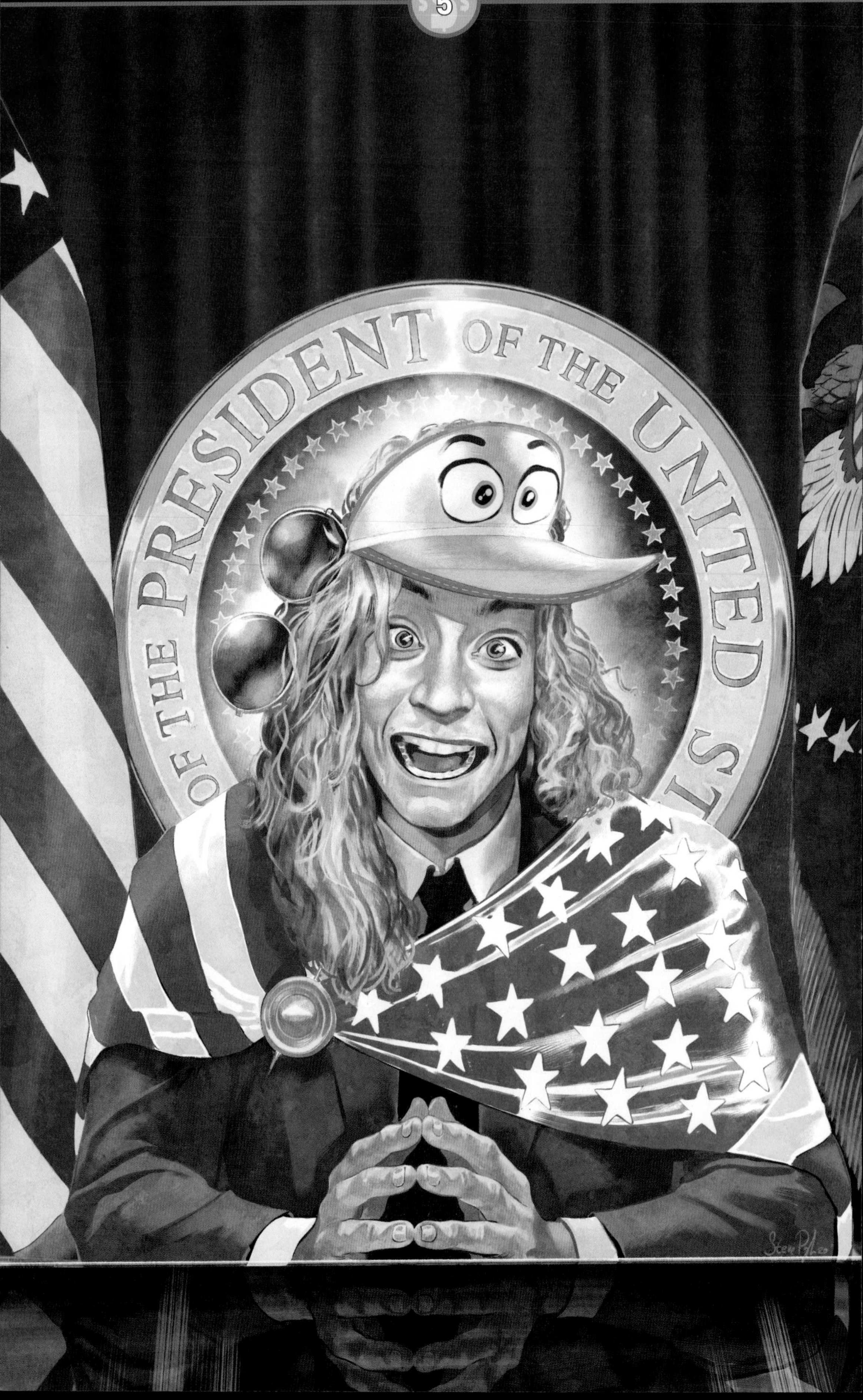
OF THE PRESIDENT OF THE UNITED ST

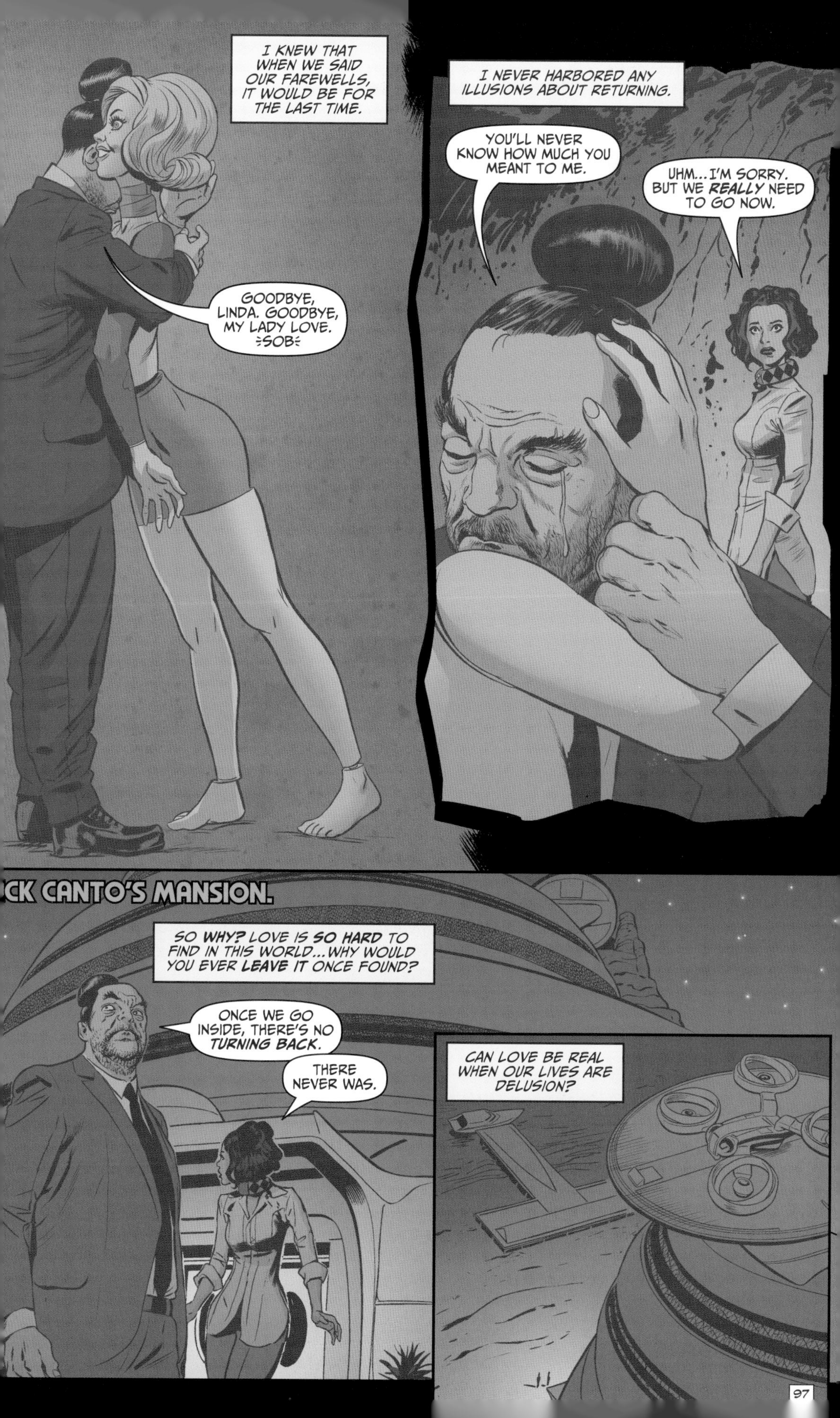
I KNEW THAT WHEN WE SAID OUR FAREWELLS, IT WOULD BE FOR THE LAST TIME.
GOODBYE, LINDA. GOODBYE, MY LADY LOVE. ≷SOB≶
I NEVER HARBORED ANY ILLUSIONS ABOUT RETURNING.
YOU'LL NEVER KNOW HOW MUCH YOU MEANT TO ME.
UHM... I'M SORRY. BUT WE REALLY NEED TO GO NOW.
CK CANTO'S MANSION.
SO WHY? LOVE IS SO HARD TO FIND IN THIS WORLD... WHY WOULD YOU EVER LEAVE IT ONCE FOUND?
ONCE WE GO INSIDE, THERE'S NO TURNING BACK.
THERE NEVER WAS.
CAN LOVE BE REAL WHEN OUR LIVES ARE DELUSION?

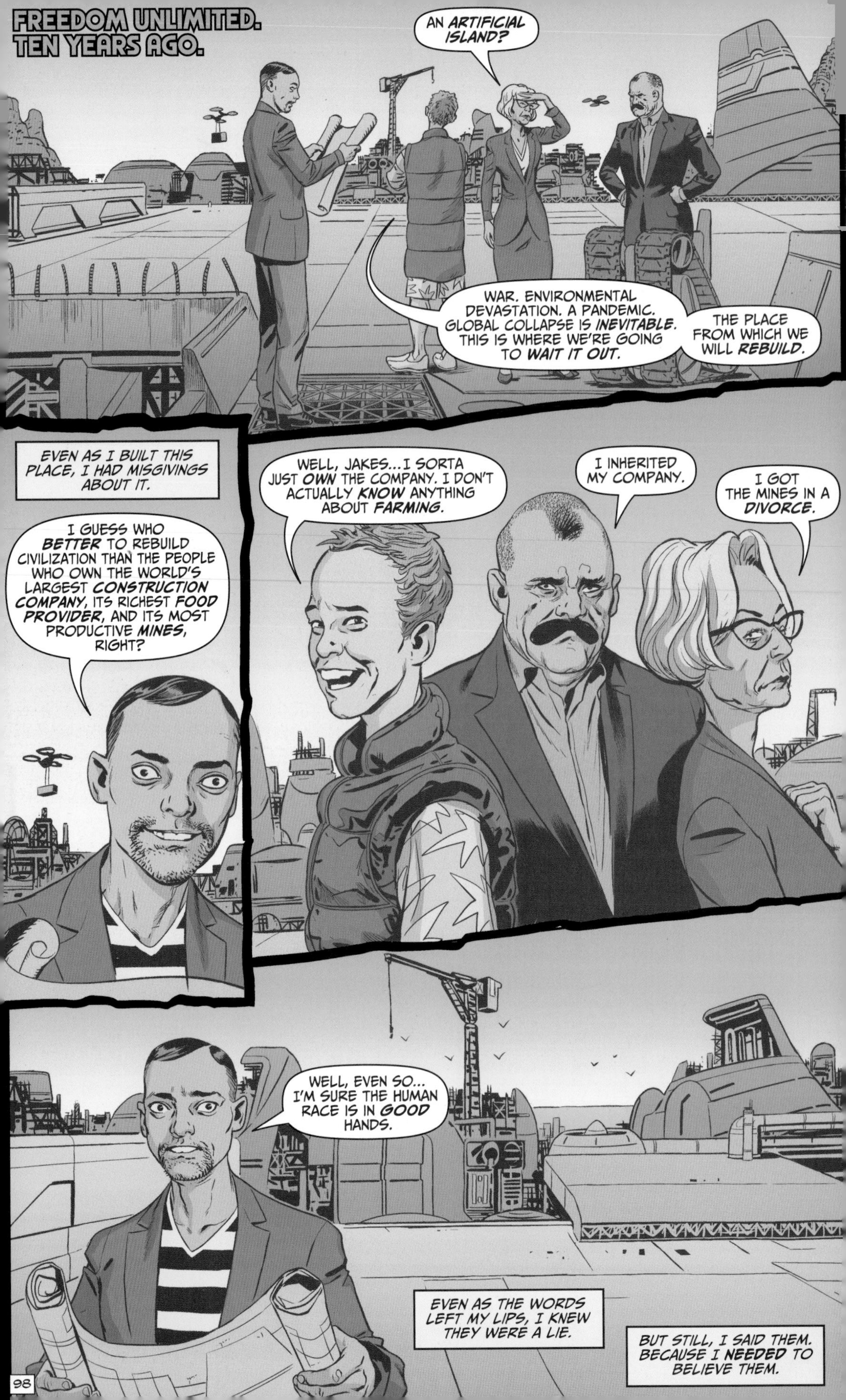

FREEDOM UNLIMITED. TEN YEARS AGO.
AN ARTIFICIAL ISLAND?
WAR. ENVIRONMENTAL DEVASTATION. A PANDEMIC. GLOBAL COLLAPSE IS INEVITABLE. THIS IS WHERE WE'RE GOING TO WAIT IT OUT.
THE PLACE FROM WHICH WE WILL REBUILD.
EVEN AS I BUILT THIS PLACE, I HAD MISGIVINGS ABOUT IT.
I GUESS WHO BETTER TO REBUILD CIVILIZATION THAN THE PEOPLE WHO OWN THE WORLD'S LARGEST CONSTRUCTION COMPANY, ITS RICHEST FOOD PROVIDER, AND ITS MOST PRODUCTIVE MINES, RIGHT?
WELL, JAKES...I SORTA JUST OWN THE COMPANY. I DON'T ACTUALLY KNOW ANYTHING ABOUT FARMING.
I INHERITED MY COMPANY.
I GOT THE MINES IN A DIVORCE.
WELL, EVEN SO... I'M SURE THE HUMAN RACE IS IN GOOD HANDS.
EVEN AS THE WORDS LEFT MY LIPS, I KNEW THEY WERE A LIE.
BUT STILL, I SAID THEM. BECAUSE I NEEDED TO BELIEVE THEM.

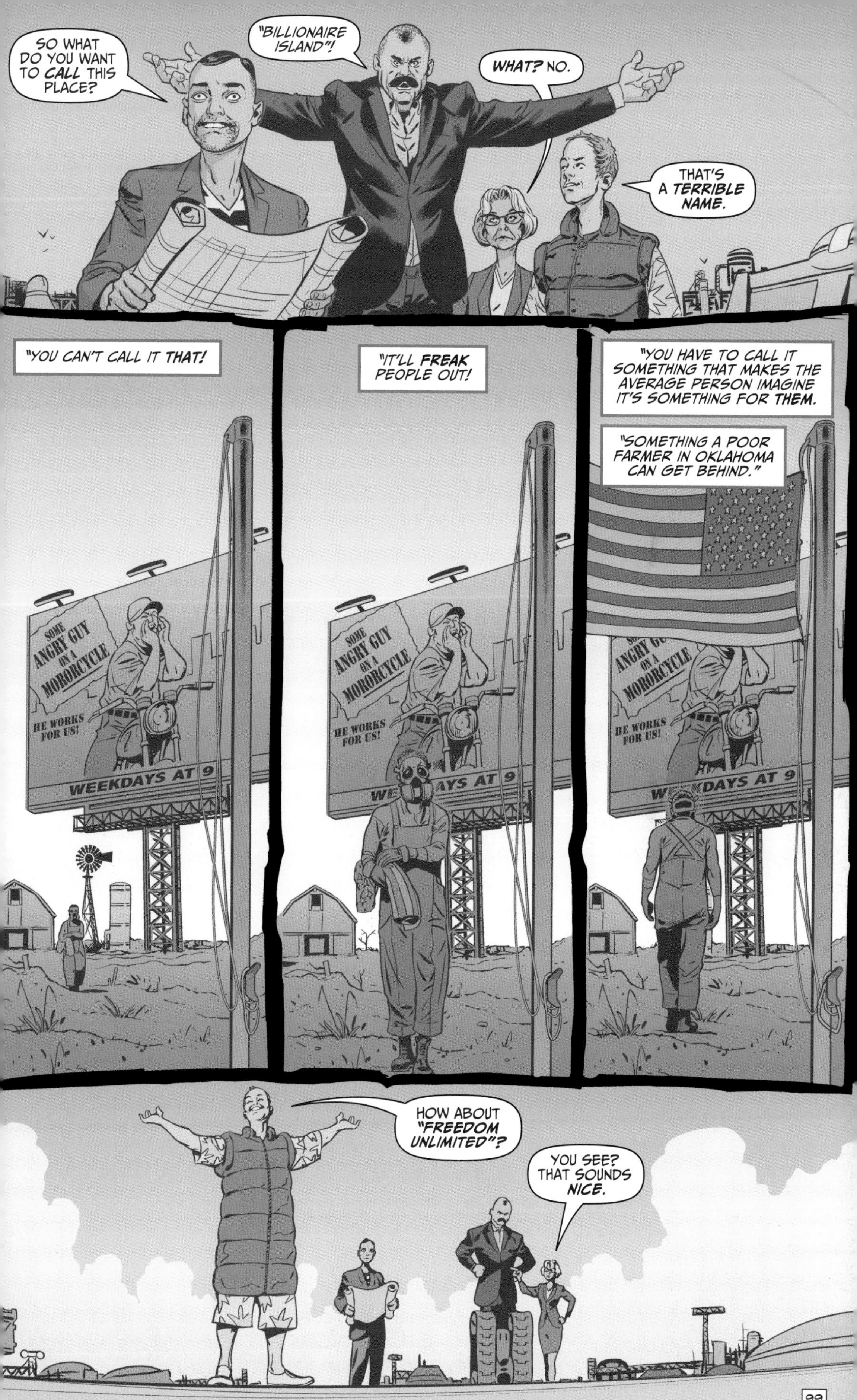

SO WHAT DO YOU WANT TO CALL THIS PLACE?
"BILLIONAIRE ISLAND"!
WHAT? NO.
THAT'S A TERRIBLE NAME.
"YOU CAN'T CALL IT THAT!
"IT'LL FREAK PEOPLE OUT!
"YOU HAVE TO CALL IT SOMETHING THAT MAKES THE AVERAGE PERSON IMAGINE IT'S SOMETHING FOR THEM.
"SOMETHING A POOR FARMER IN OKLAHOMA CAN GET BEHIND."
SOME ANGRY GUY ON A MORORCYCLE
HE WORKS FOR US!
WEEKDAYS AT 9
HOW ABOUT "FREEDOM UNLIMITED"?
YOU SEE? THAT SOUNDS NICE.

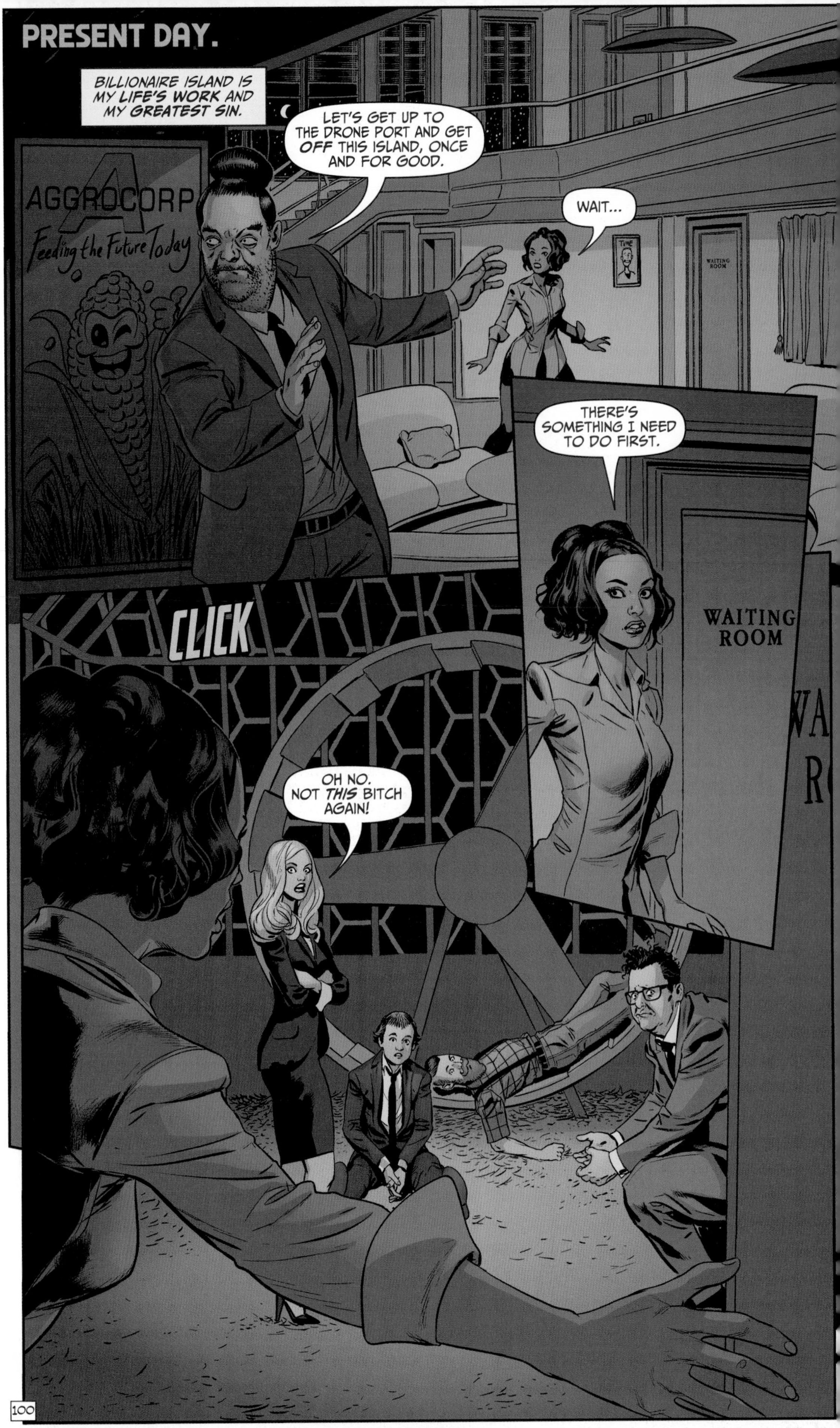
PRESENT DAY.
BILLIONAIRE ISLAND IS MY LIFE'S WORK AND MY GREATEST SIN.
AGGROCORP
Feeding the Future Today
LET'S GET UP TO THE DRONE PORT AND GET OFF THIS ISLAND, ONCE AND FOR GOOD.
WAIT...
THERE'S SOMETHING I NEED TO DO FIRST.
WAITING ROOM
CLICK
OH NO. NOT THIS BITCH AGAIN!

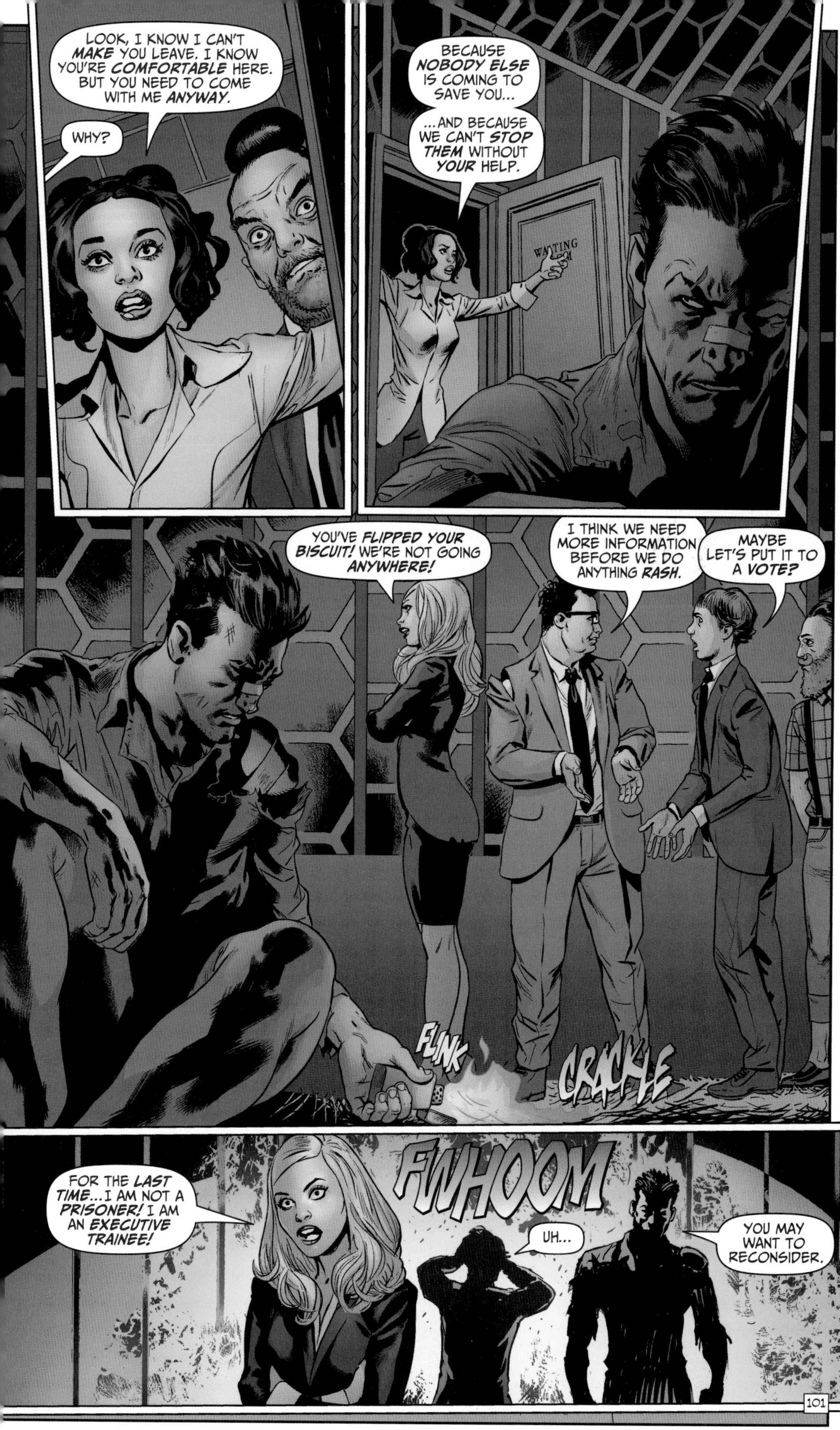
LOOK, I KNOW I CAN'T MAKE YOU LEAVE. I KNOW YOU'RE COMFORTABLE HERE. BUT YOU NEED TO COME WITH ME ANYWAY.
WHY?
BECAUSE NOBODY ELSE IS COMING TO SAVE YOU...
...AND BECAUSE WE CAN'T STOP THEM WITHOUT YOUR HELP.
WAITING ROOM
YOU'VE FLIPPED YOUR BISCUIT! WE'RE NOT GOING ANYWHERE!
I THINK WE NEED MORE INFORMATION BEFORE WE DO ANYTHING RASH.
MAYBE LET'S PUT IT TO A VOTE?
FLINK
CRACKLE
FWHOOM
FOR THE LAST TIME...I AM NOT A PRISONER! I AM AN EXECUTIVE TRAINEE!
UH...
YOU MAY WANT TO RECONSIDER.

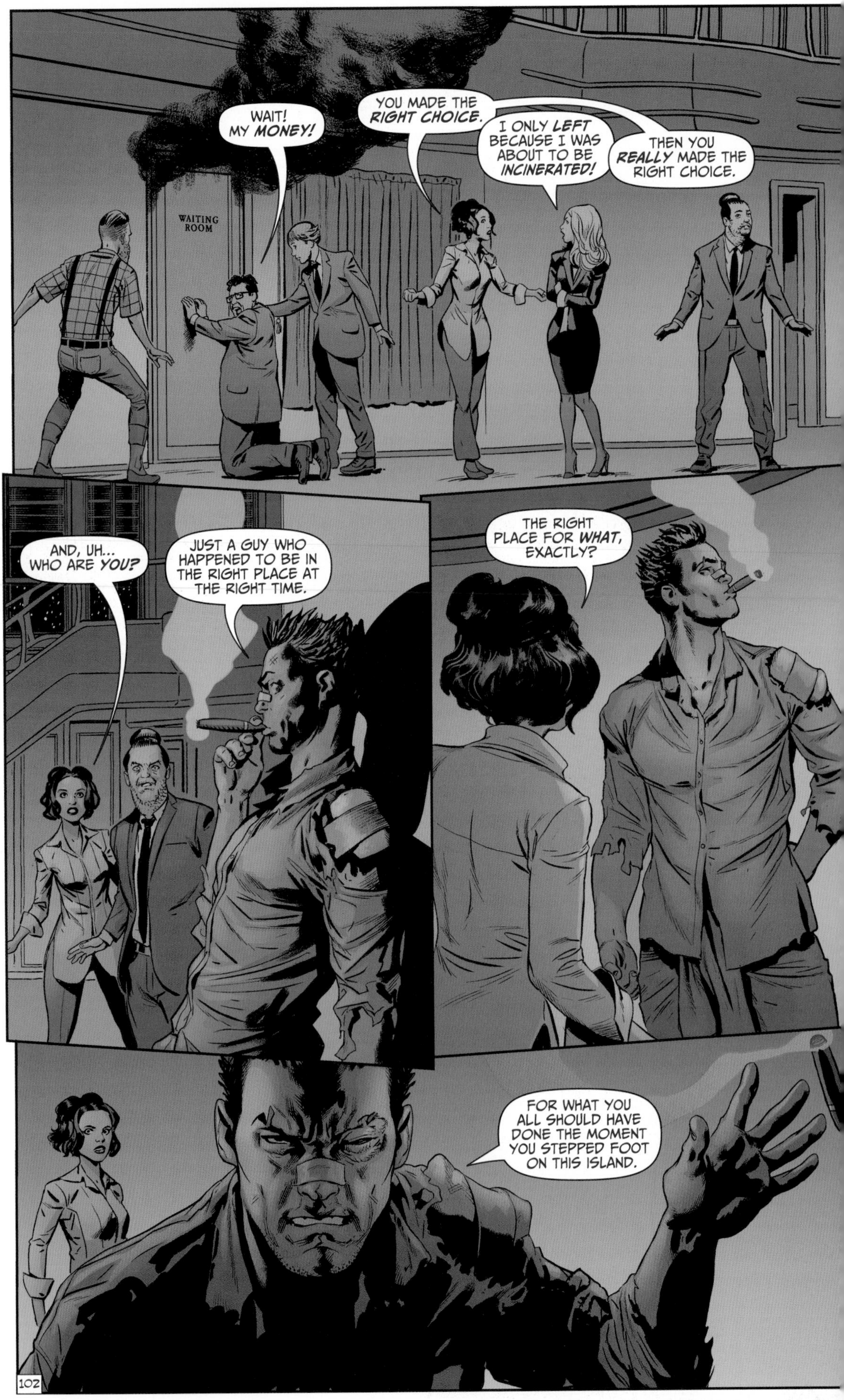
WAITING ROOM
WAIT! MY MONEY!
YOU MADE THE RIGHT CHOICE.
I ONLY LEFT BECAUSE I WAS ABOUT TO BE INCINERATED!
THEN YOU REALLY MADE THE RIGHT CHOICE.
AND, UH... WHO ARE YOU?
JUST A GUY WHO HAPPENED TO BE IN THE RIGHT PLACE AT THE RIGHT TIME.
THE RIGHT PLACE FOR WHAT, EXACTLY?
FOR WHAT YOU ALL SHOULD HAVE DONE THE MOMENT YOU STEPPED FOOT ON THIS ISLAND.

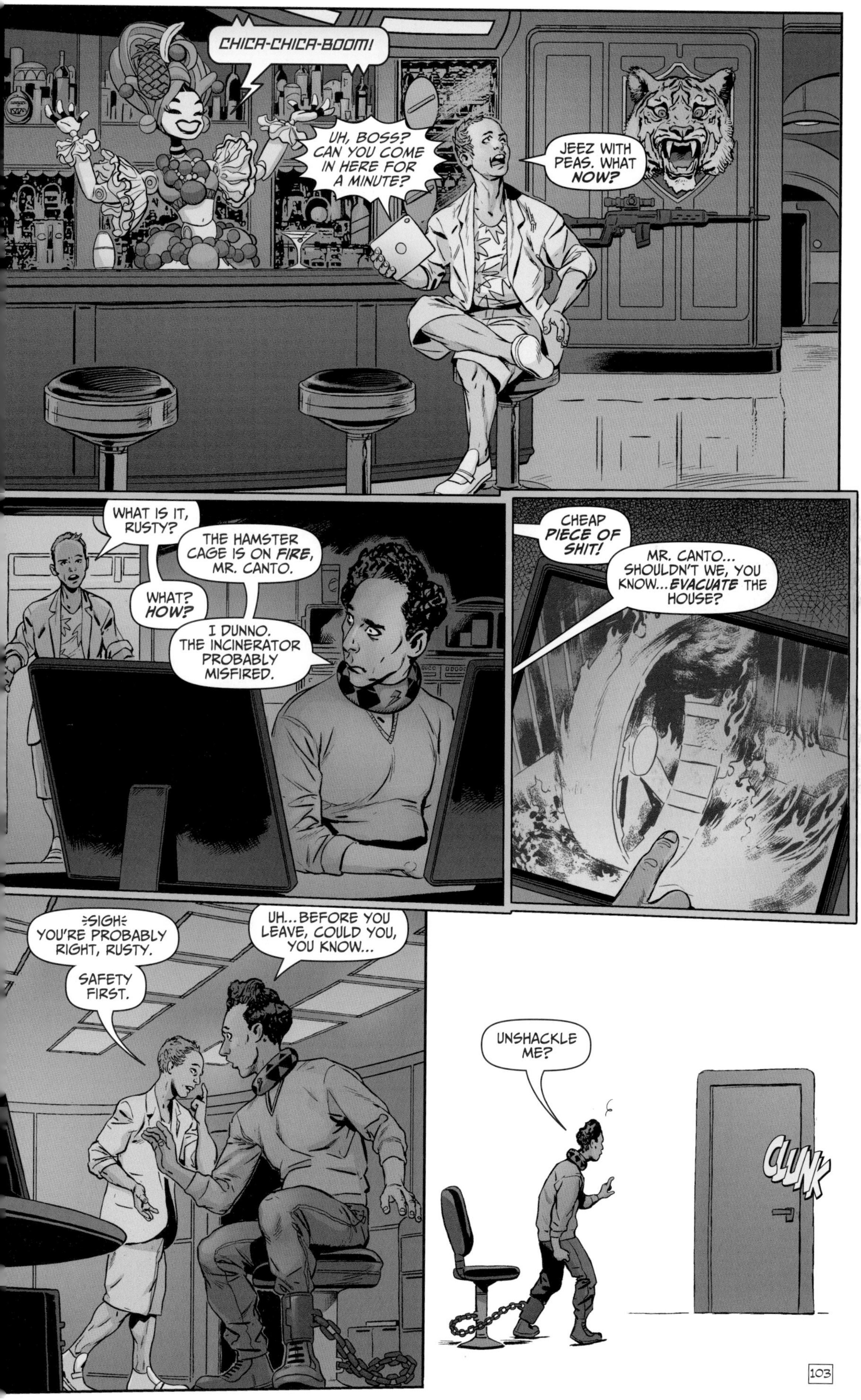

CHICA-CHICA-BOOM!
UH, BOSS? CAN YOU COME IN HERE FOR A MINUTE?
JEEZ WITH PEAS. WHAT NOW?
WHAT IS IT, RUSTY?
THE HAMSTER CAGE IS ON FIRE, MR. CANTO.
WHAT? HOW?
I DUNNO. THE INCINERATOR PROBABLY MISFIRED.
CHEAP PIECE OF SHIT!
MR. CANTO... SHOULDN'T WE, YOU KNOW...EVACUATE THE HOUSE?
=SIGH= YOU'RE PROBABLY RIGHT, RUSTY.
SAFETY FIRST.
UH...BEFORE YOU LEAVE, COULD YOU, YOU KNOW...
UNSHACKLE ME?
CLUNK

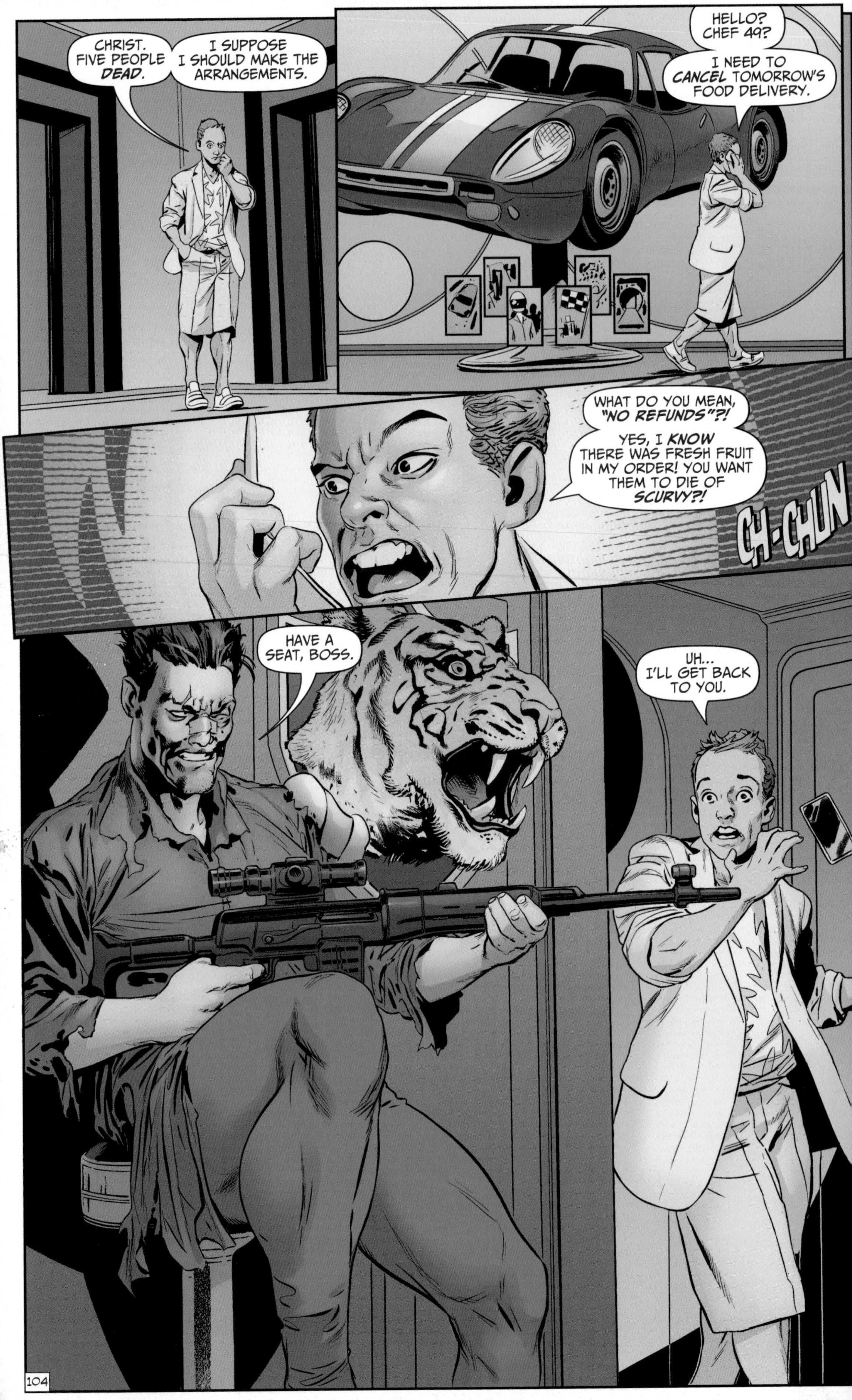

CHRIST. FIVE PEOPLE ***DEAD***.
I SUPPOSE I SHOULD MAKE THE ARRANGEMENTS.
HELLO? CHEF 49?
I NEED TO ***CANCEL*** TOMORROW'S FOOD DELIVERY.
WHAT DO YOU MEAN, ***"NO REFUNDS"?!***
YES, I ***KNOW*** THERE WAS FRESH FRUIT IN MY ORDER! YOU WANT THEM TO DIE OF ***SCURVY?!***
CH-CHUN
HAVE A SEAT, BOSS.
UH... I'LL GET BACK TO YOU.

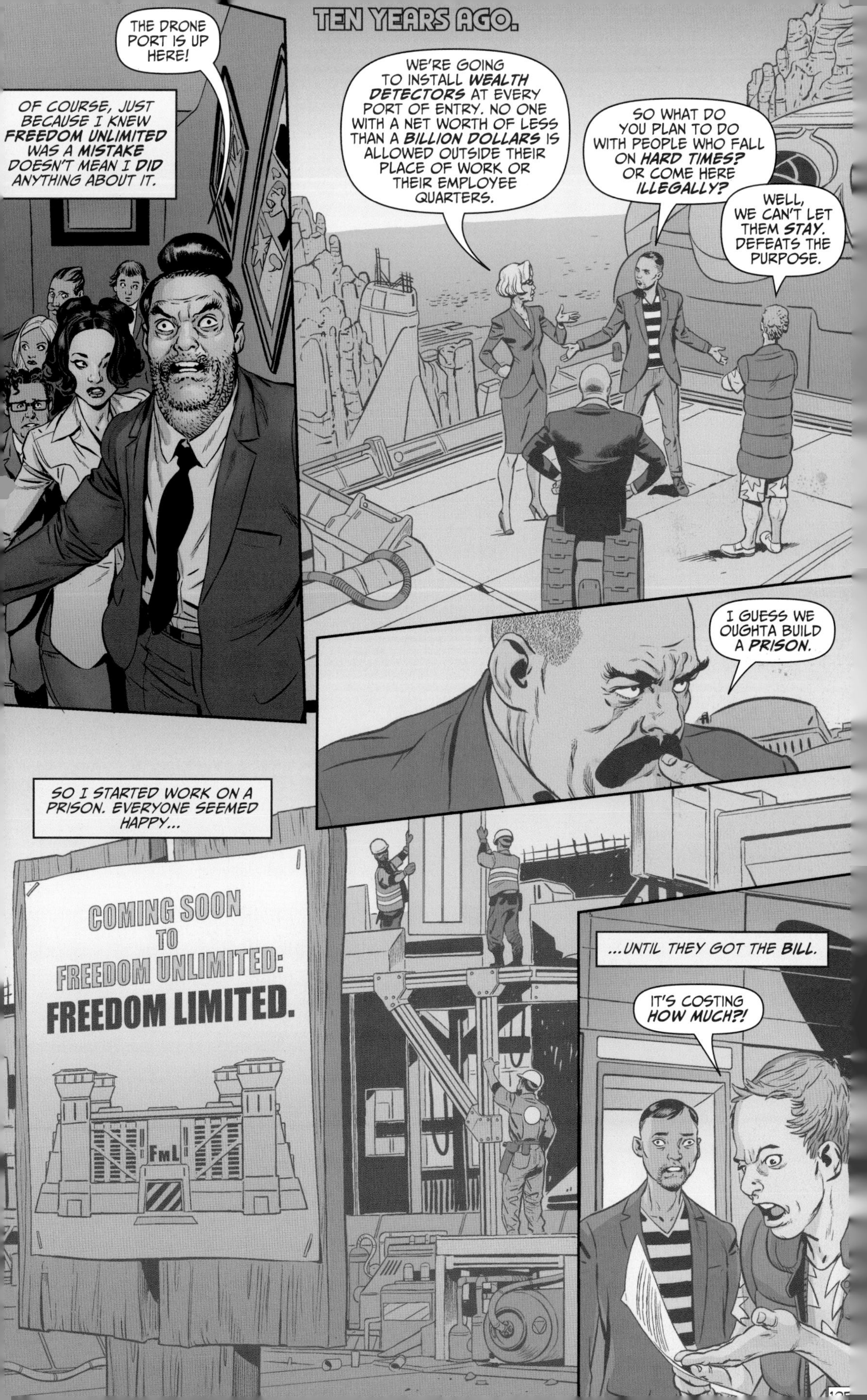
TEN YEARS AGO.
THE DRONE PORT IS UP HERE!
OF COURSE, JUST BECAUSE I KNEW FREEDOM UNLIMITED WAS A MISTAKE DOESN'T MEAN I DID ANYTHING ABOUT IT.
WE'RE GOING TO INSTALL WEALTH DETECTORS AT EVERY PORT OF ENTRY. NO ONE WITH A NET WORTH OF LESS THAN A BILLION DOLLARS IS ALLOWED OUTSIDE THEIR PLACE OF WORK OR THEIR EMPLOYEE QUARTERS.
SO WHAT DO YOU PLAN TO DO WITH PEOPLE WHO FALL ON HARD TIMES? OR COME HERE ILLEGALLY?
WELL, WE CAN'T LET THEM STAY. DEFEATS THE PURPOSE.
I GUESS WE OUGHTA BUILD A PRISON.
SO I STARTED WORK ON A PRISON. EVERYONE SEEMED HAPPY...
COMING SOON TO FREEDOM UNLIMITED:
FREEDOM LIMITED.
FmL
...UNTIL THEY GOT THE BILL.
IT'S COSTING HOW MUCH?!

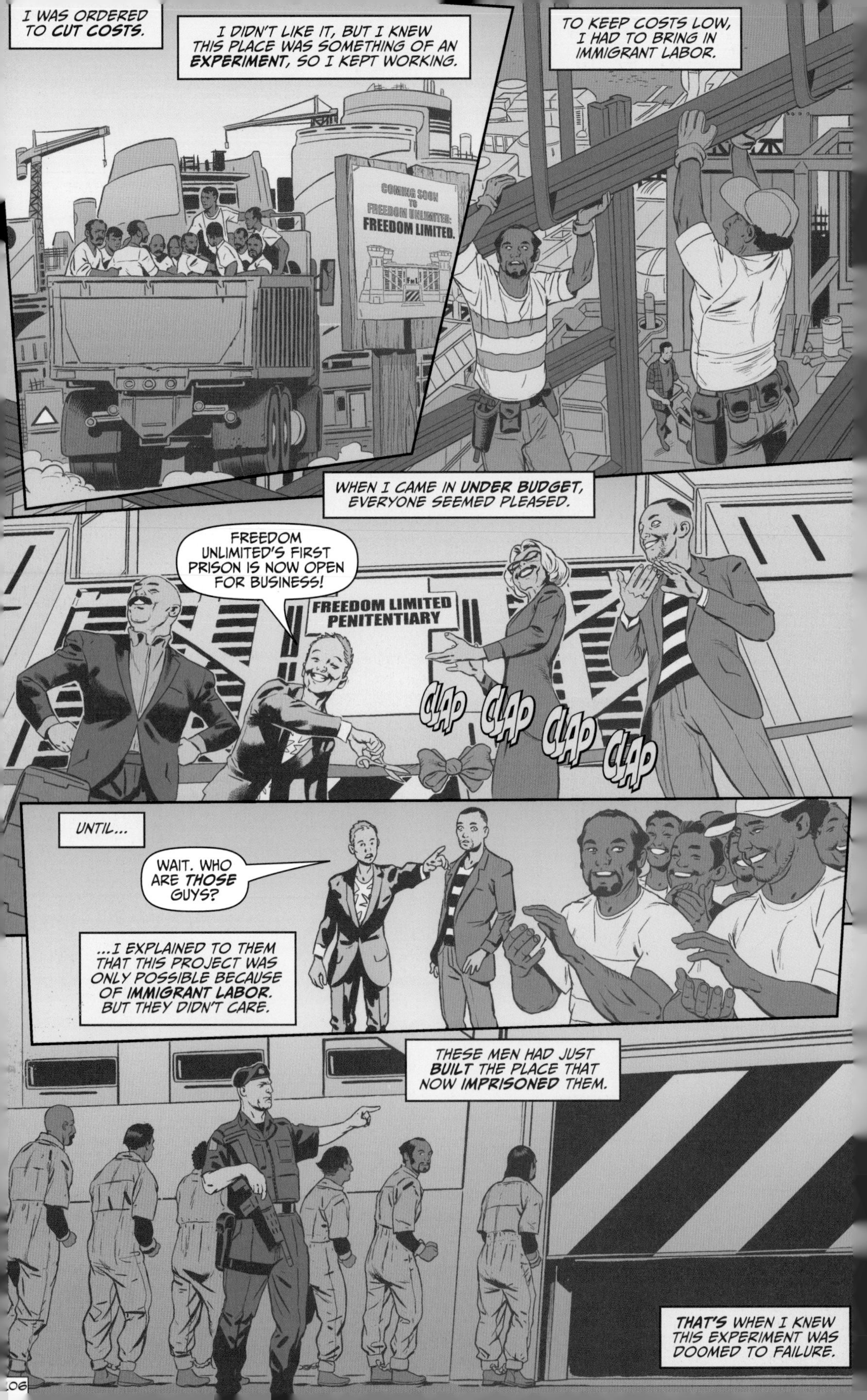
I WAS ORDERED TO CUT COSTS.
I DIDN'T LIKE IT, BUT I KNEW THIS PLACE WAS SOMETHING OF AN EXPERIMENT, SO I KEPT WORKING.
COMING SOON TO FREEDOM UNLIMITED: FREEDOM LIMITED.
TO KEEP COSTS LOW, I HAD TO BRING IN IMMIGRANT LABOR.
WHEN I CAME IN UNDER BUDGET, EVERYONE SEEMED PLEASED.
FREEDOM UNLIMITED'S FIRST PRISON IS NOW OPEN FOR BUSINESS!
FREEDOM LIMITED PENITENTIARY
CLAP CLAP CLAP CLAP
UNTIL...
WAIT. WHO ARE THOSE GUYS?
...I EXPLAINED TO THEM THAT THIS PROJECT WAS ONLY POSSIBLE BECAUSE OF IMMIGRANT LABOR. BUT THEY DIDN'T CARE.
THESE MEN HAD JUST BUILT THE PLACE THAT NOW IMPRISONED THEM.
THAT'S WHEN I KNEW THIS EXPERIMENT WAS DOOMED TO FAILURE.

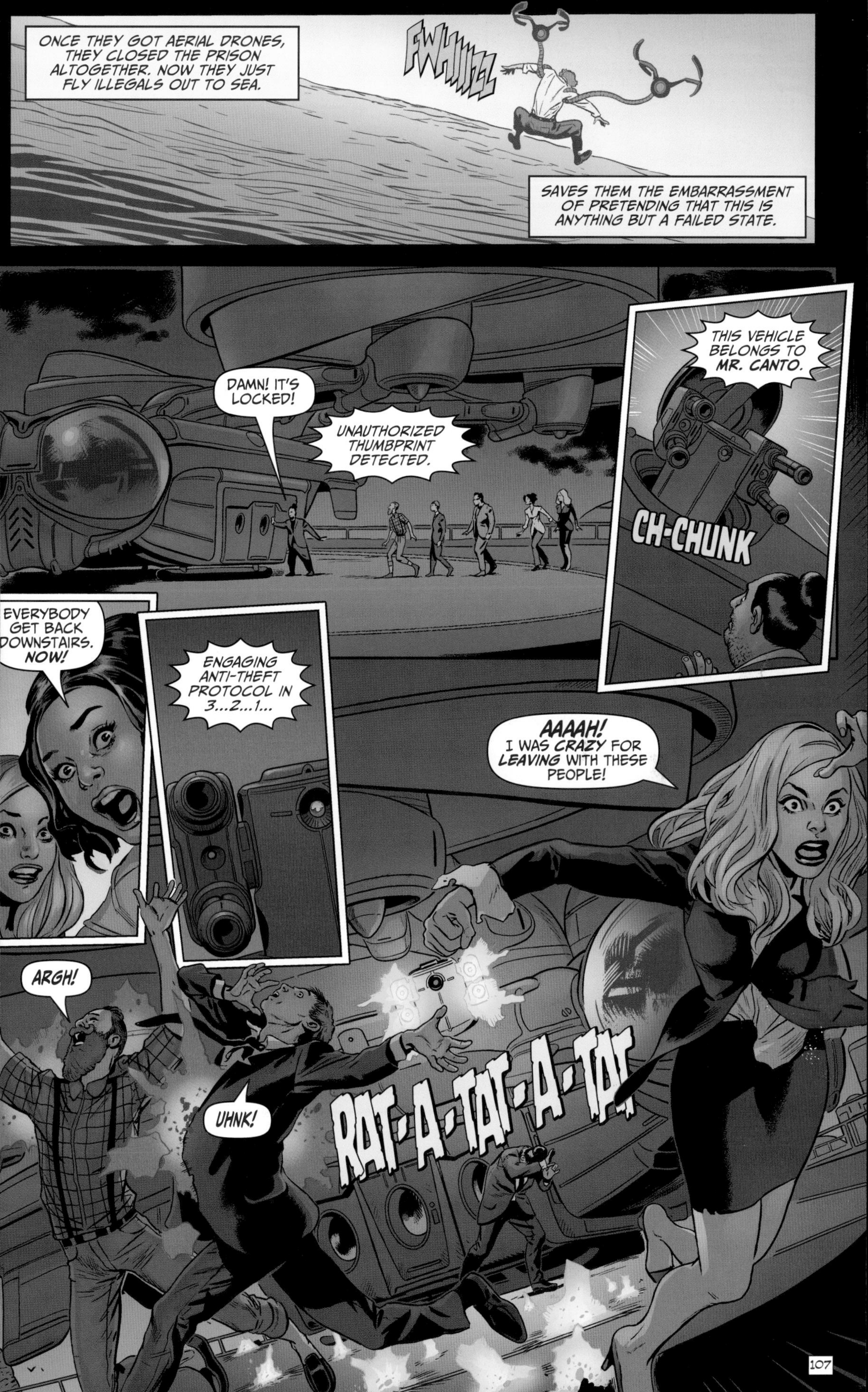

ONCE THEY GOT AERIAL DRONES, THEY CLOSED THE PRISON ALTOGETHER. NOW THEY JUST FLY ILLEGALS OUT TO SEA.
FWHIIZZ
SAVES THEM THE EMBARRASSMENT OF PRETENDING THAT THIS IS ANYTHING BUT A FAILED STATE.
DAMN! IT'S LOCKED!
UNAUTHORIZED THUMBPRINT DETECTED.
THIS VEHICLE BELONGS TO MR. CANTO.
CH-CHUNK
EVERYBODY GET BACK DOWNSTAIRS. NOW!
ENGAGING ANTI-THEFT PROTOCOL IN 3...2...1...
AAAAH! I WAS CRAZY FOR LEAVING WITH THESE PEOPLE!
ARGH!
UHNK!
RAT-A-TAT-A-TAT

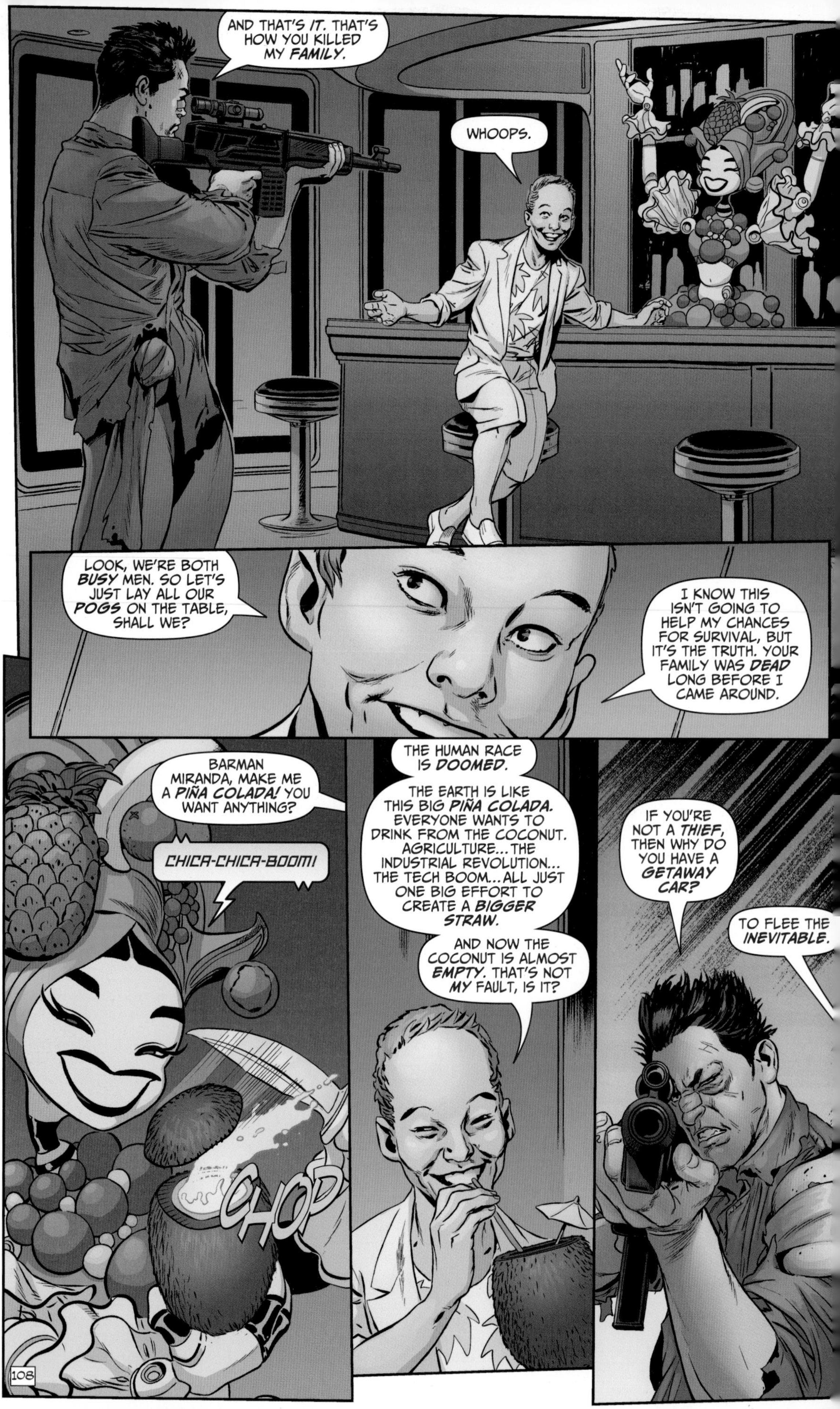
AND THAT'S IT. THAT'S HOW YOU KILLED MY FAMILY.
WHOOPS.
LOOK, WE'RE BOTH BUSY MEN. SO LET'S JUST LAY ALL OUR POGS ON THE TABLE, SHALL WE?
I KNOW THIS ISN'T GOING TO HELP MY CHANCES FOR SURVIVAL, BUT IT'S THE TRUTH. YOUR FAMILY WAS DEAD LONG BEFORE I CAME AROUND.
BARMAN MIRANDA, MAKE ME A PIÑA COLADA! YOU WANT ANYTHING?
CHICA-CHICA-BOOM!
CHOP
THE HUMAN RACE IS DOOMED.
THE EARTH IS LIKE THIS BIG PIÑA COLADA. EVERYONE WANTS TO DRINK FROM THE COCONUT. AGRICULTURE... THE INDUSTRIAL REVOLUTION... THE TECH BOOM... ALL JUST ONE BIG EFFORT TO CREATE A BIGGER STRAW.
AND NOW THE COCONUT IS ALMOST EMPTY. THAT'S NOT MY FAULT, IS IT?
IF YOU'RE NOT A THIEF, THEN WHY DO YOU HAVE A GETAWAY CAR?
TO FLEE THE INEVITABLE.

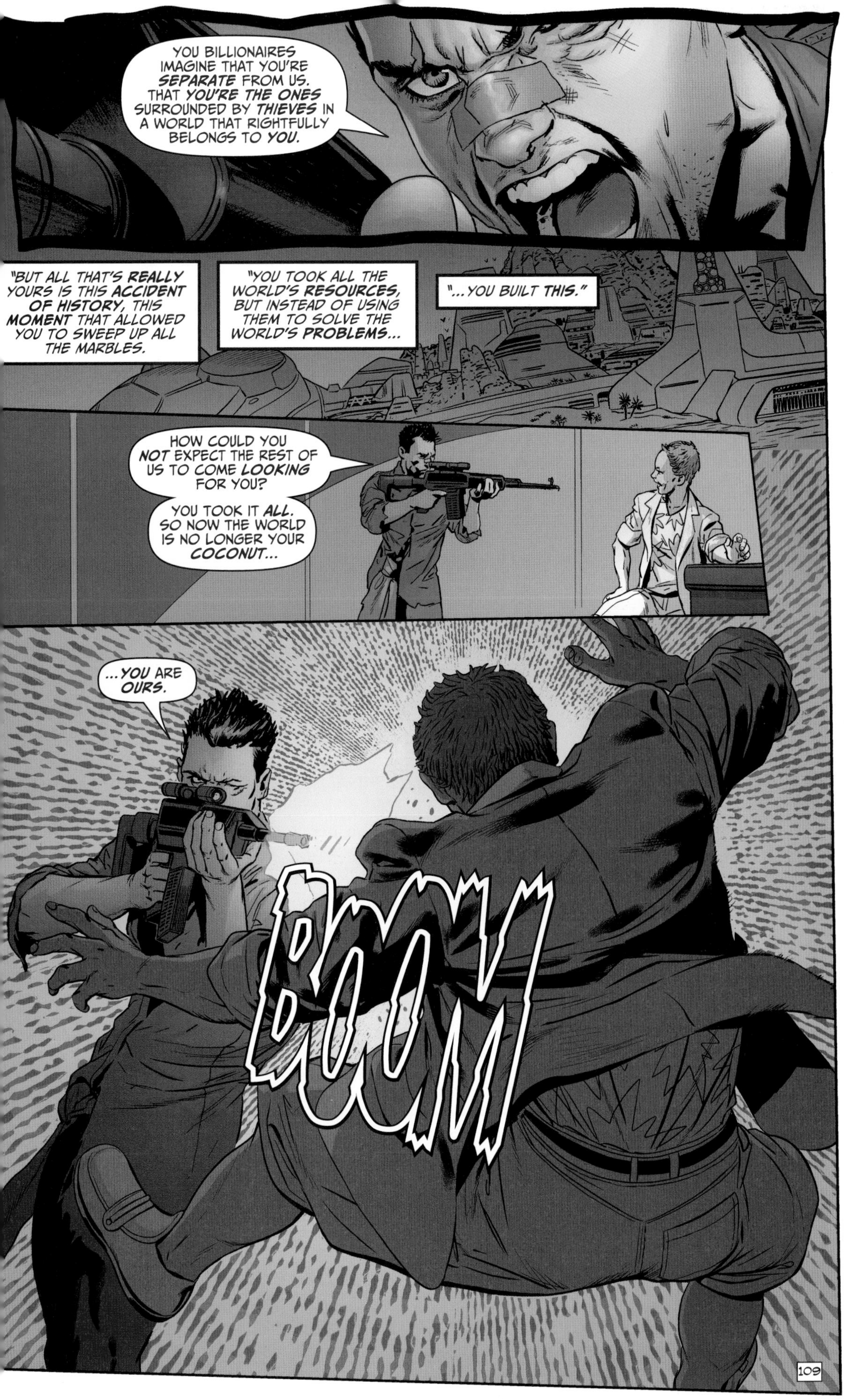
YOU BILLIONAIRES IMAGINE THAT YOU'RE SEPARATE FROM US. THAT YOU'RE THE ONES SURROUNDED BY THIEVES IN A WORLD THAT RIGHTFULLY BELONGS TO YOU.
"BUT ALL THAT'S REALLY YOURS IS THIS ACCIDENT OF HISTORY, THIS MOMENT THAT ALLOWED YOU TO SWEEP UP ALL THE MARBLES.
"YOU TOOK ALL THE WORLD'S RESOURCES, BUT INSTEAD OF USING THEM TO SOLVE THE WORLD'S PROBLEMS...
"...YOU BUILT THIS."
HOW COULD YOU NOT EXPECT THE REST OF US TO COME LOOKING FOR YOU?
YOU TOOK IT ALL. SO NOW THE WORLD IS NO LONGER YOUR COCONUT...
...YOU ARE OURS.
BOOM

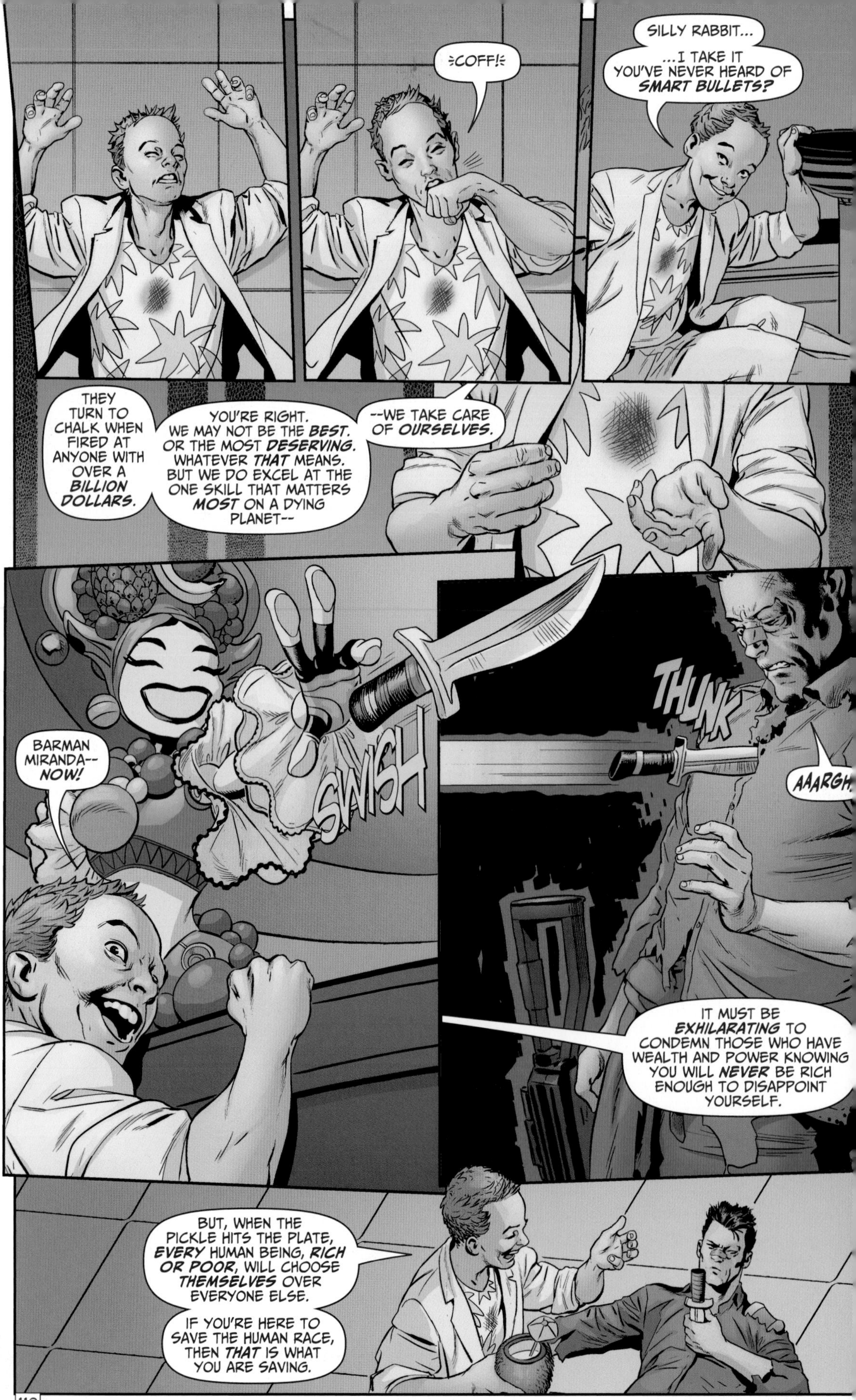

COFF!
SILLY RABBIT...
...I TAKE IT YOU'VE NEVER HEARD OF SMART BULLETS?
THEY TURN TO CHALK WHEN FIRED AT ANYONE WITH OVER A BILLION DOLLARS.
YOU'RE RIGHT. WE MAY NOT BE THE BEST. OR THE MOST DESERVING. WHATEVER THAT MEANS. BUT WE DO EXCEL AT THE ONE SKILL THAT MATTERS MOST ON A DYING PLANET--
--WE TAKE CARE OF OURSELVES.
BARMAN MIRANDA-- NOW!
SWISH
THUNK
AAARGH
IT MUST BE EXHILARATING TO CONDEMN THOSE WHO HAVE WEALTH AND POWER KNOWING YOU WILL NEVER BE RICH ENOUGH TO DISAPPOINT YOURSELF.
BUT, WHEN THE PICKLE HITS THE PLATE, EVERY HUMAN BEING, RICH OR POOR, WILL CHOOSE THEMSELVES OVER EVERYONE ELSE.
IF YOU'RE HERE TO SAVE THE HUMAN RACE, THEN THAT IS WHAT YOU ARE SAVING.

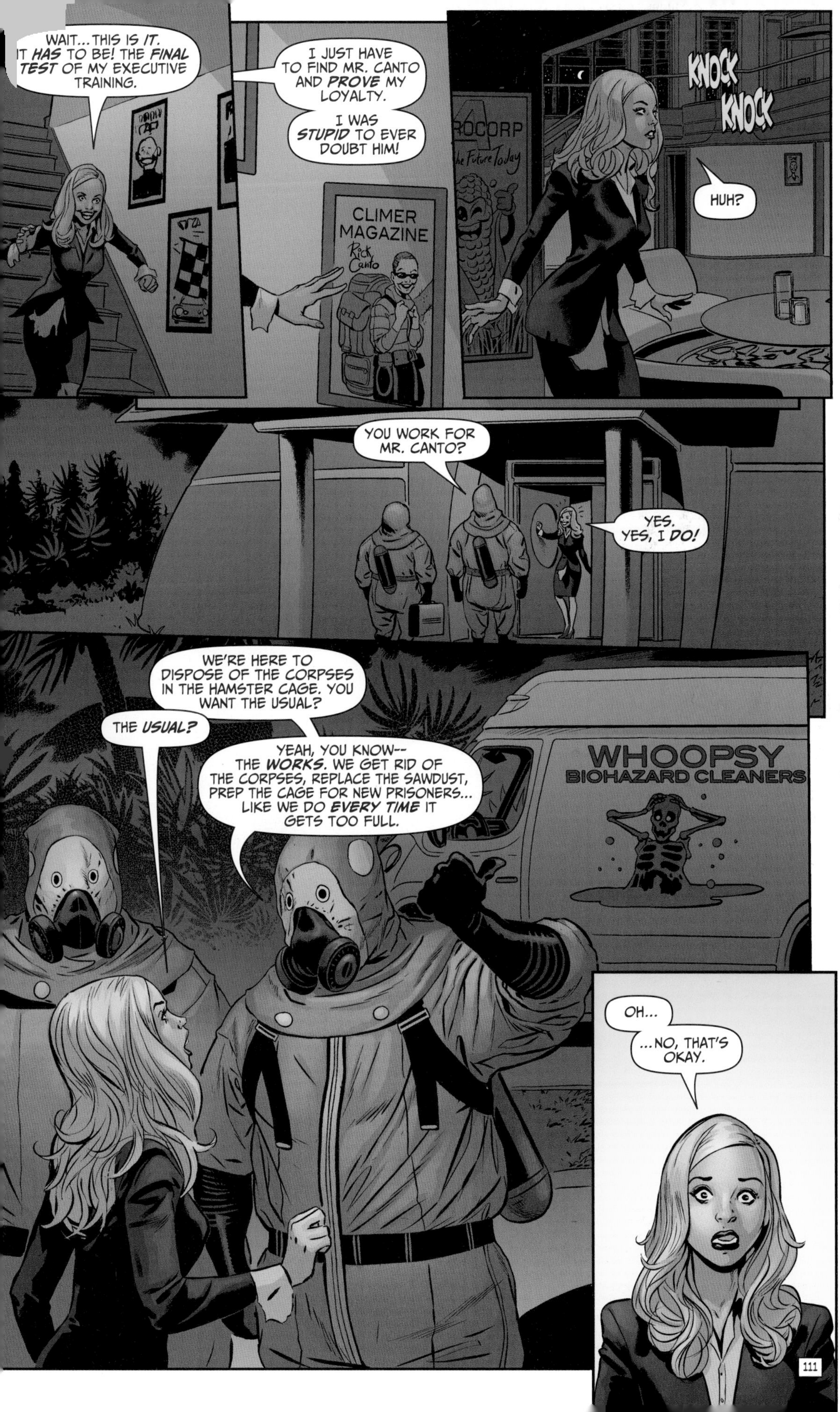

WAIT... THIS IS IT. IT HAS TO BE! THE FINAL TEST OF MY EXECUTIVE TRAINING.
I JUST HAVE TO FIND MR. CANTO AND PROVE MY LOYALTY.
I WAS STUPID TO EVER DOUBT HIM!
CLIMER MAGAZINE
Rick Canto
ROCORP
The Future Today
KNOCK KNOCK
HUH?
YOU WORK FOR MR. CANTO?
YES. YES, I DO!
WE'RE HERE TO DISPOSE OF THE CORPSES IN THE HAMSTER CAGE. YOU WANT THE USUAL?
THE USUAL?
YEAH, YOU KNOW-- THE WORKS. WE GET RID OF THE CORPSES, REPLACE THE SAWDUST, PREP THE CAGE FOR NEW PRISONERS... LIKE WE DO EVERY TIME IT GETS TOO FULL.
WHOOPSY
BIOHAZARD CLEANERS
OH...
...NO, THAT'S OKAY.

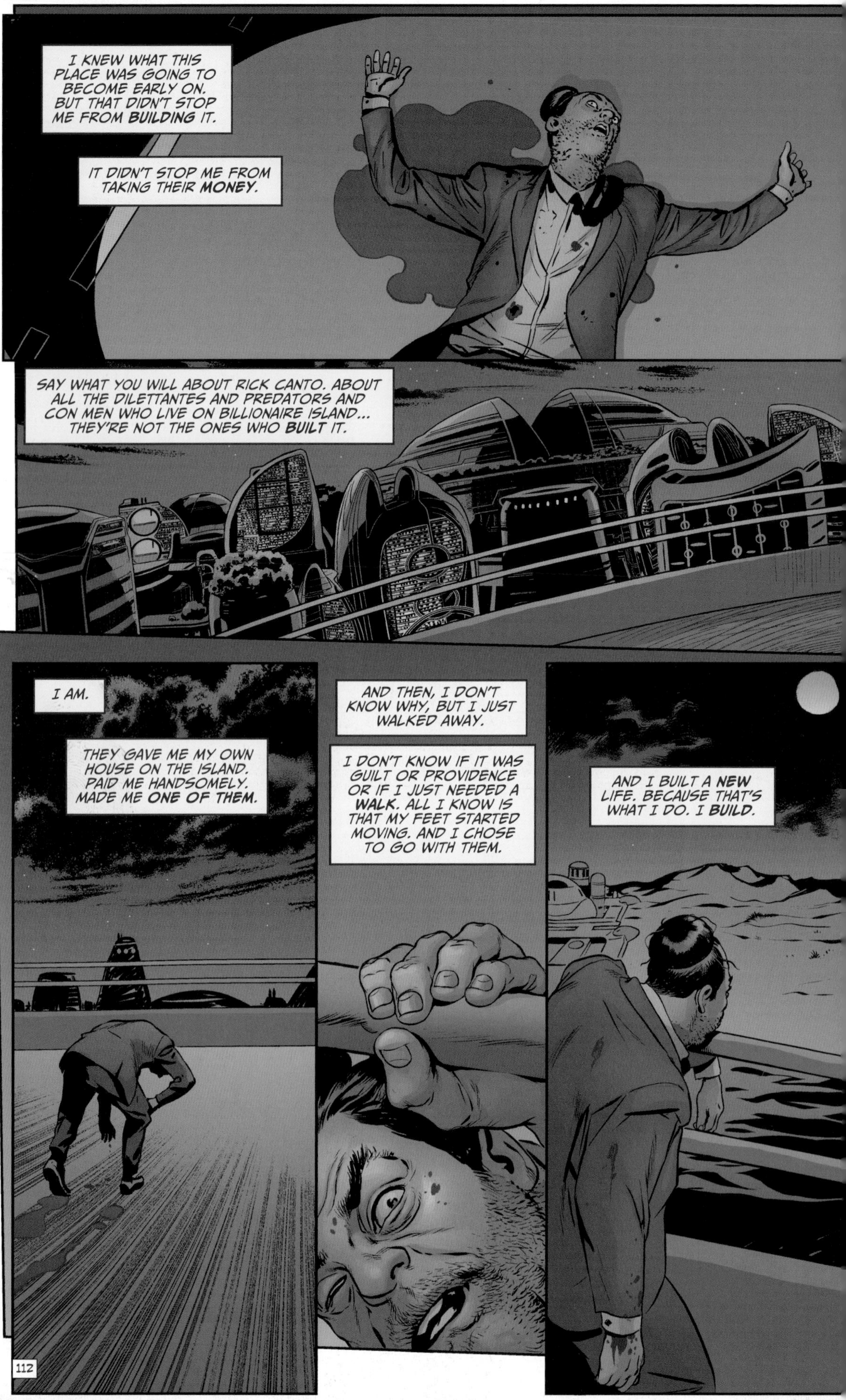
I KNEW WHAT THIS PLACE WAS GOING TO BECOME EARLY ON. BUT THAT DIDN'T STOP ME FROM **BUILDING** IT.
IT DIDN'T STOP ME FROM TAKING THEIR **MONEY**.
SAY WHAT YOU WILL ABOUT RICK CANTO. ABOUT ALL THE DILETTANTES AND PREDATORS AND CON MEN WHO LIVE ON BILLIONAIRE ISLAND... THEY'RE NOT THE ONES WHO **BUILT** IT.
I AM.
THEY GAVE ME MY OWN HOUSE ON THE ISLAND. PAID ME HANDSOMELY. MADE ME **ONE OF THEM**.
AND THEN, I DON'T KNOW WHY, BUT I JUST WALKED AWAY.
I DON'T KNOW IF IT WAS GUILT OR PROVIDENCE OR IF I JUST NEEDED A **WALK**. ALL I KNOW IS THAT MY FEET STARTED MOVING. AND I CHOSE TO GO WITH THEM.
AND I BUILT A **NEW** LIFE. BECAUSE THAT'S WHAT I DO. I **BUILD**.

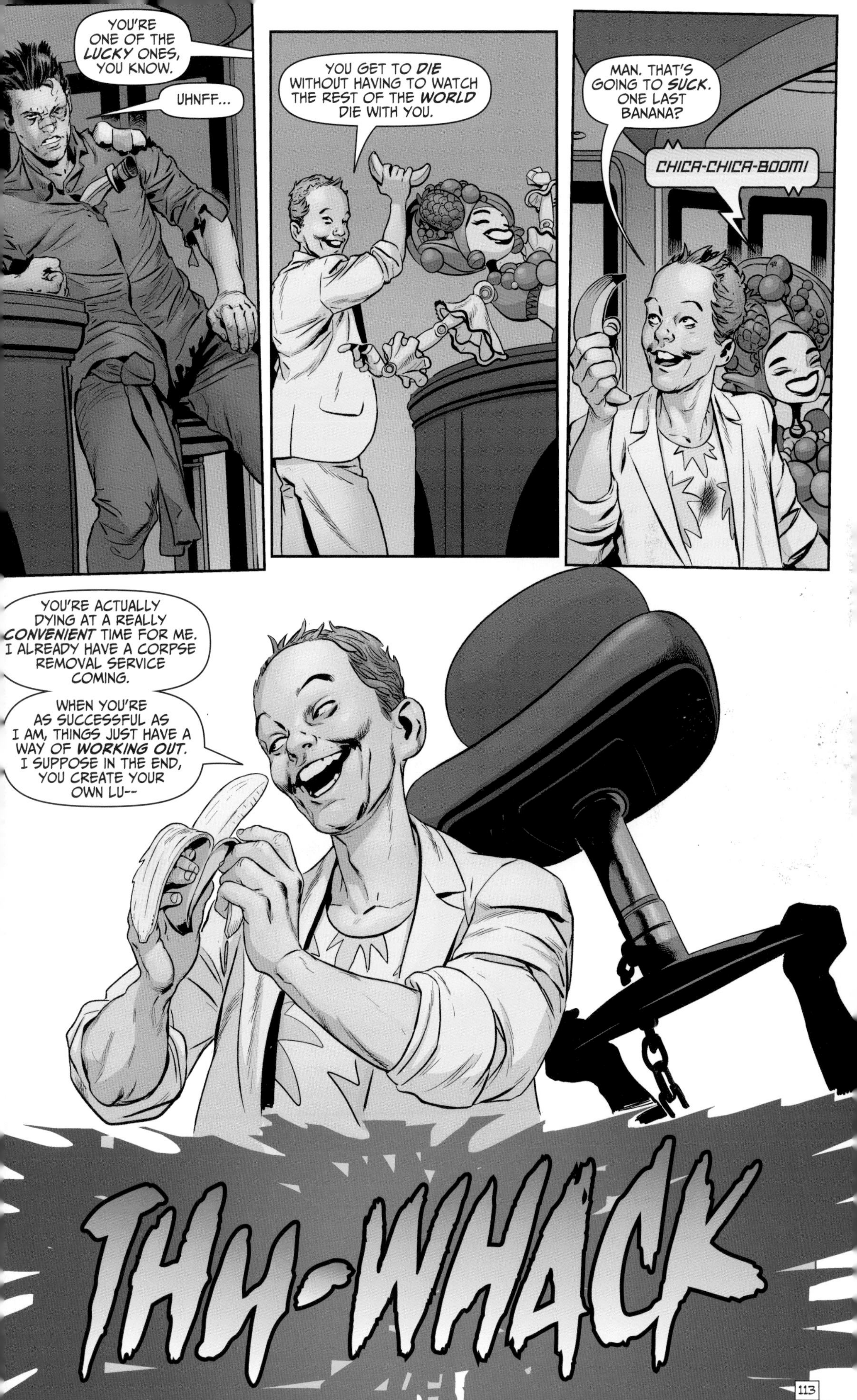
YOU'RE ONE OF THE LUCKY ONES, YOU KNOW.
UHNFF...
YOU GET TO DIE WITHOUT HAVING TO WATCH THE REST OF THE WORLD DIE WITH YOU.
MAN. THAT'S GOING TO SUCK. ONE LAST BANANA?
CHICA-CHICA-BOOM!
YOU'RE ACTUALLY DYING AT A REALLY CONVENIENT TIME FOR ME. I ALREADY HAVE A CORPSE REMOVAL SERVICE COMING.
WHEN YOU'RE AS SUCCESSFUL AS I AM, THINGS JUST HAVE A WAY OF WORKING OUT. I SUPPOSE IN THE END, YOU CREATE YOUR OWN LU--
THU-WHACK

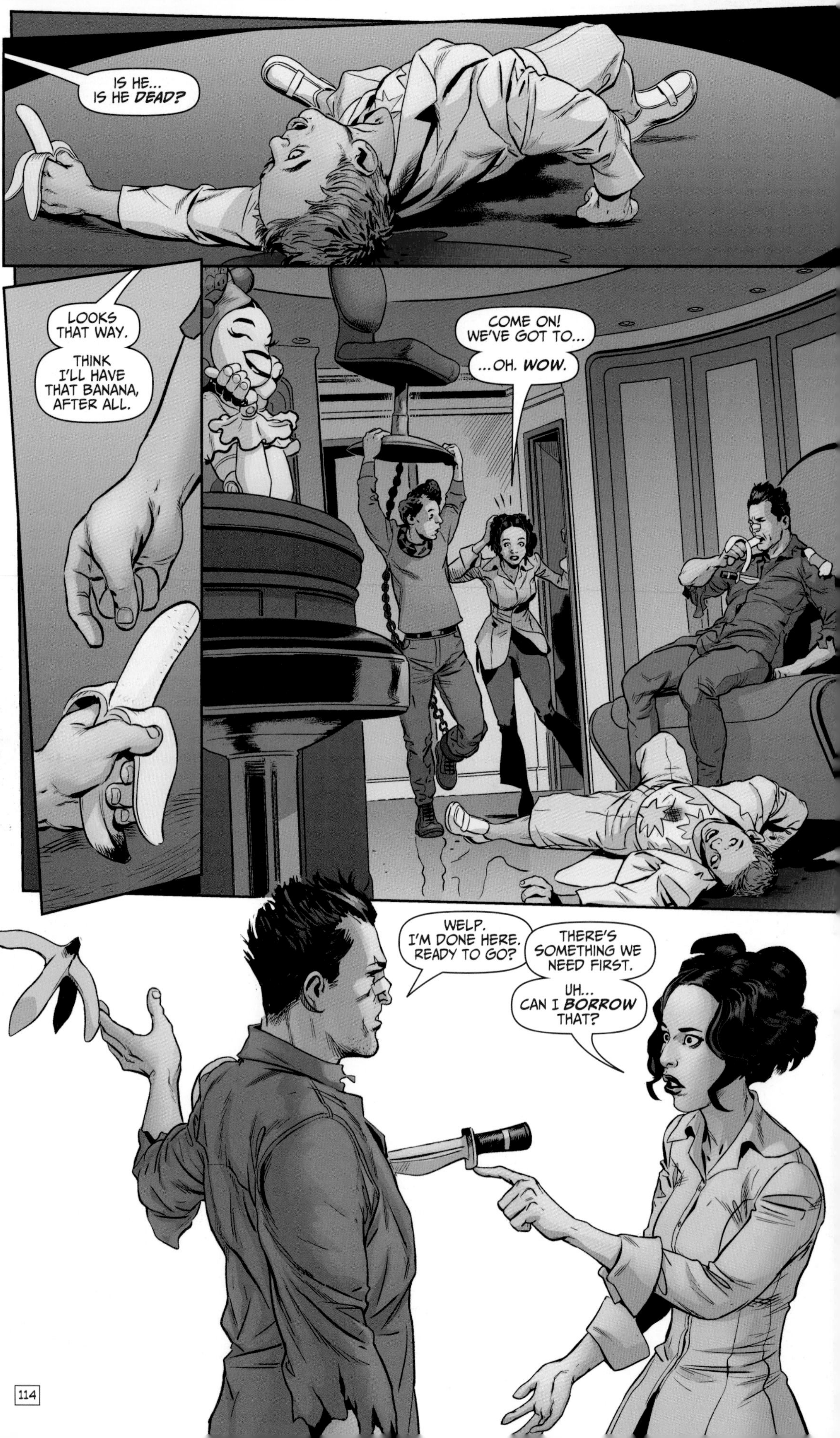
IS HE...
IS HE DEAD?
LOOKS THAT WAY.
THINK I'LL HAVE THAT BANANA, AFTER ALL.
COME ON! WE'VE GOT TO...
...OH. WOW.
WELP. I'M DONE HERE. READY TO GO?
THERE'S SOMETHING WE NEED FIRST.
UH... CAN I BORROW THAT?

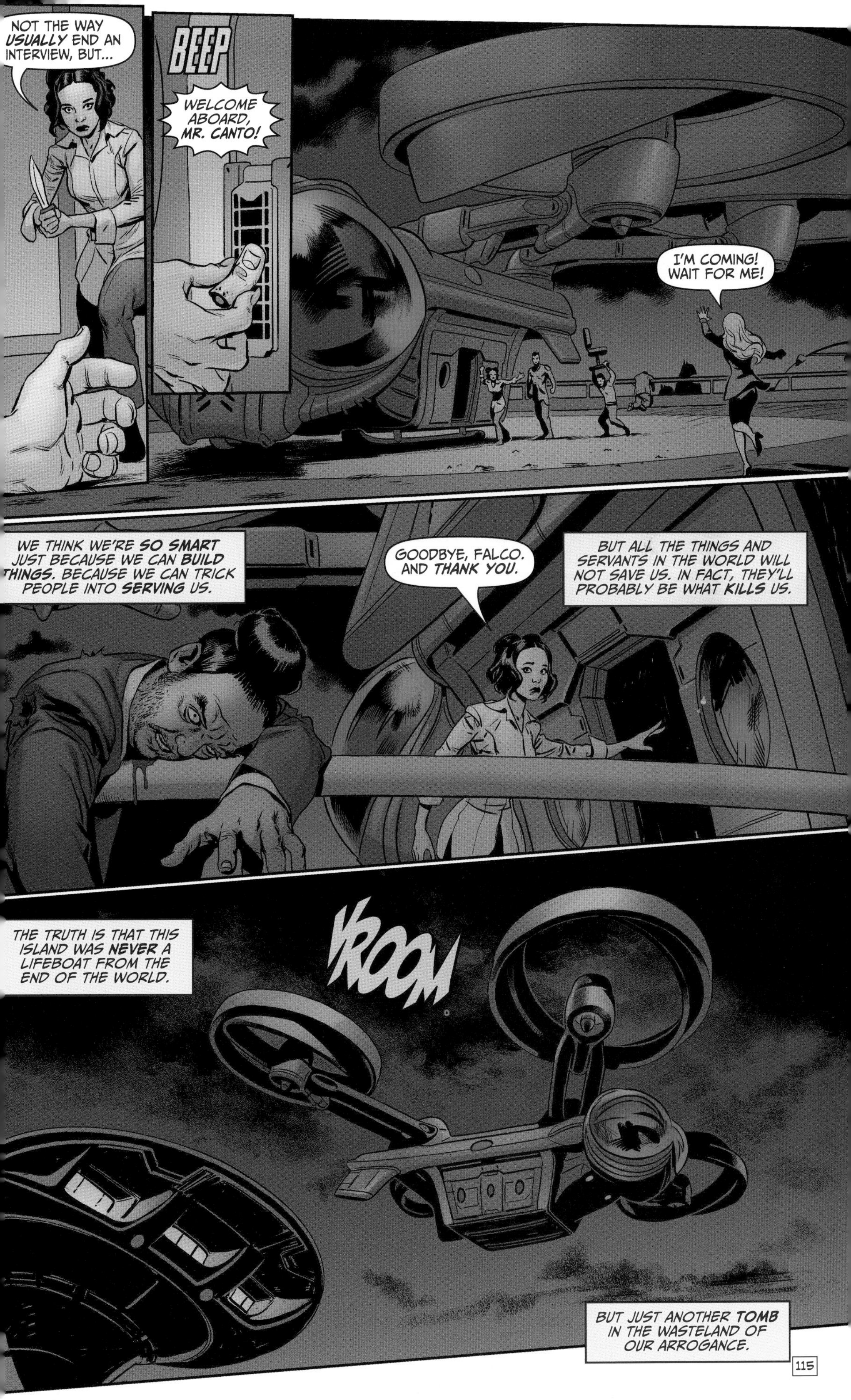
NOT THE WAY USUALLY END AN INTERVIEW, BUT...
BEEP
WELCOME ABOARD, MR. CANTO!
I'M COMING! WAIT FOR ME!
WE THINK WE'RE SO SMART JUST BECAUSE WE CAN BUILD THINGS. BECAUSE WE CAN TRICK PEOPLE INTO SERVING US.
GOODBYE, FALCO. AND THANK YOU.
BUT ALL THE THINGS AND SERVANTS IN THE WORLD WILL NOT SAVE US. IN FACT, THEY'LL PROBABLY BE WHAT KILLS US.
THE TRUTH IS THAT THIS ISLAND WAS NEVER A LIFEBOAT FROM THE END OF THE WORLD.
VROOM
BUT JUST ANOTHER TOMB IN THE WASTELAND OF OUR ARROGANCE.

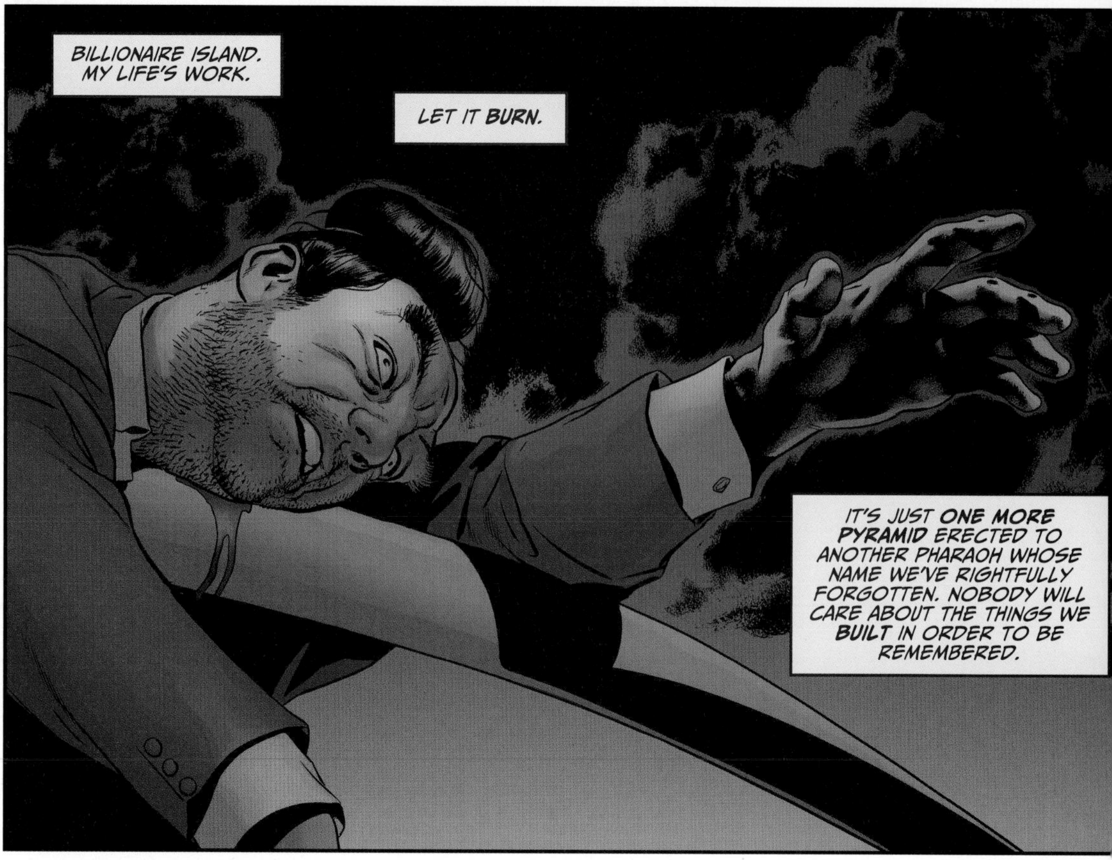
BILLIONAIRE ISLAND. MY LIFE'S WORK.
LET IT BURN.
IT'S JUST ONE MORE PYRAMID ERECTED TO ANOTHER PHARAOH WHOSE NAME WE'VE RIGHTFULLY FORGOTTEN. NOBODY WILL CARE ABOUT THE THINGS WE BUILT IN ORDER TO BE REMEMBERED.

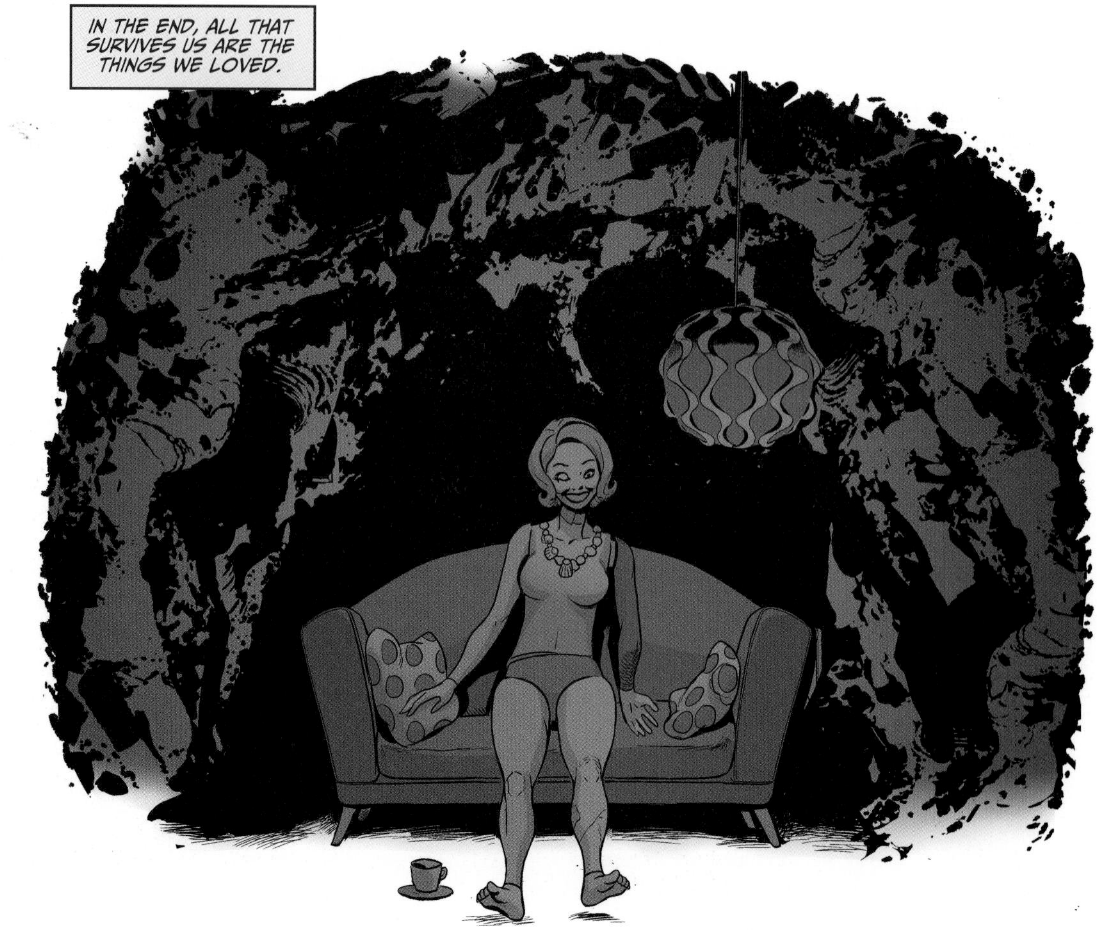
IN THE END, ALL THAT SURVIVES US ARE THE THINGS WE LOVED.

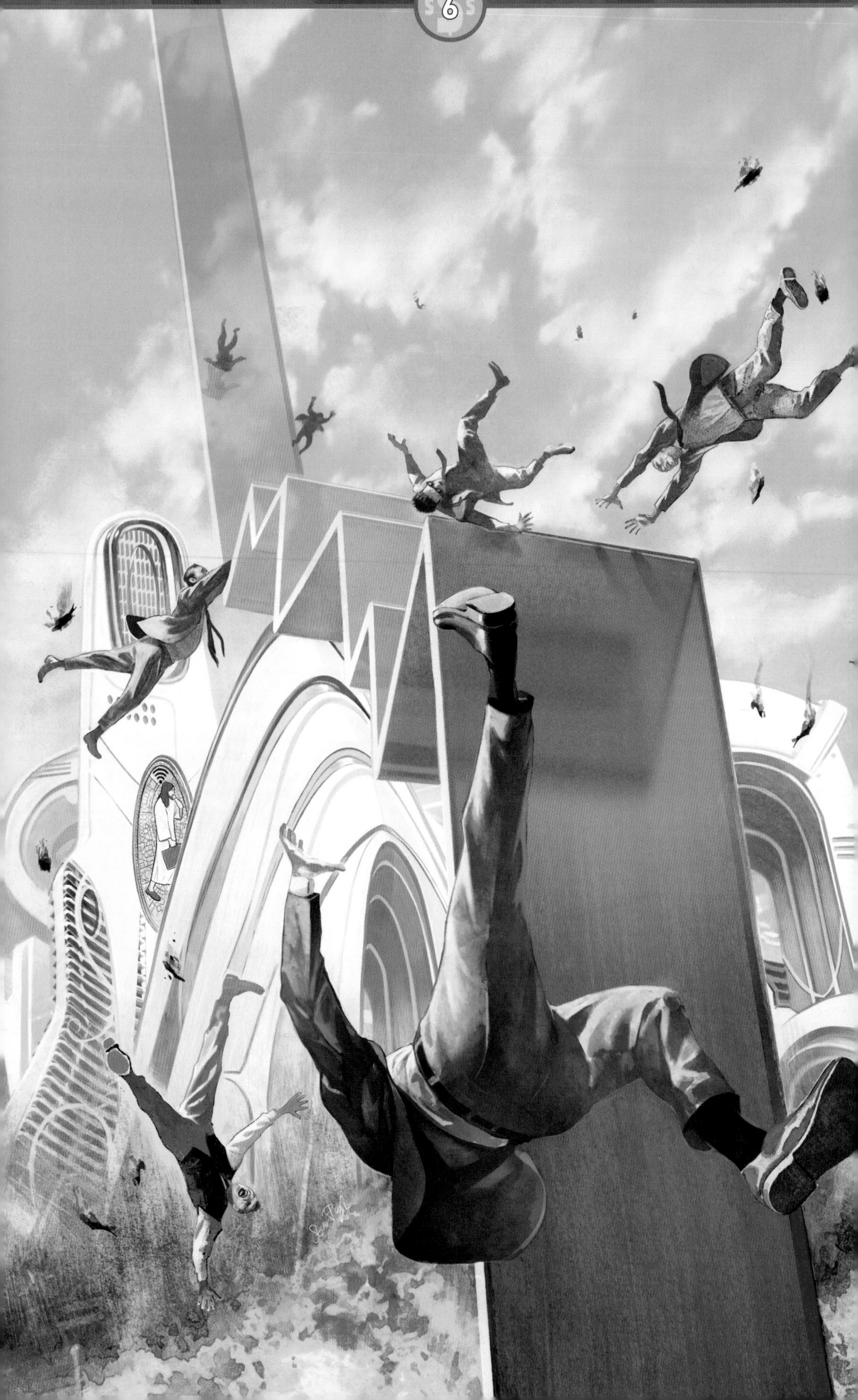

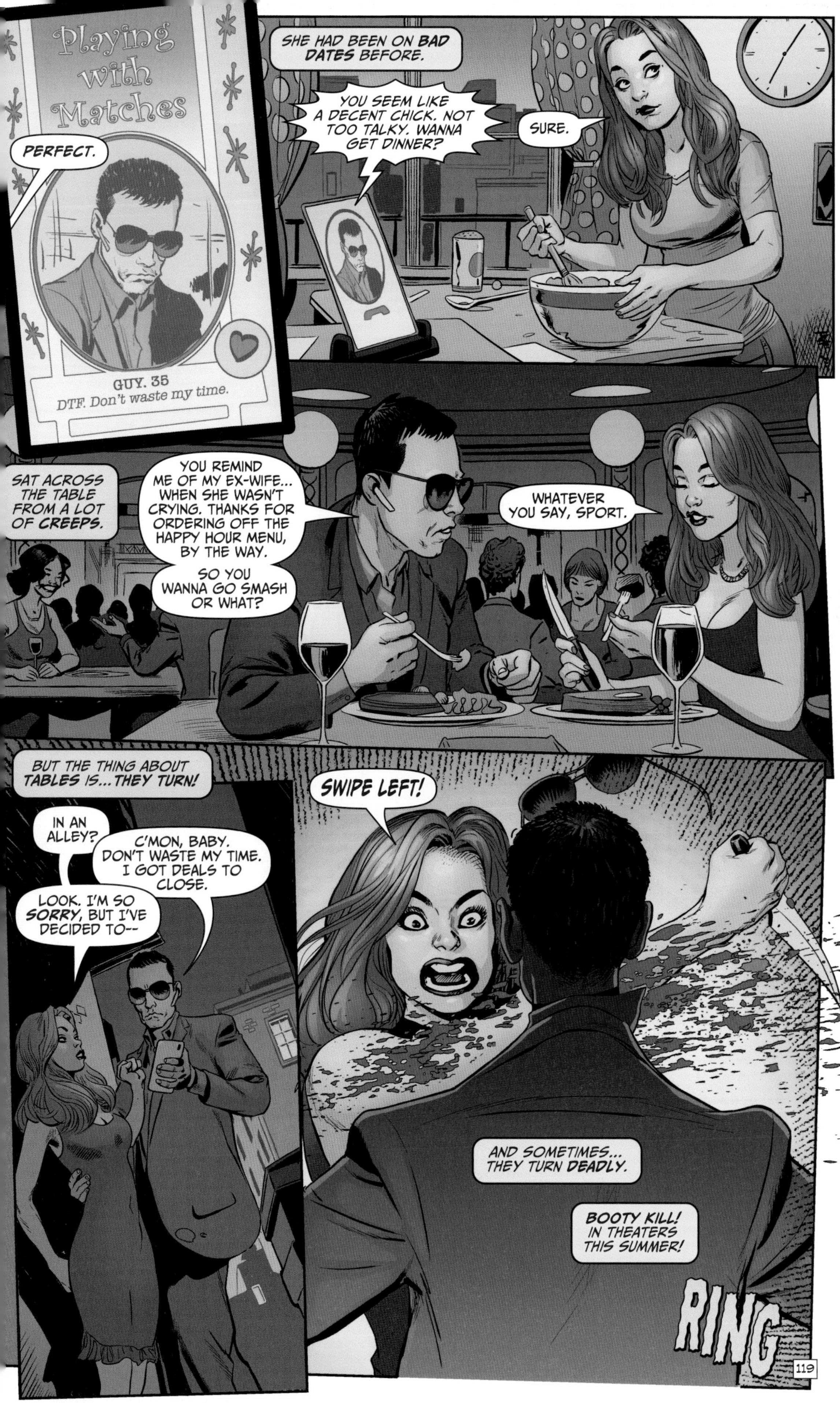
Playing with Matches
PERFECT.
GUY. 35
DTF. Don't waste my time.
SHE HAD BEEN ON BAD DATES BEFORE.
YOU SEEM LIKE A DECENT CHICK. NOT TOO TALKY. WANNA GET DINNER?
SURE.
SAT ACROSS THE TABLE FROM A LOT OF CREEPS.
YOU REMIND ME OF MY EX-WIFE... WHEN SHE WASN'T CRYING. THANKS FOR ORDERING OFF THE HAPPY HOUR MENU, BY THE WAY.
SO YOU WANNA GO SMASH OR WHAT?
WHATEVER YOU SAY, SPORT.
BUT THE THING ABOUT TABLES IS...THEY TURN!
IN AN ALLEY?
C'MON, BABY. DON'T WASTE MY TIME. I GOT DEALS TO CLOSE.
LOOK. I'M SO SORRY, BUT I'VE DECIDED TO--
SWIPE LEFT!
AND SOMETIMES... THEY TURN DEADLY.
BOOTY KILL! IN THEATERS THIS SUMMER!
RING

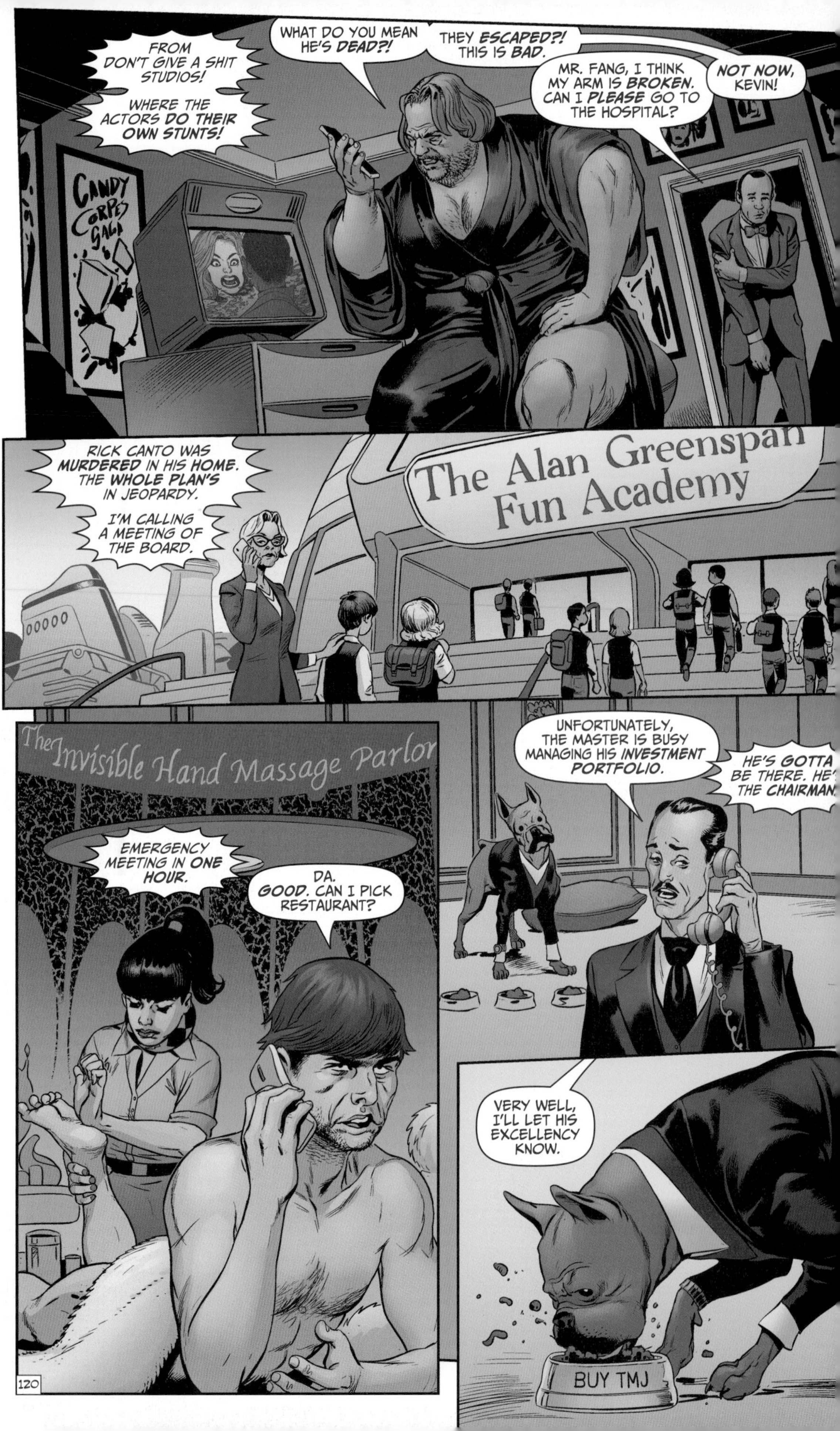
FROM DON'T GIVE A SHIT STUDIOS!
WHERE THE ACTORS DO THEIR OWN STUNTS!
WHAT DO YOU MEAN HE'S DEAD?!
THEY ESCAPED?! THIS IS BAD.
MR. FANG, I THINK MY ARM IS BROKEN. CAN I PLEASE GO TO THE HOSPITAL?
NOT NOW, KEVIN!
CANDY CORPSES GALA
RICK CANTO WAS MURDERED IN HIS HOME. THE WHOLE PLAN'S IN JEOPARDY.
I'M CALLING A MEETING OF THE BOARD.
The Alan Greenspan Fun Academy
The Invisible Hand Massage Parlor
EMERGENCY MEETING IN ONE HOUR.
DA. GOOD. CAN I PICK RESTAURANT?
UNFORTUNATELY, THE MASTER IS BUSY MANAGING HIS INVESTMENT PORTFOLIO.
HE'S GOTTA BE THERE. HE'S THE CHAIRMAN.
VERY WELL, I'LL LET HIS EXCELLENCY KNOW.
BUY TMJ

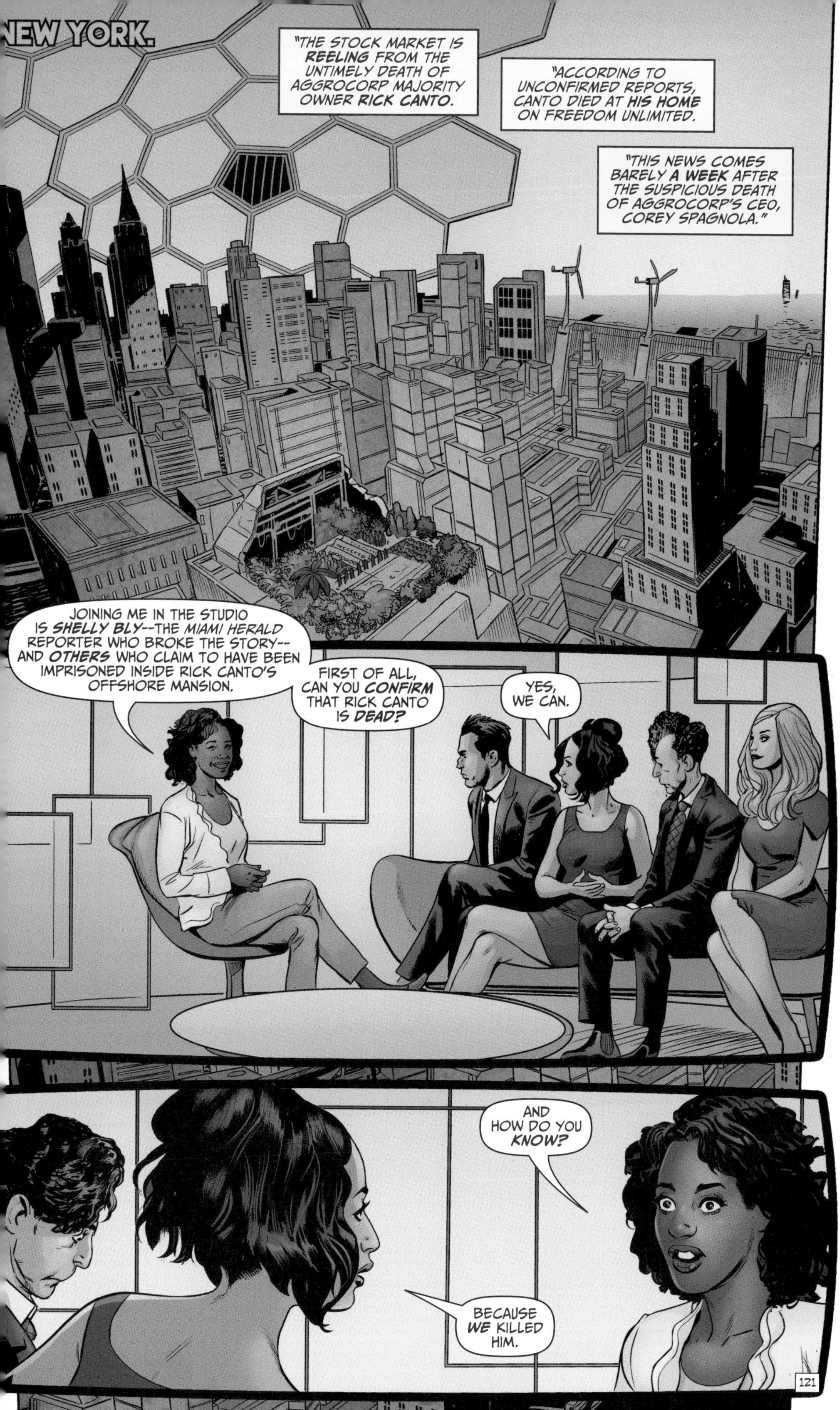
NEW YORK.
"THE STOCK MARKET IS REELING FROM THE UNTIMELY DEATH OF AGGROCORP MAJORITY OWNER RICK CANTO.
"ACCORDING TO UNCONFIRMED REPORTS, CANTO DIED AT HIS HOME ON FREEDOM UNLIMITED.
"THIS NEWS COMES BARELY A WEEK AFTER THE SUSPICIOUS DEATH OF AGGROCORP'S CEO, COREY SPAGNOLA."
JOINING ME IN THE STUDIO IS SHELLY BLY--THE MIAMI HERALD REPORTER WHO BROKE THE STORY--AND OTHERS WHO CLAIM TO HAVE BEEN IMPRISONED INSIDE RICK CANTO'S OFFSHORE MANSION.
FIRST OF ALL, CAN YOU CONFIRM THAT RICK CANTO IS DEAD?
YES, WE CAN.
AND HOW DO YOU KNOW?
BECAUSE WE KILLED HIM.

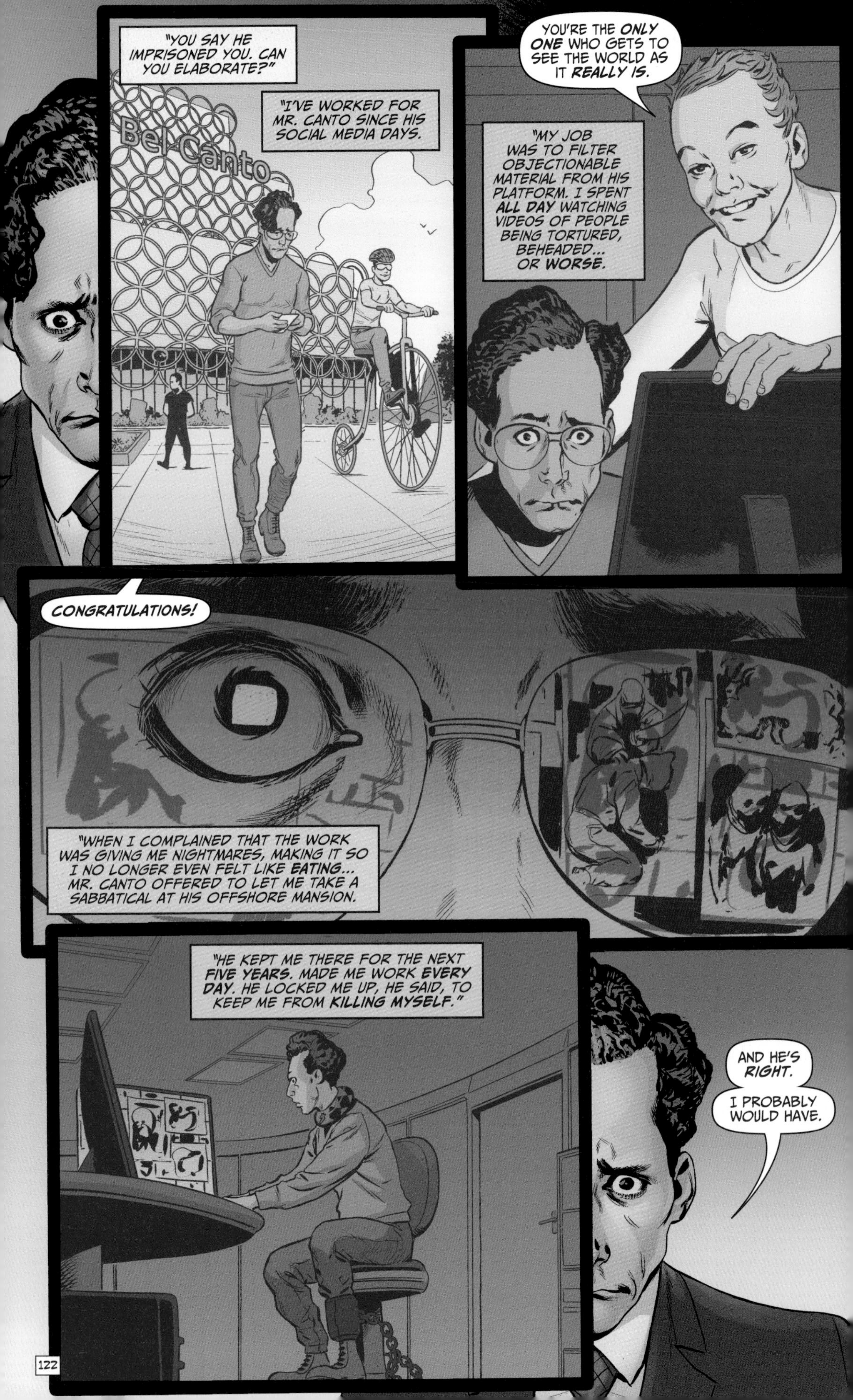
"YOU SAY HE IMPRISONED YOU. CAN YOU ELABORATE?"
"I'VE WORKED FOR MR. CANTO SINCE HIS SOCIAL MEDIA DAYS.
Bel Canto
YOU'RE THE ONLY ONE WHO GETS TO SEE THE WORLD AS IT REALLY IS.
"MY JOB WAS TO FILTER OBJECTIONABLE MATERIAL FROM HIS PLATFORM. I SPENT ALL DAY WATCHING VIDEOS OF PEOPLE BEING TORTURED, BEHEADED... OR WORSE.
CONGRATULATIONS!
"WHEN I COMPLAINED THAT THE WORK WAS GIVING ME NIGHTMARES, MAKING IT SO I NO LONGER EVEN FELT LIKE EATING... MR. CANTO OFFERED TO LET ME TAKE A SABBATICAL AT HIS OFFSHORE MANSION.
"HE KEPT ME THERE FOR THE NEXT FIVE YEARS. MADE ME WORK EVERY DAY. HE LOCKED ME UP, HE SAID, TO KEEP ME FROM KILLING MYSELF."
AND HE'S RIGHT.
I PROBABLY WOULD HAVE.

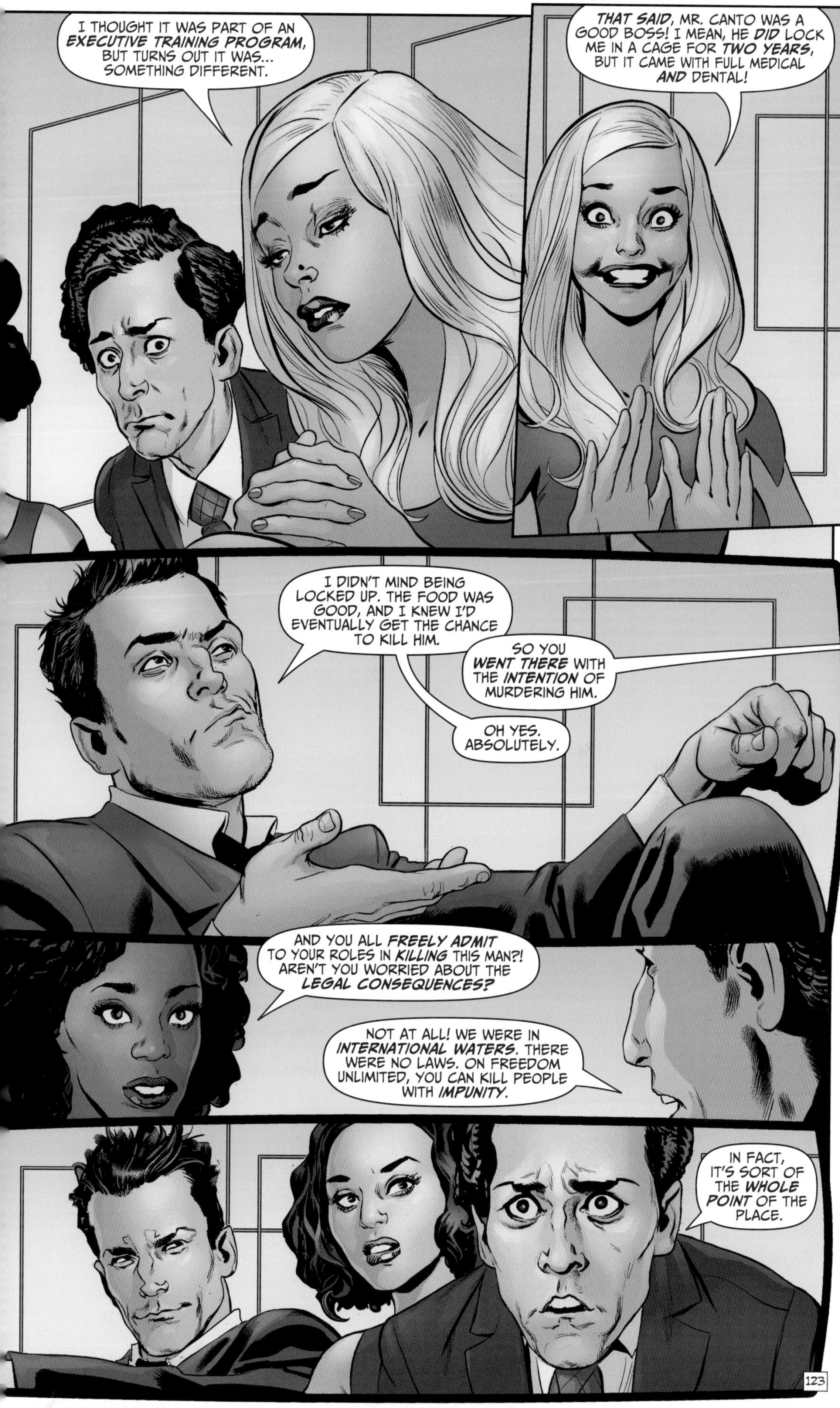
I THOUGHT IT WAS PART OF AN EXECUTIVE TRAINING PROGRAM, BUT TURNS OUT IT WAS... SOMETHING DIFFERENT.
THAT SAID, MR. CANTO WAS A GOOD BOSS! I MEAN, HE DID LOCK ME IN A CAGE FOR TWO YEARS, BUT IT CAME WITH FULL MEDICAL AND DENTAL!
I DIDN'T MIND BEING LOCKED UP. THE FOOD WAS GOOD, AND I KNEW I'D EVENTUALLY GET THE CHANCE TO KILL HIM.
SO YOU WENT THERE WITH THE INTENTION OF MURDERING HIM.
OH YES. ABSOLUTELY.
AND YOU ALL FREELY ADMIT TO YOUR ROLES IN KILLING THIS MAN?! AREN'T YOU WORRIED ABOUT THE LEGAL CONSEQUENCES?
NOT AT ALL! WE WERE IN INTERNATIONAL WATERS. THERE WERE NO LAWS. ON FREEDOM UNLIMITED, YOU CAN KILL PEOPLE WITH IMPUNITY.
IN FACT, IT'S SORT OF THE WHOLE POINT OF THE PLACE.

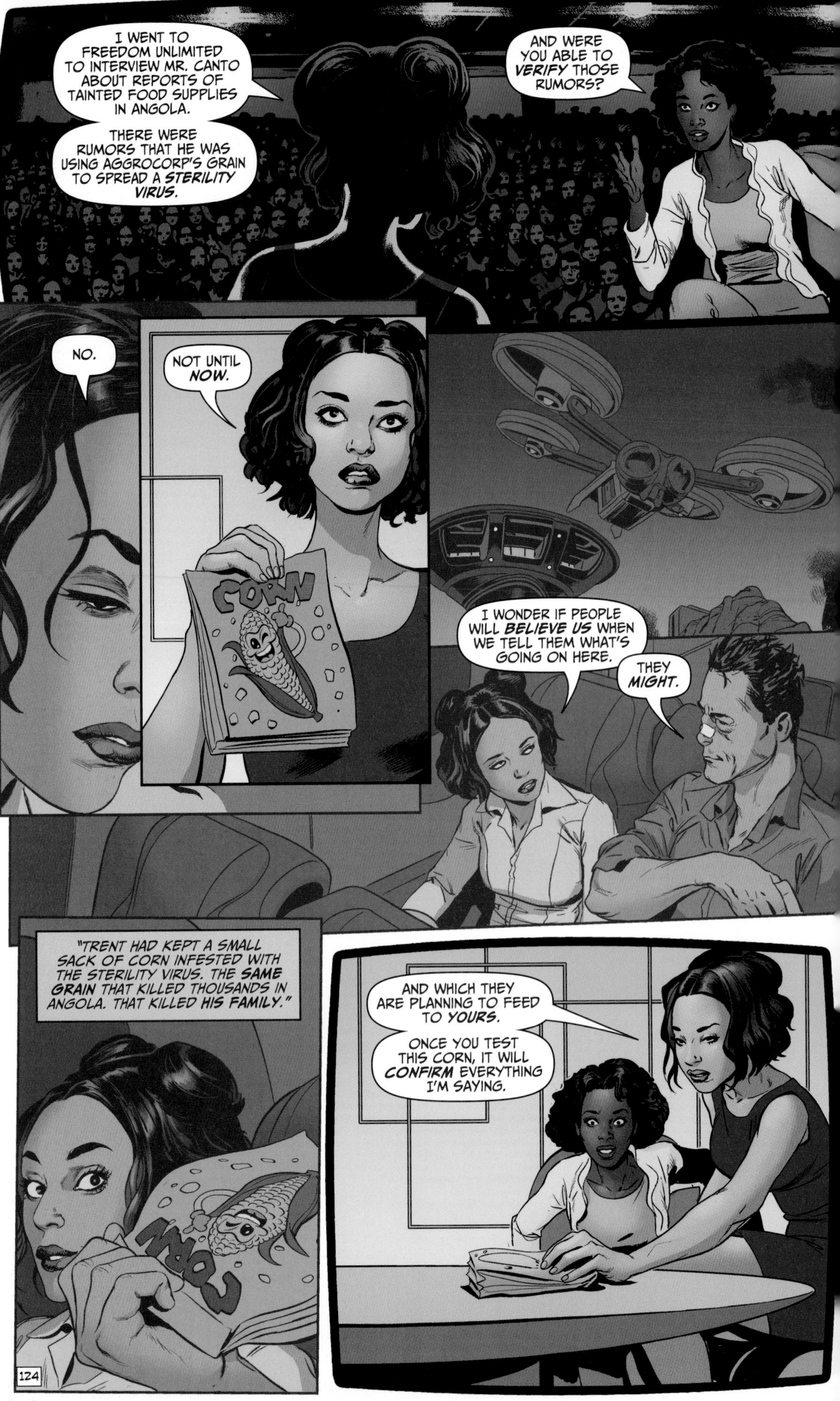
I WENT TO FREEDOM UNLIMITED TO INTERVIEW MR. CANTO ABOUT REPORTS OF TAINTED FOOD SUPPLIES IN ANGOLA.
THERE WERE RUMORS THAT HE WAS USING AGGROCORP'S GRAIN TO SPREAD A STERILITY VIRUS.
AND WERE YOU ABLE TO VERIFY THOSE RUMORS?
NO.
NOT UNTIL NOW.
CORN
I WONDER IF PEOPLE WILL BELIEVE US WHEN WE TELL THEM WHAT'S GOING ON HERE.
THEY MIGHT.
"TRENT HAD KEPT A SMALL SACK OF CORN INFESTED WITH THE STERILITY VIRUS. THE SAME GRAIN THAT KILLED THOUSANDS IN ANGOLA. THAT KILLED HIS FAMILY."
AND WHICH THEY ARE PLANNING TO FEED TO YOURS.
ONCE YOU TEST THIS CORN, IT WILL CONFIRM EVERYTHING I'M SAYING.

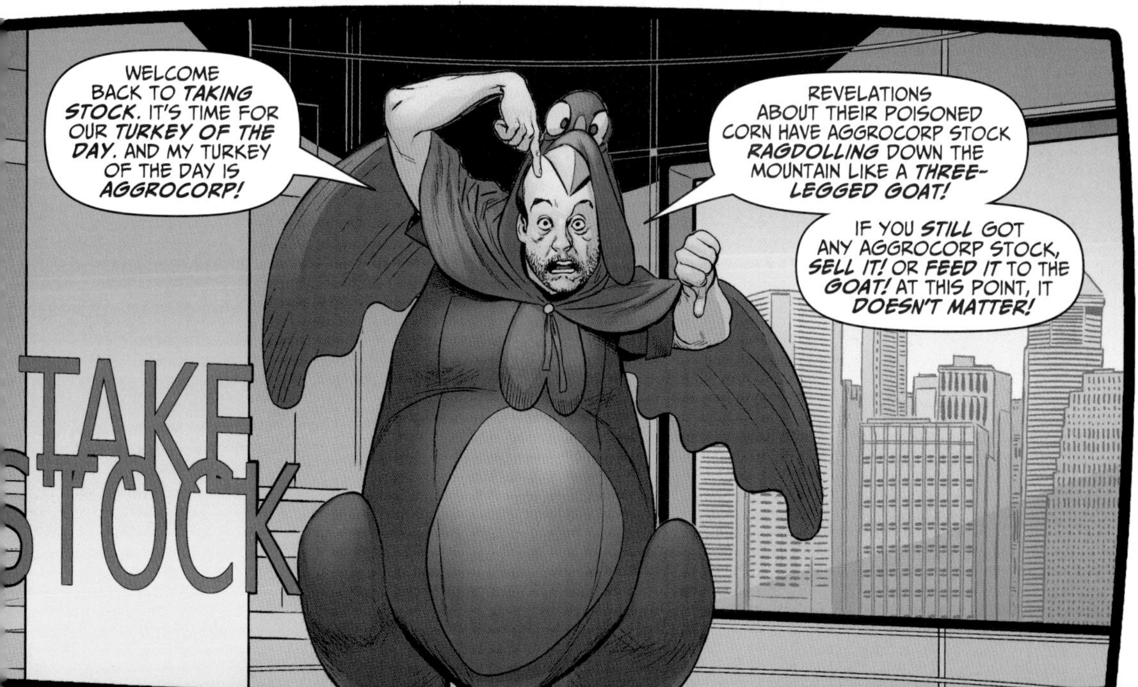
WELCOME BACK TO TAKING STOCK. IT'S TIME FOR OUR TURKEY OF THE DAY. AND MY TURKEY OF THE DAY IS AGGROCORP!
REVELATIONS ABOUT THEIR POISONED CORN HAVE AGGROCORP STOCK RAGDOLLING DOWN THE MOUNTAIN LIKE A THREE-LEGGED GOAT!
IF YOU STILL GOT ANY AGGROCORP STOCK, SELL IT! OR FEED IT TO THE GOAT! AT THIS POINT, IT DOESN'T MATTER!
TAKE STOCK

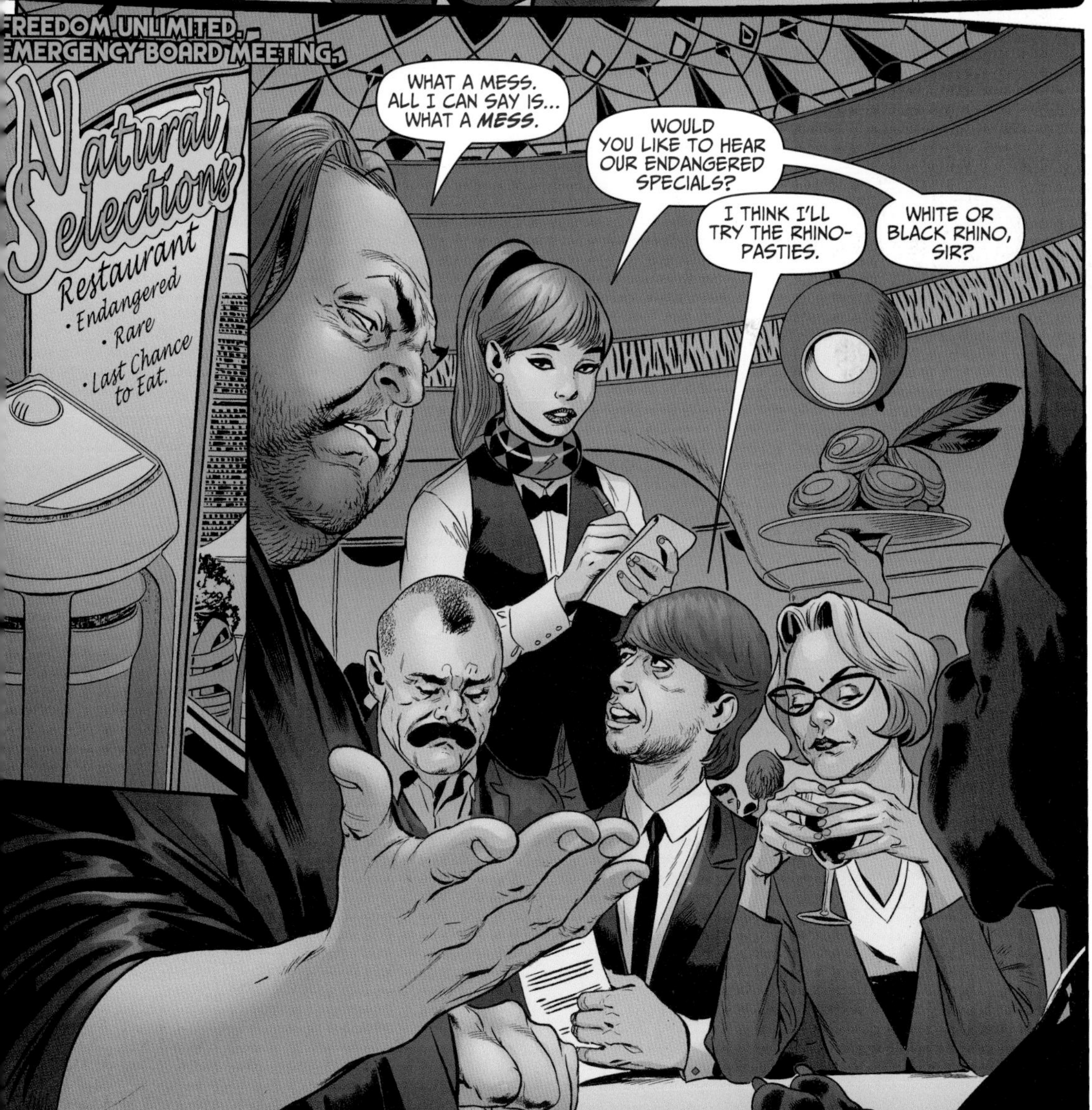
FREEDOM UNLIMITED. EMERGENCY BOARD MEETING.
Natural Selections
Restaurant
• Endangered
• Rare
• Last Chance to Eat.
WHAT A MESS. ALL I CAN SAY IS... WHAT A MESS.
WOULD YOU LIKE TO HEAR OUR ENDANGERED SPECIALS?
I THINK I'LL TRY THE RHINO-PASTIES.
WHITE OR BLACK RHINO, SIR?

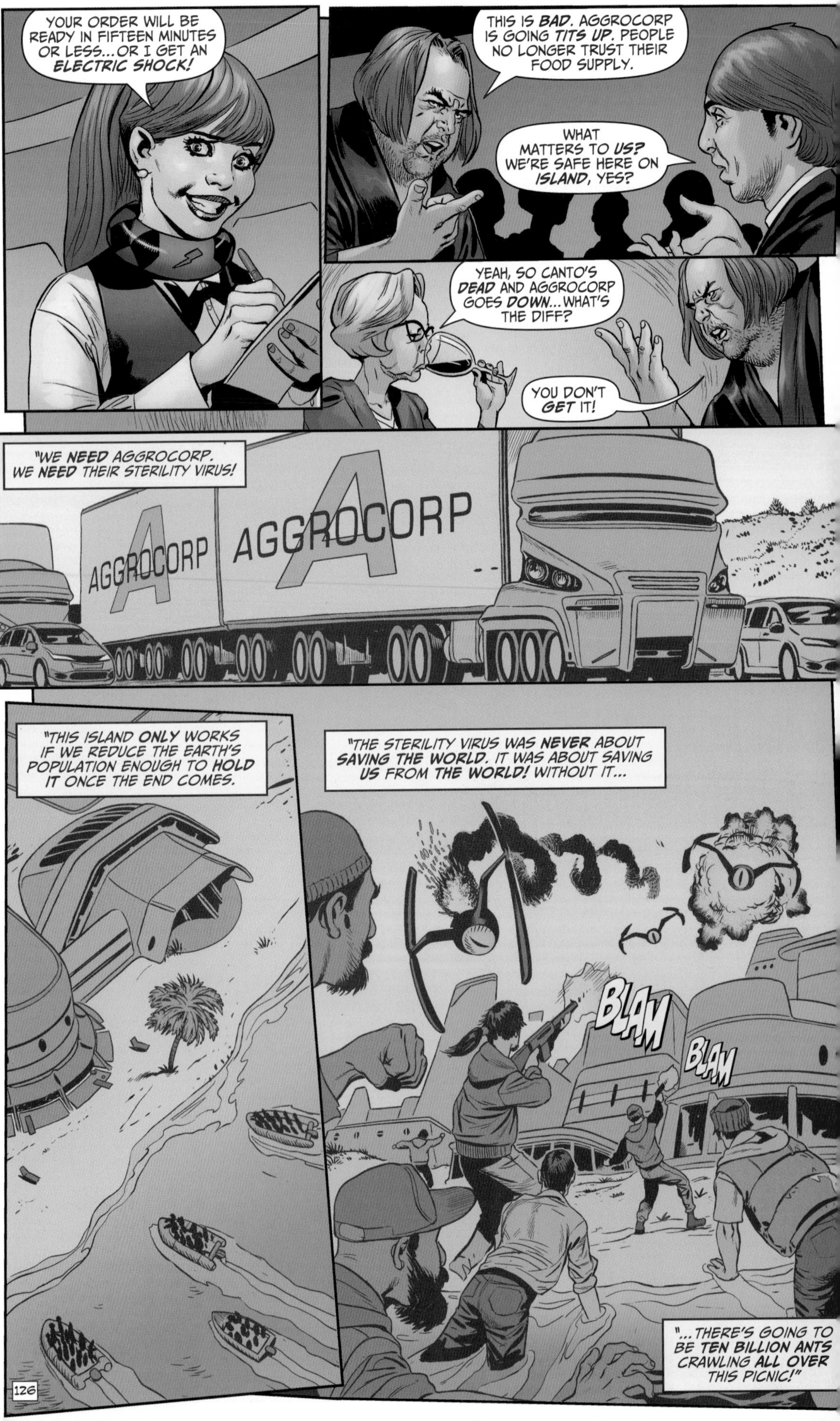
YOUR ORDER WILL BE READY IN FIFTEEN MINUTES OR LESS...OR I GET AN ELECTRIC SHOCK!
THIS IS BAD. AGGROCORP IS GOING TITS UP. PEOPLE NO LONGER TRUST THEIR FOOD SUPPLY.
WHAT MATTERS TO US? WE'RE SAFE HERE ON ISLAND, YES?
YEAH, SO CANTO'S DEAD AND AGGROCORP GOES DOWN...WHAT'S THE DIFF?
YOU DON'T GET IT!
"WE NEED AGGROCORP. WE NEED THEIR STERILITY VIRUS!
AGGROCORP
AGGROCORP
"THIS ISLAND ONLY WORKS IF WE REDUCE THE EARTH'S POPULATION ENOUGH TO HOLD IT ONCE THE END COMES.
"THE STERILITY VIRUS WAS NEVER ABOUT SAVING THE WORLD. IT WAS ABOUT SAVING US FROM THE WORLD! WITHOUT IT...
BLAM
BLAM
"...THERE'S GOING TO BE TEN BILLION ANTS CRAWLING ALL OVER THIS PICNIC!"

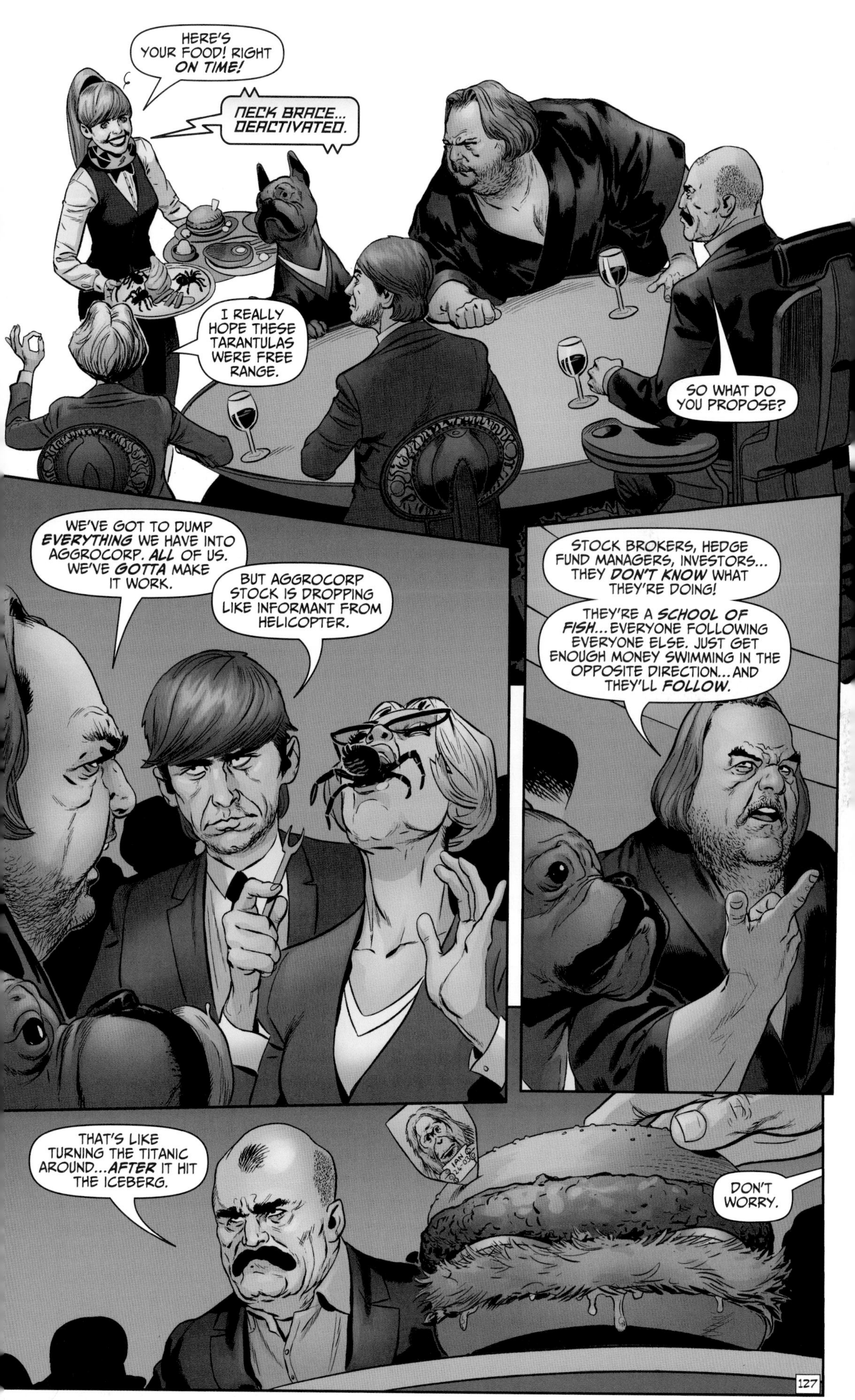

HERE'S YOUR FOOD! RIGHT ON TIME!
NECK BRACE... DEACTIVATED.
I REALLY HOPE THESE TARANTULAS WERE FREE RANGE.
SO WHAT DO YOU PROPOSE?
WE'VE GOT TO DUMP EVERYTHING WE HAVE INTO AGGROCORP. ALL OF US. WE'VE GOTTA MAKE IT WORK.
BUT AGGROCORP STOCK IS DROPPING LIKE INFORMANT FROM HELICOPTER.
STOCK BROKERS, HEDGE FUND MANAGERS, INVESTORS... THEY DON'T KNOW WHAT THEY'RE DOING!
THEY'RE A SCHOOL OF FISH... EVERYONE FOLLOWING EVERYONE ELSE. JUST GET ENOUGH MONEY SWIMMING IN THE OPPOSITE DIRECTION... AND THEY'LL FOLLOW.
THAT'S LIKE TURNING THE TITANIC AROUND... AFTER IT HIT THE ICEBERG.
DON'T WORRY.

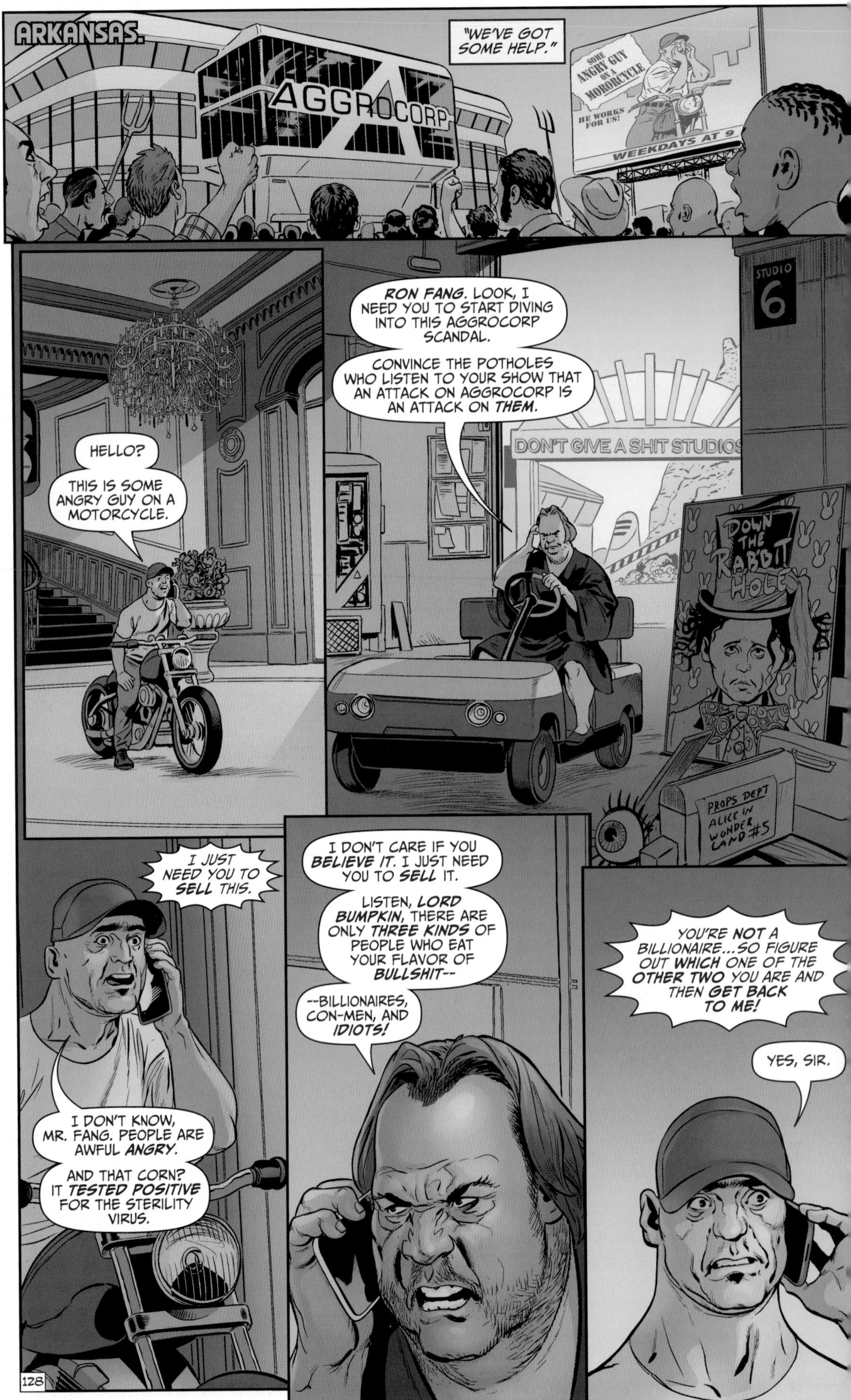
ARKANSAS.
"WE'VE GOT SOME HELP."
AGGROCORP
SOME ANGRY GUY ON A MORORCYCLE
HE WORKS FOR US!
WEEKDAYS AT 9
STUDIO 6
RON FANG. LOOK, I NEED YOU TO START DIVING INTO THIS AGGROCORP SCANDAL.
CONVINCE THE POTHOLES WHO LISTEN TO YOUR SHOW THAT AN ATTACK ON AGGROCORP IS AN ATTACK ON THEM.
HELLO?
THIS IS SOME ANGRY GUY ON A MOTORCYCLE.
DON'T GIVE A SHIT STUDIOS
DOWN THE RABBIT HOLE
PROPS DEPT ALICE IN WONDER LAND #5
I JUST NEED YOU TO SELL THIS.
I DON'T KNOW, MR. FANG. PEOPLE ARE AWFUL ANGRY.
AND THAT CORN? IT TESTED POSITIVE FOR THE STERILITY VIRUS.
I DON'T CARE IF YOU BELIEVE IT. I JUST NEED YOU TO SELL IT.
LISTEN, LORD BUMPKIN, THERE ARE ONLY THREE KINDS OF PEOPLE WHO EAT YOUR FLAVOR OF BULLSHIT--
--BILLIONAIRES, CON-MEN, AND IDIOTS!
YOU'RE NOT A BILLIONAIRE...SO FIGURE OUT WHICH ONE OF THE OTHER TWO YOU ARE AND THEN GET BACK TO ME!
YES, SIR.

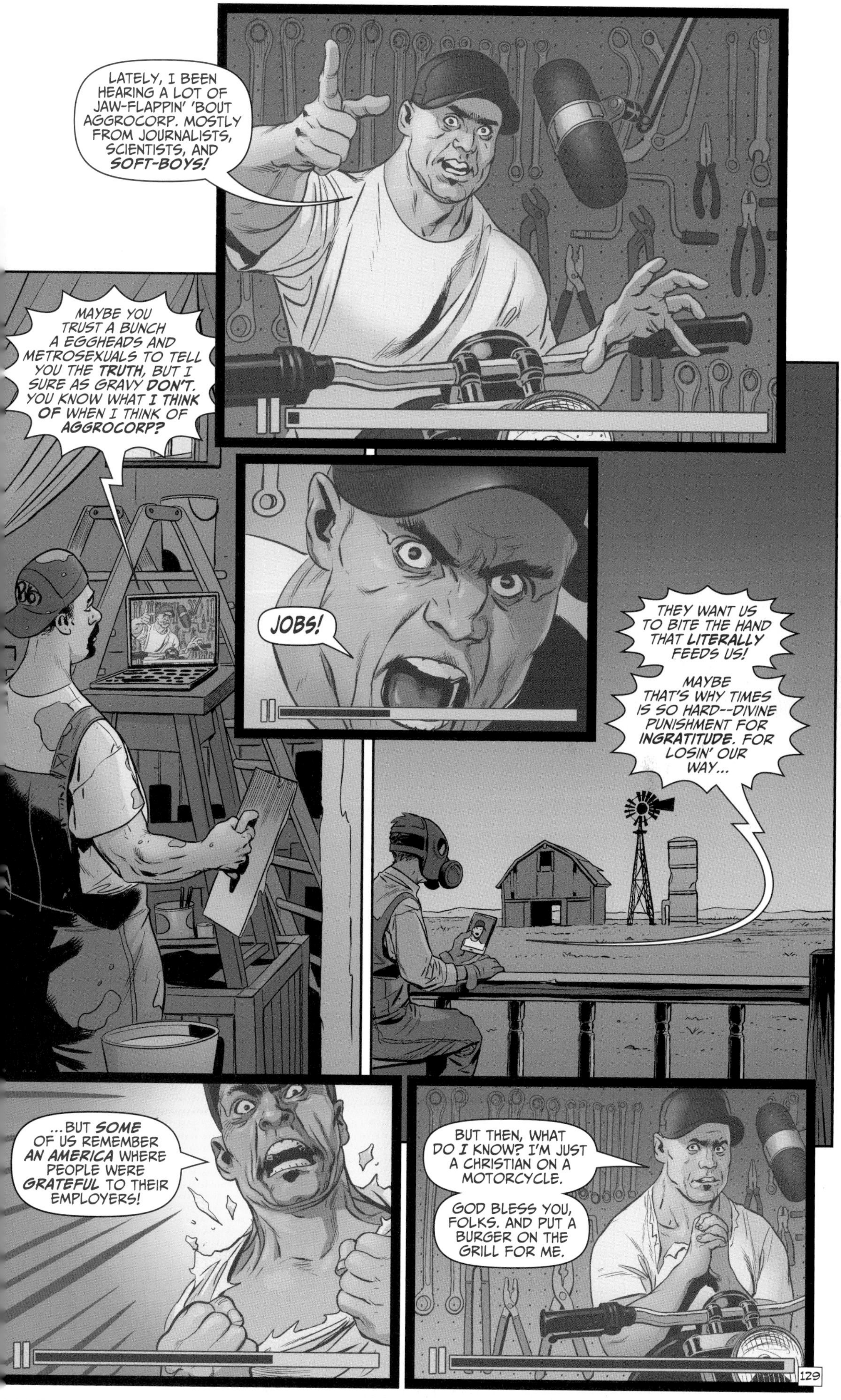
LATELY, I BEEN HEARING A LOT OF JAW-FLAPPIN' 'BOUT AGGROCORP. MOSTLY FROM JOURNALISTS, SCIENTISTS, AND SOFT-BOYS!
MAYBE YOU TRUST A BUNCH A EGGHEADS AND METROSEXUALS TO TELL YOU THE TRUTH, BUT I SURE AS GRAVY DON'T. YOU KNOW WHAT I THINK OF WHEN I THINK OF AGGROCORP?
JOBS!
THEY WANT US TO BITE THE HAND THAT LITERALLY FEEDS US!
MAYBE THAT'S WHY TIMES IS SO HARD--DIVINE PUNISHMENT FOR INGRATITUDE. FOR LOSIN' OUR WAY...
...BUT SOME OF US REMEMBER AN AMERICA WHERE PEOPLE WERE GRATEFUL TO THEIR EMPLOYERS!
BUT THEN, WHAT DO I KNOW? I'M JUST A CHRISTIAN ON A MOTORCYCLE.
GOD BLESS YOU, FOLKS. AND PUT A BURGER ON THE GRILL FOR ME.

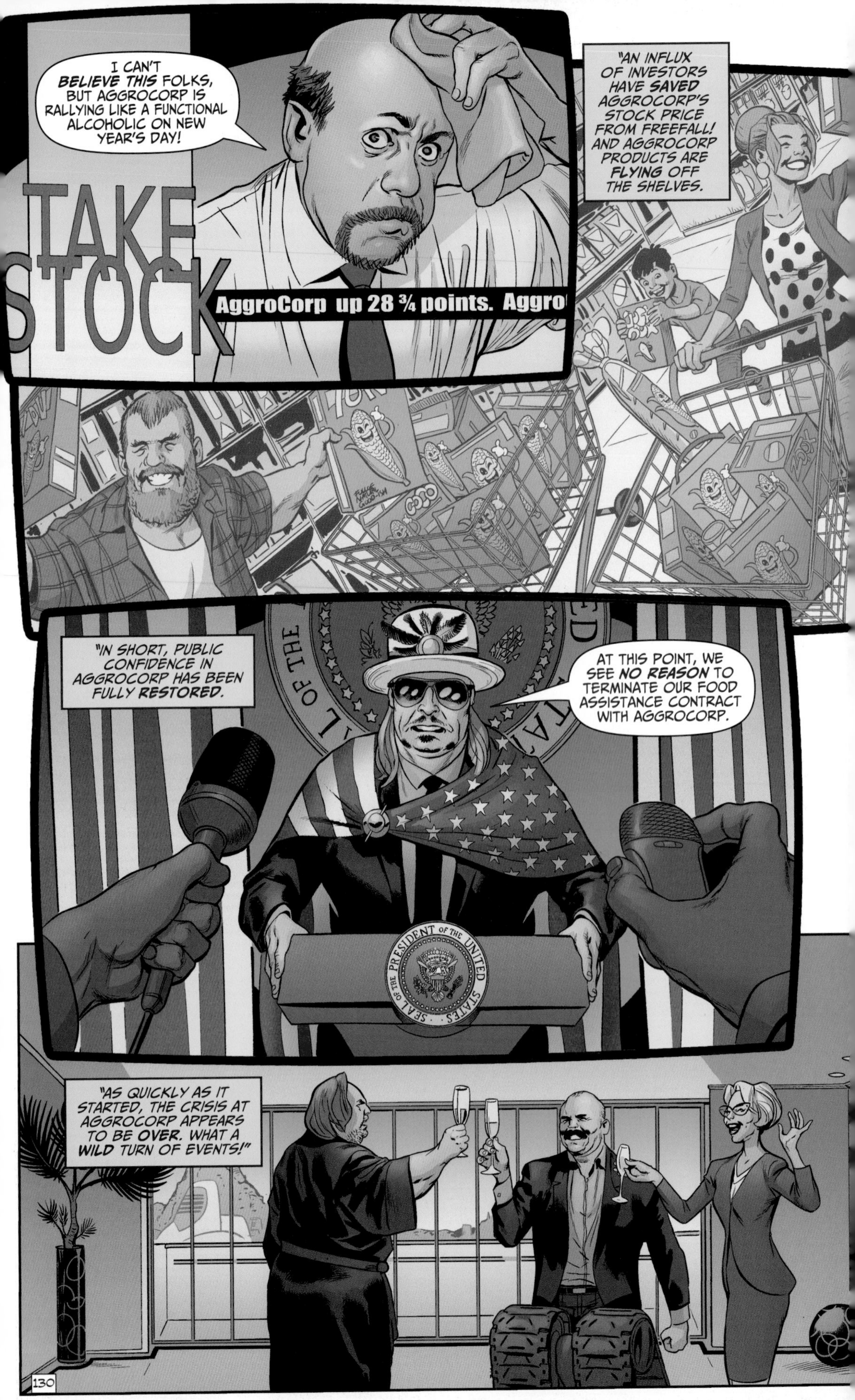
I CAN'T BELIEVE THIS FOLKS, BUT AGGROCORP IS RALLYING LIKE A FUNCTIONAL ALCOHOLIC ON NEW YEAR'S DAY!
TAKE STOCK
AggroCorp up 28 ¾ points. Aggro
"AN INFLUX OF INVESTORS HAVE SAVED AGGROCORP'S STOCK PRICE FROM FREEFALL! AND AGGROCORP PRODUCTS ARE FLYING OFF THE SHELVES.
"IN SHORT, PUBLIC CONFIDENCE IN AGGROCORP HAS BEEN FULLY RESTORED.
AT THIS POINT, WE SEE NO REASON TO TERMINATE OUR FOOD ASSISTANCE CONTRACT WITH AGGROCORP.
SEAL OF THE PRESIDENT OF THE UNITED STATES
"AS QUICKLY AS IT STARTED, THE CRISIS AT AGGROCORP APPEARS TO BE OVER. WHAT A WILD TURN OF EVENTS!"

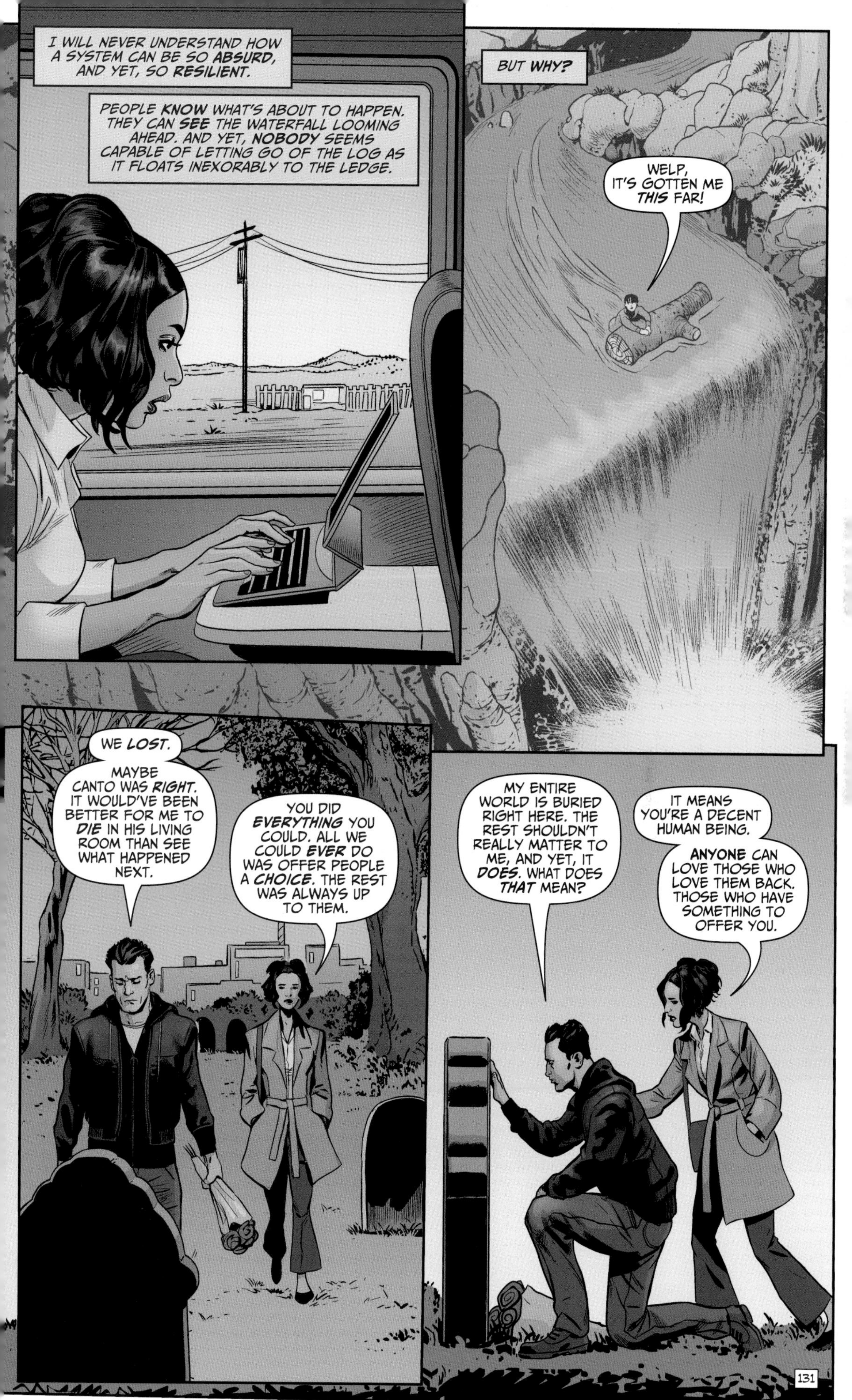
I WILL NEVER UNDERSTAND HOW A SYSTEM CAN BE SO ABSURD, AND YET, SO RESILIENT.
PEOPLE KNOW WHAT'S ABOUT TO HAPPEN. THEY CAN SEE THE WATERFALL LOOMING AHEAD. AND YET, NOBODY SEEMS CAPABLE OF LETTING GO OF THE LOG AS IT FLOATS INEXORABLY TO THE LEDGE.
BUT WHY?
WELP, IT'S GOTTEN ME THIS FAR!
WE LOST.
MAYBE CANTO WAS RIGHT. IT WOULD'VE BEEN BETTER FOR ME TO DIE IN HIS LIVING ROOM THAN SEE WHAT HAPPENED NEXT.
YOU DID EVERYTHING YOU COULD. ALL WE COULD EVER DO WAS OFFER PEOPLE A CHOICE. THE REST WAS ALWAYS UP TO THEM.
MY ENTIRE WORLD IS BURIED RIGHT HERE. THE REST SHOULDN'T REALLY MATTER TO ME, AND YET, IT DOES. WHAT DOES THAT MEAN?
IT MEANS YOU'RE A DECENT HUMAN BEING.
ANYONE CAN LOVE THOSE WHO LOVE THEM BACK. THOSE WHO HAVE SOMETHING TO OFFER YOU.

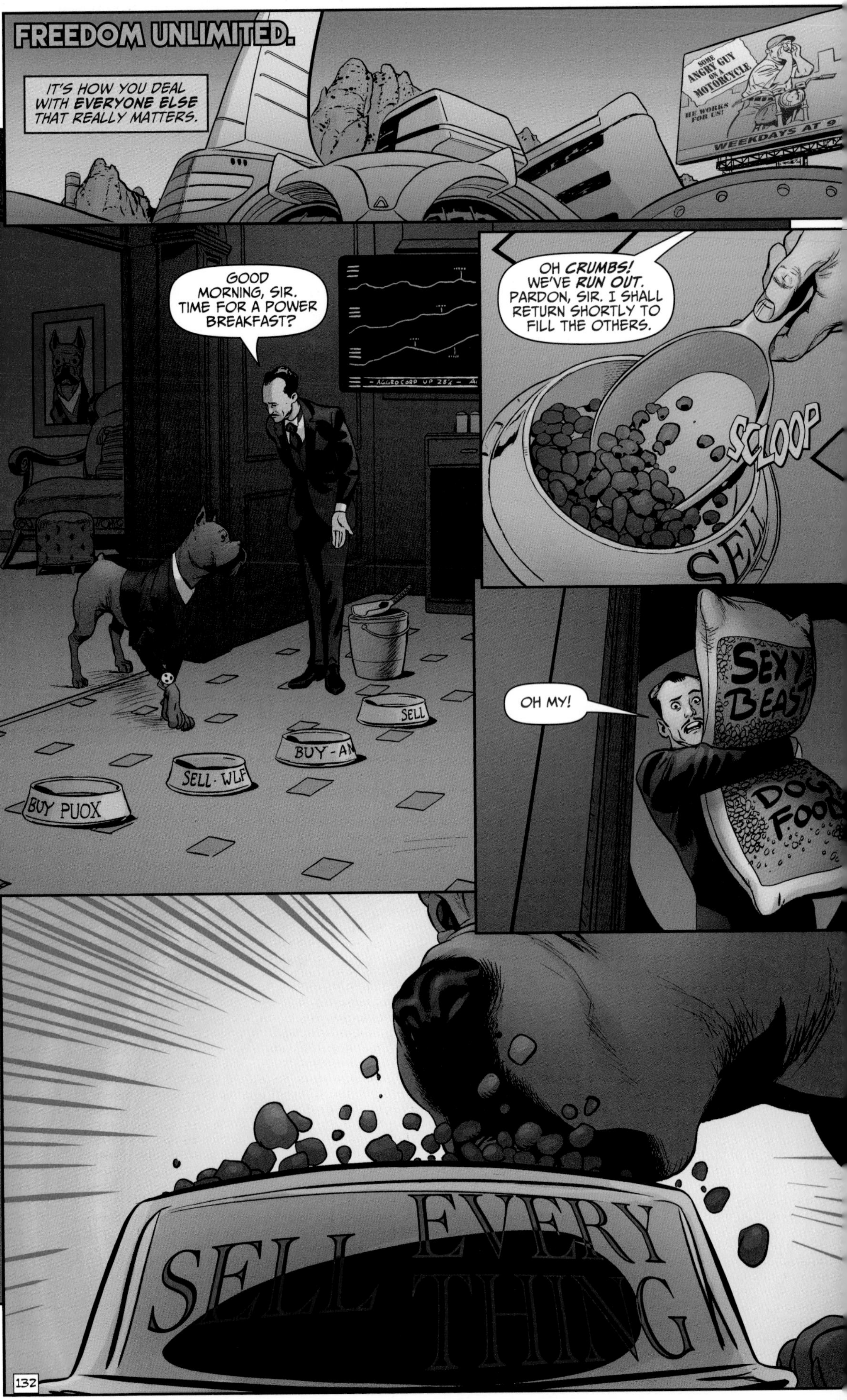
FREEDOM UNLIMITED.
IT'S HOW YOU DEAL WITH EVERYONE ELSE THAT REALLY MATTERS.
SOME ANGRY GUY ON A MOTORCYCLE
HE WORKS FOR US!
WEEKDAYS AT 9
GOOD MORNING, SIR. TIME FOR A POWER BREAKFAST?
AGGROCORP UP 28%
SELL
BUY-AM
SELL · WLF
BUY PUOX
OH CRUMBS! WE'VE RUN OUT. PARDON, SIR. I SHALL RETURN SHORTLY TO FILL THE OTHERS.
SCLOOP
SELL
OH MY!
SEXY BEAST
DOG FOOD
SELL EVERY THING

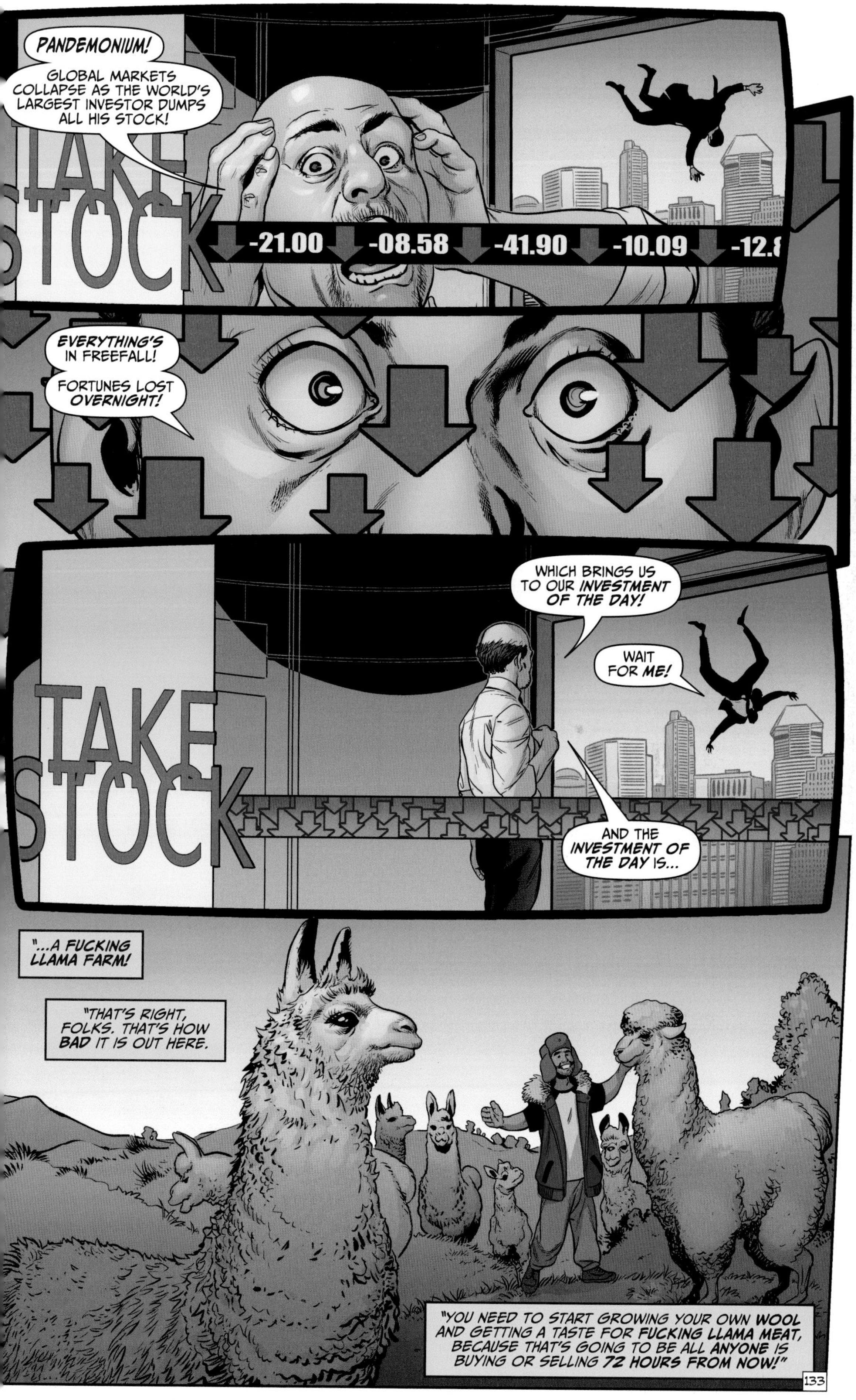
PANDEMONIUM!
GLOBAL MARKETS COLLAPSE AS THE WORLD'S LARGEST INVESTOR DUMPS ALL HIS STOCK!
TAKE STOCK
-21.00
-08.58
-41.90
-10.09
EVERYTHING'S IN FREEFALL!
FORTUNES LOST OVERNIGHT!
WHICH BRINGS US TO OUR INVESTMENT OF THE DAY!
WAIT FOR ME!
TAKE STOCK
AND THE INVESTMENT OF THE DAY IS...
"...A FUCKING LLAMA FARM!
"THAT'S RIGHT, FOLKS. THAT'S HOW BAD IT IS OUT HERE.
"YOU NEED TO START GROWING YOUR OWN WOOL AND GETTING A TASTE FOR FUCKING LLAMA MEAT, BECAUSE THAT'S GOING TO BE ALL ANYONE IS BUYING OR SELLING 72 HOURS FROM NOW!"

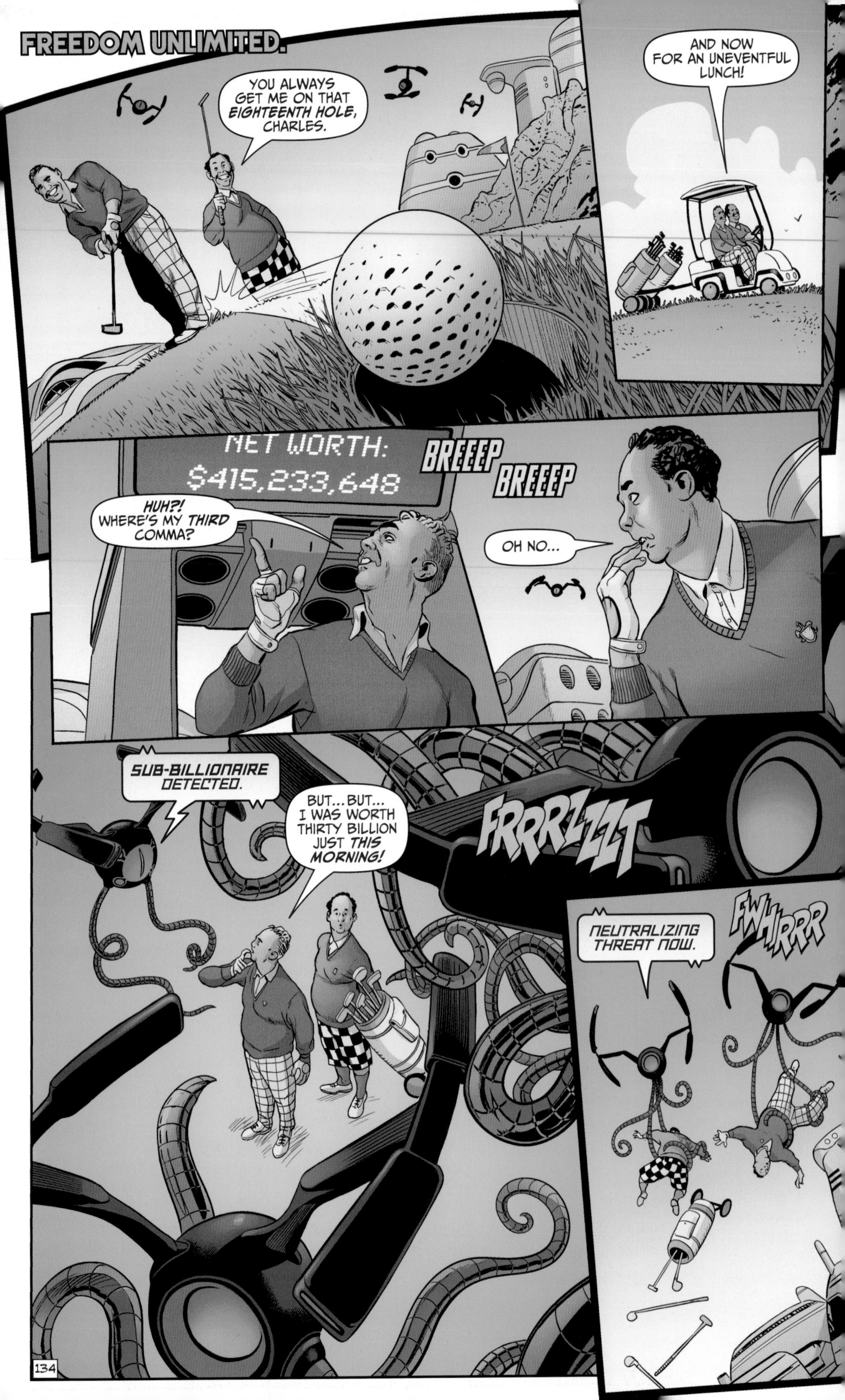
FREEDOM UNLIMITED.
YOU ALWAYS GET ME ON THAT EIGHTEENTH HOLE, CHARLES.
AND NOW FOR AN UNEVENTFUL LUNCH!
NET WORTH: $415,233,648
BREEEP BREEEP
HUH?! WHERE'S MY THIRD COMMA?
OH NO...
SUB-BILLIONAIRE DETECTED.
BUT... BUT... I WAS WORTH THIRTY BILLION JUST THIS MORNING!
FRRRZZZT
NEUTRALIZING THREAT NOW.
FWHIRRR

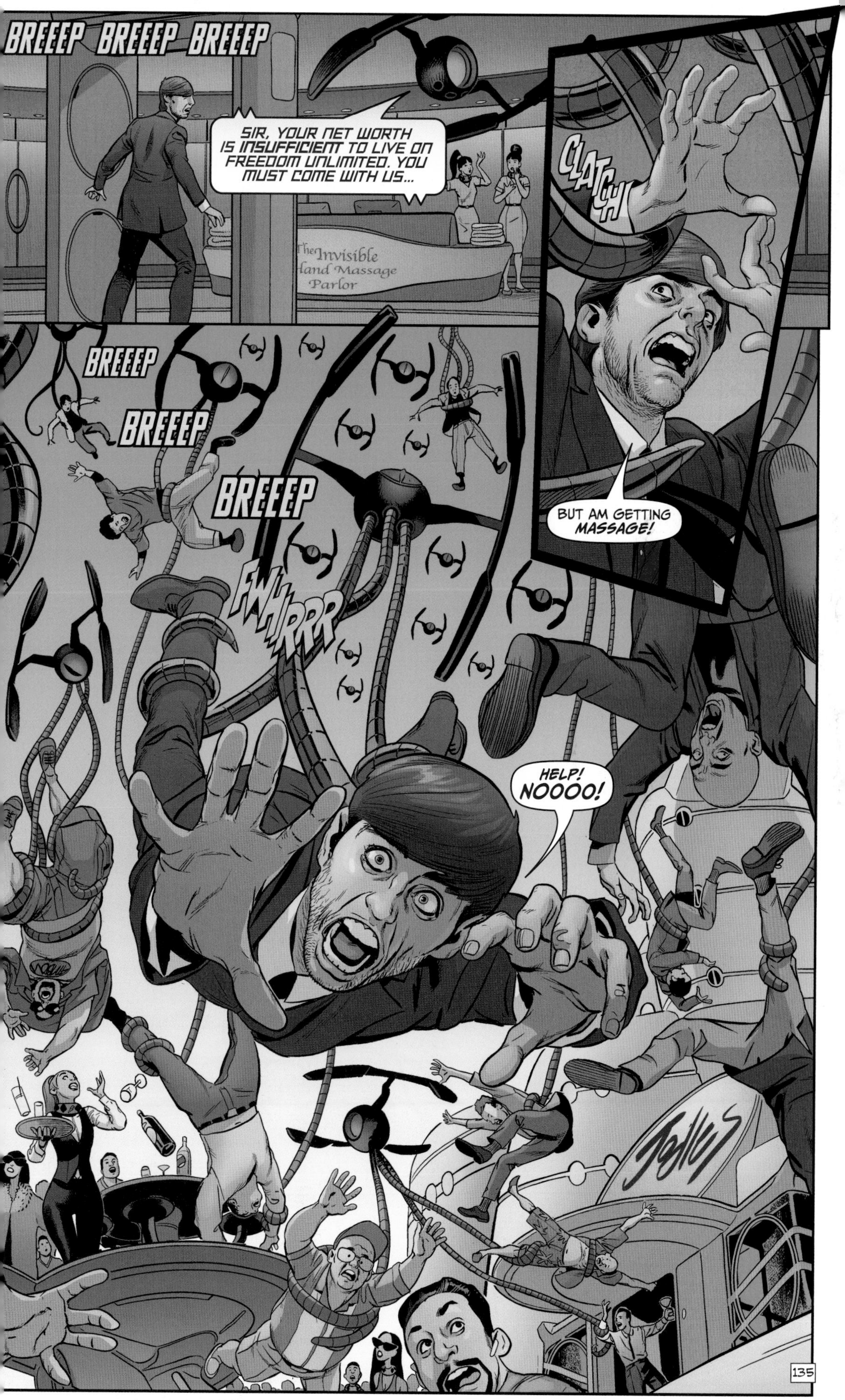
BREEEP BREEEP BREEEP
SIR, YOUR NET WORTH IS INSUFFICIENT TO LIVE ON FREEDOM UNLIMITED. YOU MUST COME WITH US...
The Invisible Hand Massage Parlor
CLATCH!
BUT AM GETTING MASSAGE!
BREEEP
BREEEP
BREEEP
FWHIRRR
HELP! NOOOO!

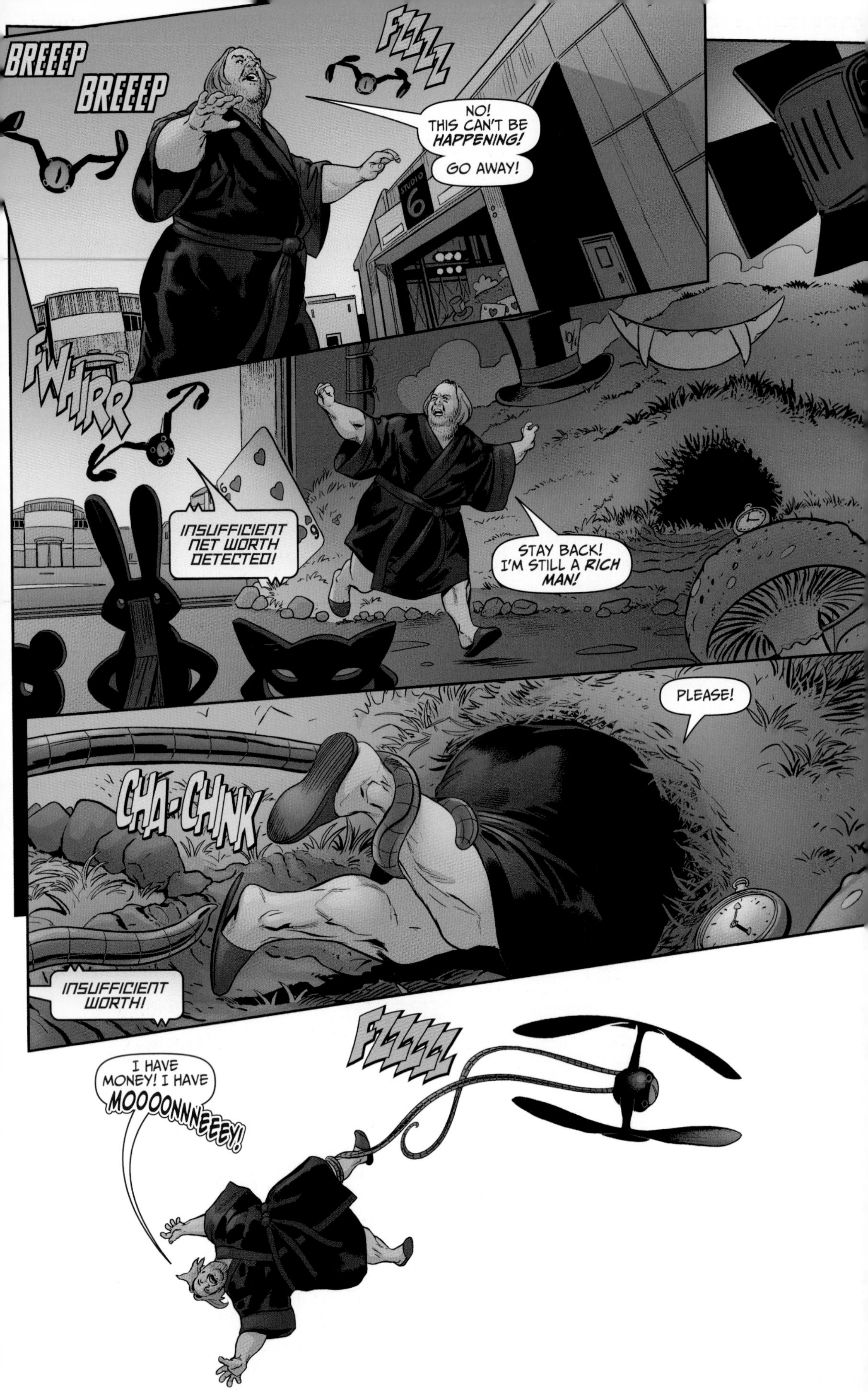
BREEEP
BREEEP
FZZZZ
NO! THIS CAN'T BE HAPPENING!
GO AWAY!
STUDIO 6
FWHIRR
INSUFFICIENT NET WORTH DETECTED!
STAY BACK! I'M STILL A RICH MAN!
PLEASE!
CHA-CHINK
INSUFFICIENT WORTH!
FZZZZ
I HAVE MONEY! I HAVE MOOOONNNEEEY!

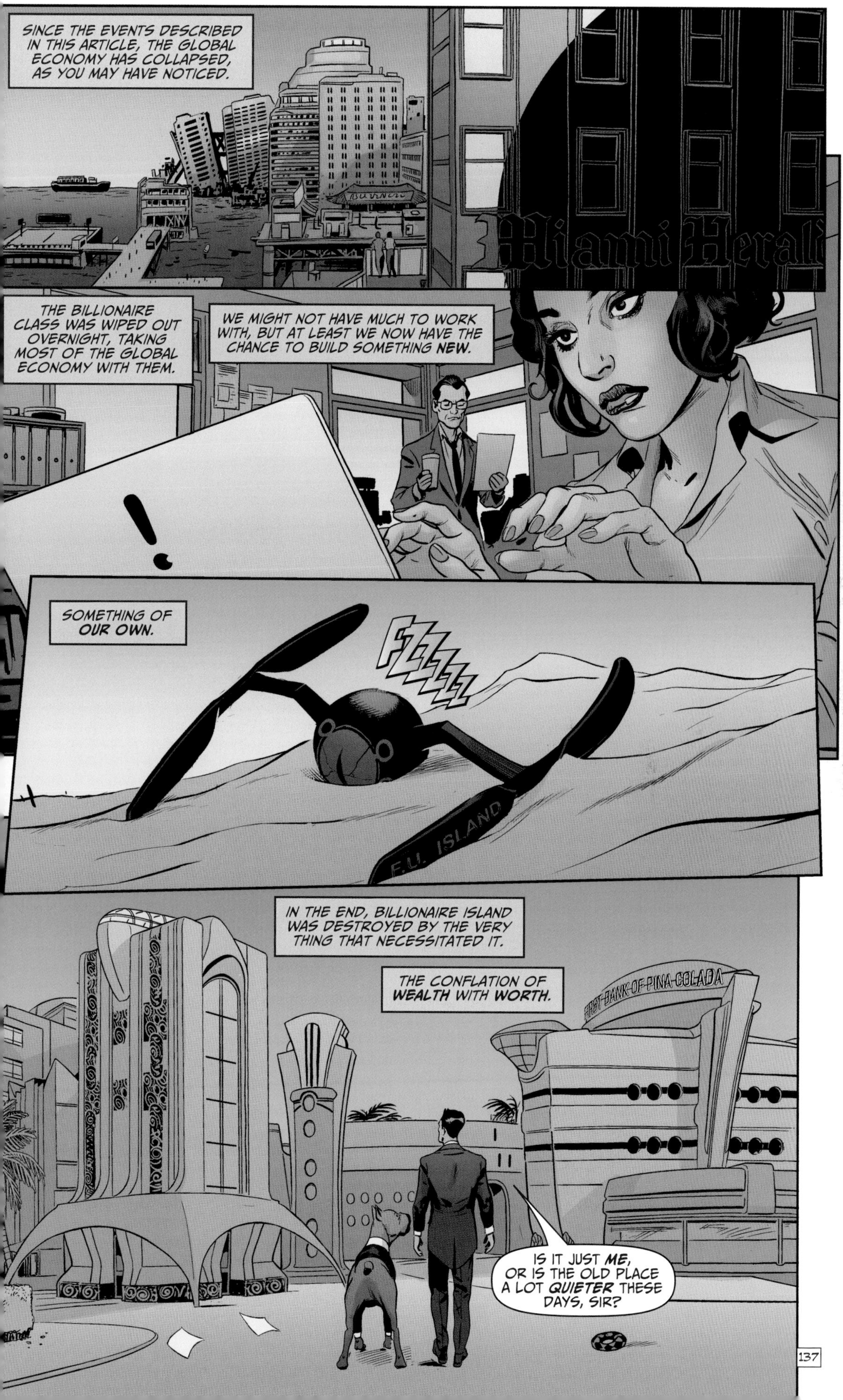

SINCE THE EVENTS DESCRIBED IN THIS ARTICLE, THE GLOBAL ECONOMY HAS COLLAPSED, AS YOU MAY HAVE NOTICED.
Miami Herald
THE BILLIONAIRE CLASS WAS WIPED OUT OVERNIGHT, TAKING MOST OF THE GLOBAL ECONOMY WITH THEM.
WE MIGHT NOT HAVE MUCH TO WORK WITH, BUT AT LEAST WE NOW HAVE THE CHANCE TO BUILD SOMETHING NEW.
!
SOMETHING OF OUR OWN.
FZZZZ
F.U. ISLAND
IN THE END, BILLIONAIRE ISLAND WAS DESTROYED BY THE VERY THING THAT NECESSITATED IT.
THE CONFLATION OF WEALTH WITH WORTH.
FIRST BANK OF PINA COLADA
IS IT JUST ME, OR IS THE OLD PLACE A LOT QUIETER THESE DAYS, SIR?

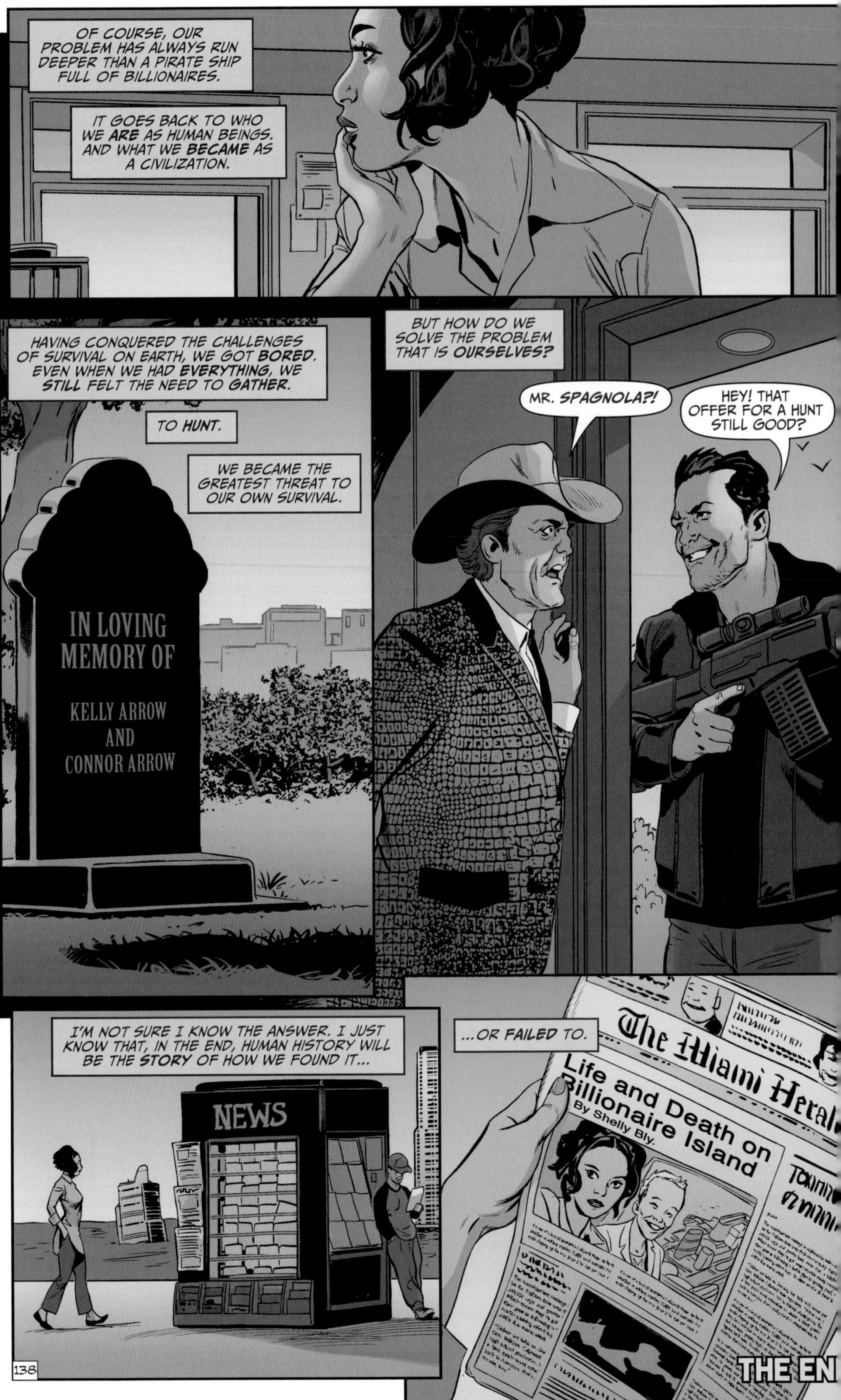
OF COURSE, OUR PROBLEM HAS ALWAYS RUN DEEPER THAN A PIRATE SHIP FULL OF BILLIONAIRES.
IT GOES BACK TO WHO WE ARE AS HUMAN BEINGS. AND WHAT WE BECAME AS A CIVILIZATION.
HAVING CONQUERED THE CHALLENGES OF SURVIVAL ON EARTH, WE GOT BORED. EVEN WHEN WE HAD EVERYTHING, WE STILL FELT THE NEED TO GATHER.
TO HUNT.
WE BECAME THE GREATEST THREAT TO OUR OWN SURVIVAL.
IN LOVING MEMORY OF
KELLY ARROW
AND
CONNOR ARROW
BUT HOW DO WE SOLVE THE PROBLEM THAT IS OURSELVES?
MR. SPAGNOLA?!
HEY! THAT OFFER FOR A HUNT STILL GOOD?
I'M NOT SURE I KNOW THE ANSWER. I JUST KNOW THAT, IN THE END, HUMAN HISTORY WILL BE THE STORY OF HOW WE FOUND IT...
NEWS
...OR FAILED TO.
The Miami Heral
Life and Death on Billionaire Island
By Shelly Bly.
THE EN

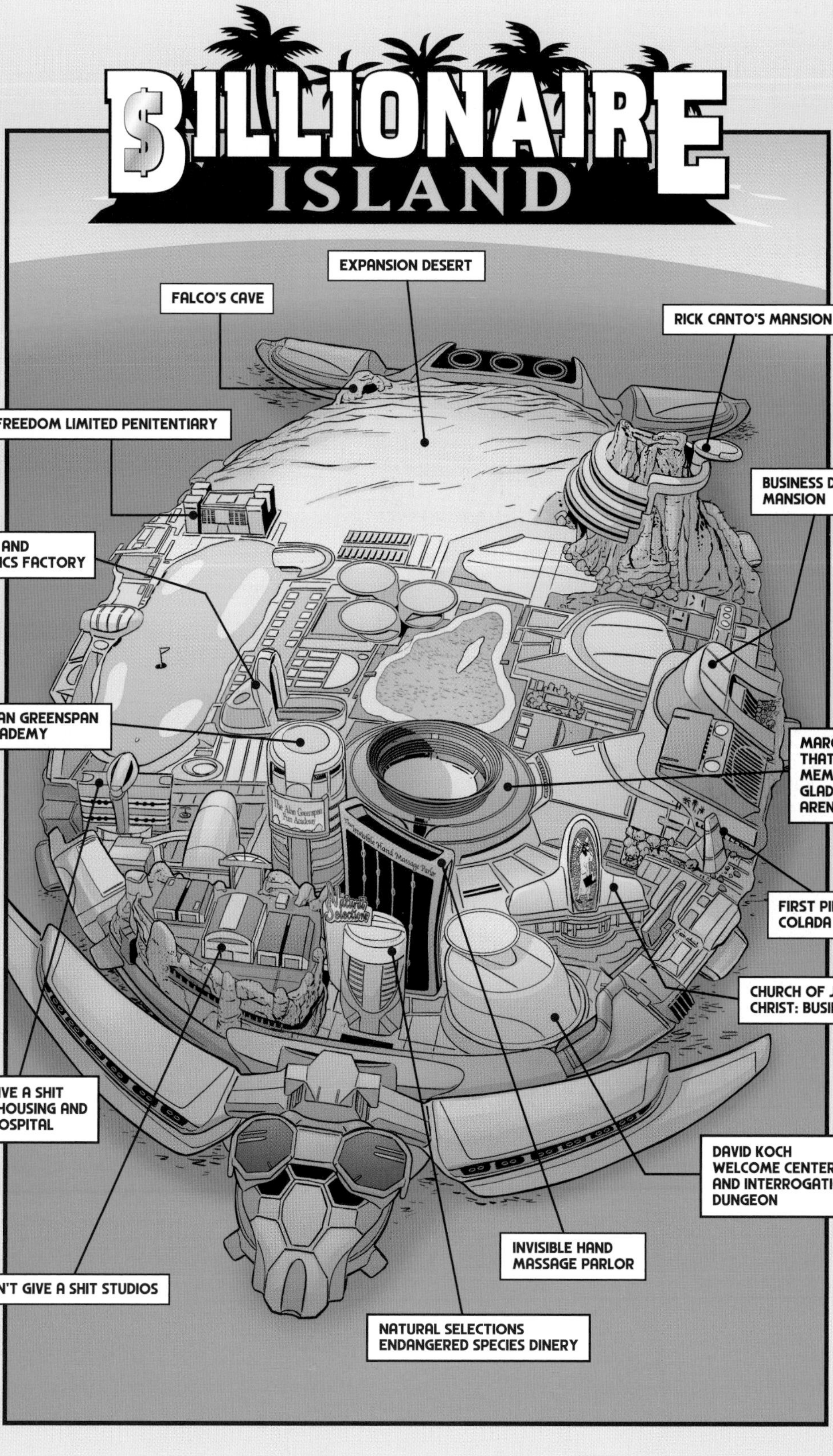
BILLIONAIRE
ISLAND
EXPANSION DESERT
FALCO'S CAVE
RICK CANTO'S MANSION
FREEDOM LIMITED PENITENTIARY
BUSINESS DOG'S MANSION
DRONE AND ROBOTICS FACTORY
THE ALAN GREENSPAN FUN ACADEMY
MARGARET THATCHER MEMORIAL GLADIATORIAL ARENA
FIRST PINA COLADA BANK
CHURCH OF JESUS CHRIST: BUSINESSMAN
DON'T GIVE A SHIT TALENT HOUSING AND STUNT HOSPITAL
DAVID KOCH WELCOME CENTER AND INTERROGATION DUNGEON
INVISIBLE HAND MASSAGE PARLOR
DON'T GIVE A SHIT STUDIOS
NATURAL SELECTIONS ENDANGERED SPECIES DINERY

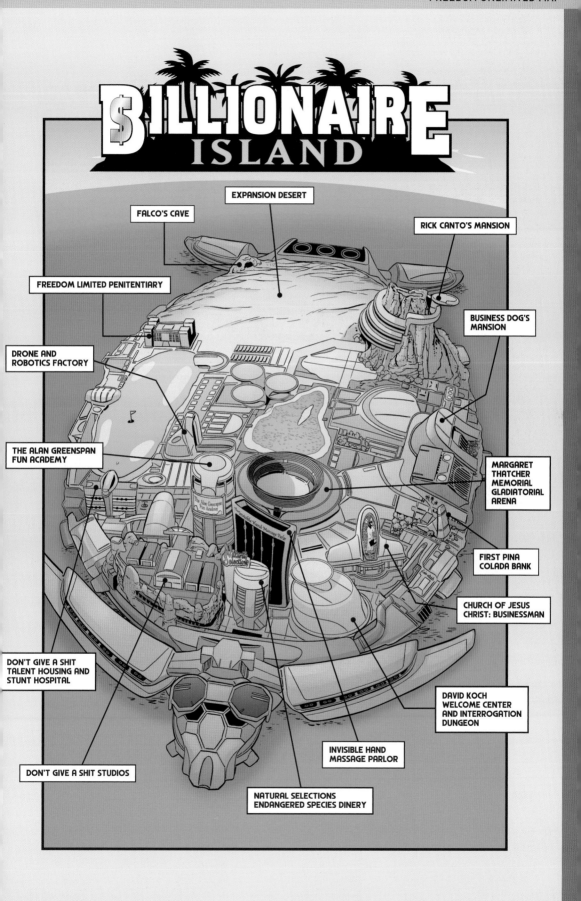

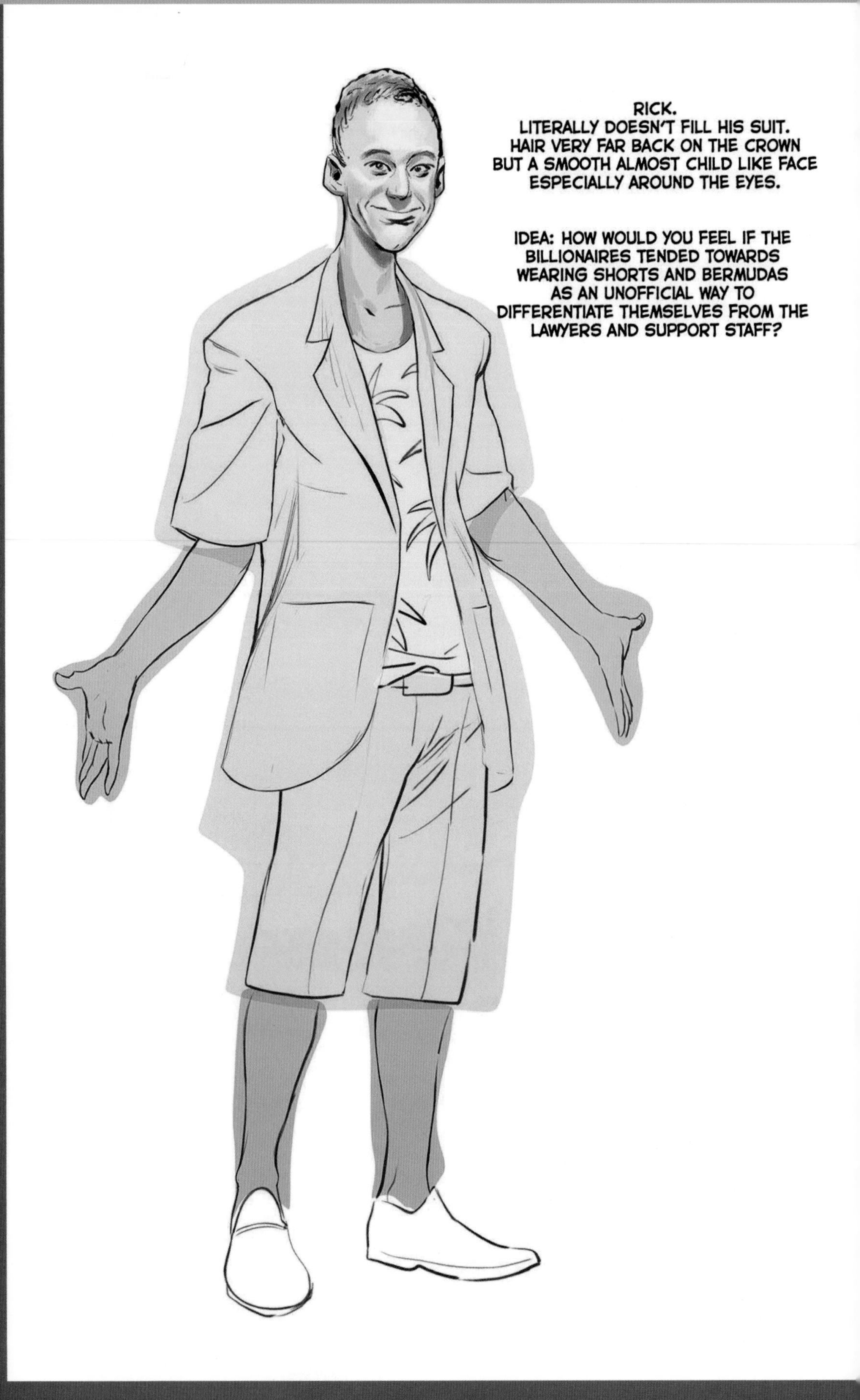
RICK.
LITERALLY DOESN'T FILL HIS SUIT.
HAIR VERY FAR BACK ON THE CROWN
BUT A SMOOTH ALMOST CHILD LIKE FACE
ESPECIALLY AROUND THE EYES.
IDEA: HOW WOULD YOU FEEL IF THE
BILLIONAIRES TENDED TOWARDS
WEARING SHORTS AND BERMUDAS
AS AN UNOFFICIAL WAY TO
DIFFERENTIATE THEMSELVES FROM THE
LAWYERS AND SUPPORT STAFF?

SAD, TIRED AND RELENTLESS

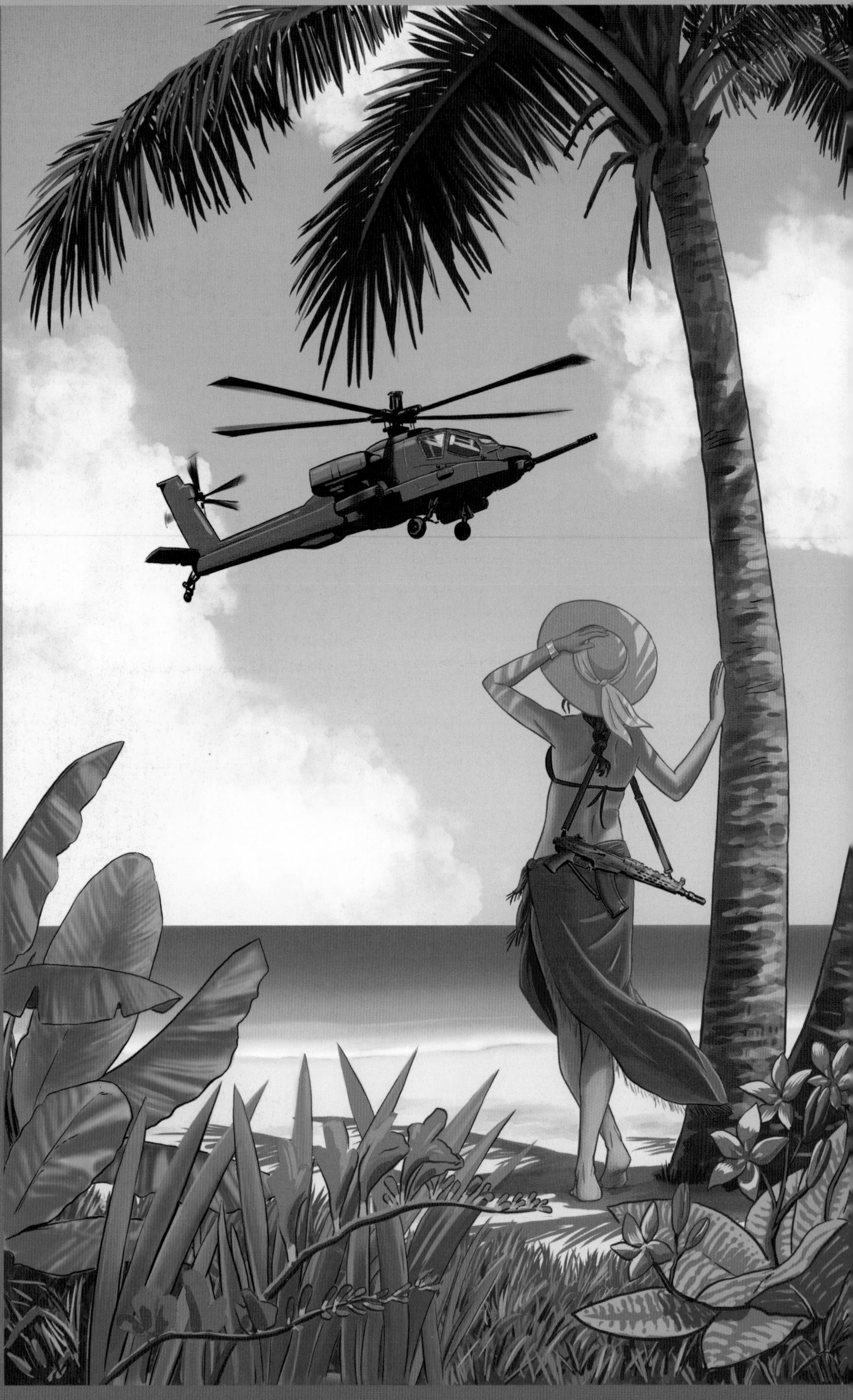

BILLIONAIRE ISLAND #2 VARIANT COVER by DARICK ROBERTSON & LEE LOUGHRIDGE

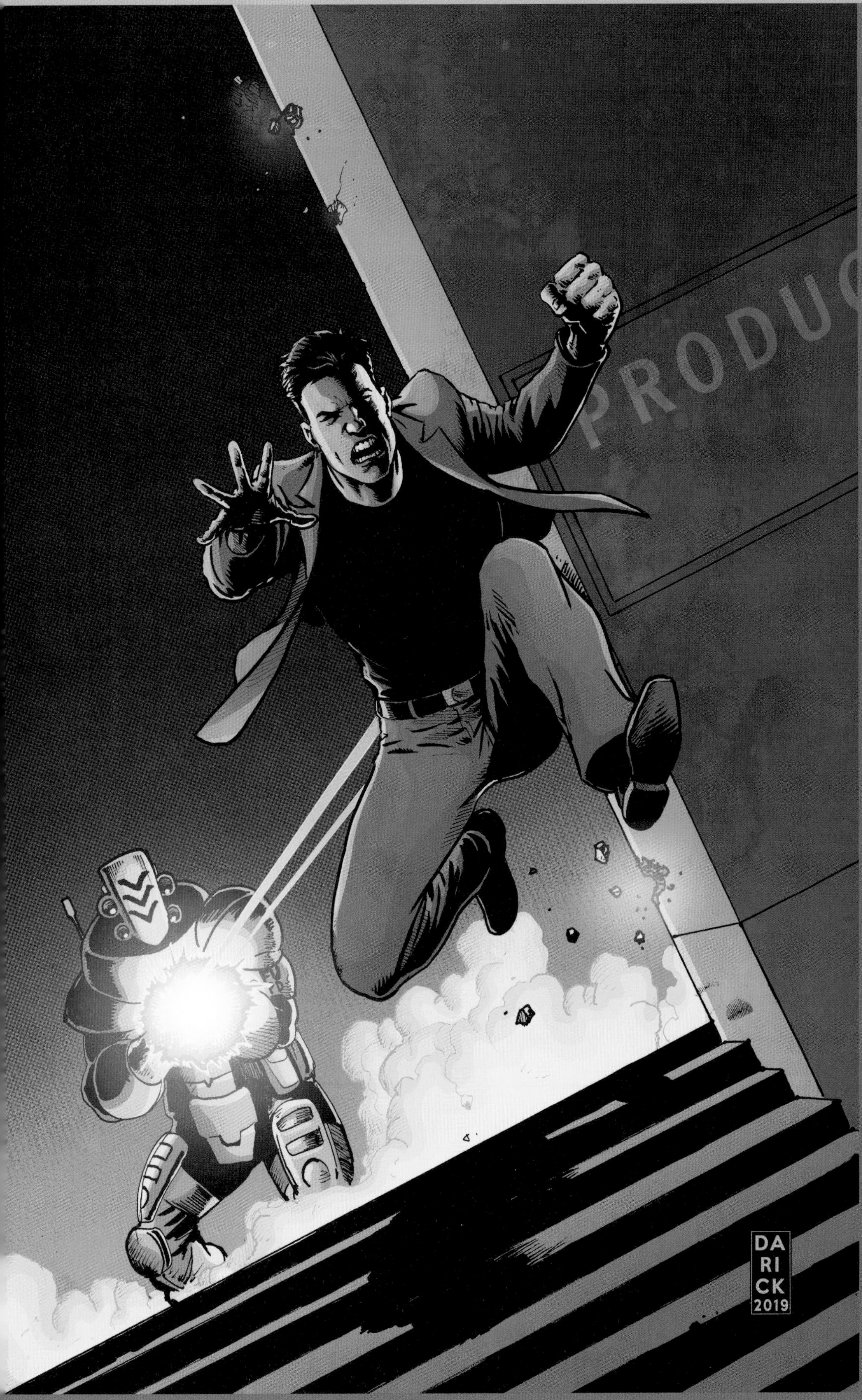
PRODUC
DA
RI
CK
2019

B I O G R A P H I E S

CHRISTOPHER CHUCKRY is a veteran colorist who has colored many comics and graphic novels for publishers throughout North America and Europe. He previously teamed up with Mark Russell and Steve Pugh on the acclaimed *Flintstones* miniseries. Also an illustrator, his work has appeared on book covers, trading cards, magazines, e-books, and juried art shows, including *Visions From The Upside Down: Stranger Things Artbook*, the World Horror Convention and the anthology *Spectrum: The Best in Contemporary Fantastic Art*. Chris lives in Winnipeg, Manitoba, Canada with his wife and two sons.

PIA GUERRA is a Canadian comic book artist and cartoonist best known for her work as penciler and co-creator of Vertigo's *Y: The Last Man* with writer Brian K. Vaughan. She has drawn editorial cartoons for *TheNib.com* and gags for *The New Yorker* written by her partner and husband, comedian Ian Boothby. She has won several awards including the comic industry's top prize, the Eisner Award. Pia has drawn stories for *Hellblazer*, *Black Canary*, *Doctor Who*, *Torchwood Magazine* and *Bart Simpson's Treehouse of Horror Comics*.

STEVE PUGH is a British artist and sometimes writer, born and based in the Midlands of England. Recruited for DC's Vertigo imprint at its inception, he worked on titles including *Hellblazer*, *Animal Man*, and *Preacher: Saint of Killers*. Later, he wrote and illustrated *Hotwire* for Radical Comics and received Eisner nominations for his art on the critically acclaimed reimaginings of *The Flintstones* and *Harley Quinn: Breaking Glass*.

DARICK ROBERTSON is an American comic book artist, writer and creator with a decades long career in the industry. Born and raised in the northern California Bay Area ans self trained as an artist, his notable works include co-creating the award winning *Transmetropolitan*, *The Boys*, *Happy!* and *Oliver*. Darick has illustrated for both Marvel and DC including work on their icons Batman, Wolverine, the Punisher and Spider-Man.

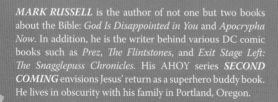

MARK RUSSELL is the author of not one but two books about the Bible: *God Is Disappointed in You* and *Apocrypha Now*. In addition, he is the writer behind various DC comic books such as *Prez*, *The Flintstones*, and *Exit Stage Left: The Snagglepuss Chronicles*. His AHOY series **SECOND COMING** envisions Jesus' return as a superhero buddy book. He lives in obscurity with his family in Portland, Oregon.

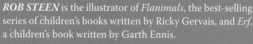

ROB STEEN is the illustrator of *Flanimals*, the best-selling series of children's books written by Ricky Gervais, and *Erf*, a children's book written by Garth Ennis.